THE FOREMAN'S
BOYS

THE STORY OF CIVILIAN CONSERVATION CORPS, COMPANY 1333, CAMP S-63, POE VALLEY

WILLIAM MARCUM

SUNBURY
P R E S S

Mechanicsburg, PA USA

Published by Sunbury Press, Inc.
Mechanicsburg, Pennsylvania

www.sunburypress.com

For information about special discounts for bulk purchases, please contact Sunbury Press Orders Dept. at (855) 338-8359 or orders@sunburypress.com.

To request one of our authors for speaking engagements or book signings, please contact Sunbury Press Publicity Dept. at publicity@sunburypress.com.

ISBN: 978-1-62006-138-1 (Trade paperback)

Library of Congress Control Number: 2019937975

FIRST SUNBURY PRESS EDITION: April 2019

Product of the United States of America
0 1 1 2 3 5 8 13 21 34 55

Set in Bookman Old Style
Designed by Crystal Devine
Cover by Terry Kennedy
Edited by Janice Rhayem

Continue the Enlightenment!

This book is dedicated to
the memory of my mother,
Mae Regie Frankenberger Marcum.
Had Mom not saved all of the
Civilian Conservation Corps memorabilia
found in my Grandfather's wooden chest
this book could not have been written.

CONTENTS

ACKNOWLEDGMENTS

This book became reality due to the support and contributions of many. My wife Mary who continued to tell me I could write a book. The many Poe Valley State Park managers who supported reunions and gatherings across the span of four decades. Jack Yarnall, and his endless support to the legacy of Civilian Conservation Corps, Company 1333. Vonnie Henninger, researcher extraordinaire. Penns Valley Historical Society. The many Civilian Conservation Corps veterans and family members who shared their stories. Gene Morris, National Archives. Mary Sorenson, Executive Director, Centre County Historical Society. Michael Wennin, Executive Director, Lumber Heritage Region of Pennsylvania. John Eastlake, Civilian Conservation Corps enthusiast.

INTRODUCTION

I **grew up in the small,** remote village of Coburn, Pennsylvania, a small town with a population of less than 200, without a traffic light, located in the rural dairy farmland of Central Pennsylvania among generational family farms. My surname is not one of the family names of the early and mostly German descendants to the area, yet mostly everyone knew I was Sum's grandson.

My grandfather lived in the nearby town of Millheim, a town of more than 800 residents with one traffic light.

I spent a lot of time with my grandfather as a young boy, and everywhere we traveled people would in most cases greet one another by their name, as mostly everyone knew each other and almost everybody greeting my grandfather would call out, "Good morning, Sum" or "Good afternoon, Sum" or simply just nod and say, "Sum." Sum, affectionately known to me as "PaPa," was Sumner Frankenberger, my grandfather.

My grandfather built and operated the local Farmer's Supply Company, a farm implement store, also located in Millheim, where most of the farmers in the region had done some level of business with my grandfather, making him well-known throughout the community.

I am not sure I knew my grandfather's full first and last name until sometime in early elementary school. One time, when required to fill out forms where family member names were required, I remember asking my teacher to tell me my grandparents' names, and of course she knew who they were and how to spell their names.

Sum, born in 1900, was a farmer's son growing up on one of the generational, community family farms situated not more than three miles from the town of Millheim, where he resided all his life after leaving the farm.

By the time my grandfather was thirty-three years old, his resume stated he had experience as a crewman in a lumber mill, crewman on a thrashing machine, tractor operator, heavy highway machine operator, carpenter, and owner of a sawmill and thrashing machine business.

In the springtime of 1933, these experiences were what supported his being selected by the Pennsylvania Department of Forest and Waters to be a foreman in a local Civilian Conservation Corps camp.

The Civilian Conservation Corps camp he was selected to work in would be Civilian Conservation Corps Company 1333, Camp S-63 Poe Valley with a Coburn, Pennsylvania, mailing address.

The Poe Valley Civilian Conservation Corps camp where he served was situated approximately seven miles as the crow flies from the farm where he was born and raised.

My grandfather lived to be seventy-seven years old, and right up until the time of his passing he enjoyed telling anyone who would give him a bit of their time about his work and time in the CCC camps. Among the many experiences and paths taken in my grandfather's life, the one experience I believe my grandfather was most proud to have been part of and would share with anyone was his experience in the Civilian Conservation Corp.

It is said The Great Depression of the 1930s following the stock market crash of 1929 affected every American in one way or another. Banks closed their doors, depositors lost most or all of their saving deposits, possessions acquired on credit were repossessed, and some level of economic loss affected everyone.

Many lost homes, automobiles, and anything on loan was lost when unable to pay the called-in debts. Industry and employment opportunity slowed to a crawl or halted altogether. Job prospects were severely limited and in many locations nonexistent.

The resultant joblessness affected all ages, some of those most affected were young, unmarried men in their late teens through their middle twenties, as jobs were most unavailable to this eighteen- to twenty-five year old age group.

These young men found themselves on the street without much prospect in life, feeling the hurt of being a burden to their families, not being able to contribute in general and finding themselves doing anything to get by. Getting by, unfortunately, sometimes would not always be within the confines of common laws. Petty crimes were committed to have something to eat or a pair of shoes on their feet all too often.

During this time in American history, there were no social assistance programs in place to provide help with the basic substances of life. No such thing as social services, food stamps, unemployment compensation, etc.

A newly elected president had a plan to address the joblessness being experienced by these young men. President Franklin D. Roosevelt addressed the nation immediately after taking the oath of office in 1933, proposing a bold plan to tackle the economic plight gripping the country. This plan would commonly become known as the New Deal. One of the parts of this plan was to put the growing number of unemployed young men to work throughout the country in forest and land management projects.

This part of the New Deal plan initially was called "Emergency Conservation Work." The plan was to put these young, unemployed men to work in the forested lands of the country performing conservation measures to address the conservation and reforestation needs of lands all across America where unmanaged lumbering and abuse had gone unchecked for preceding decades.

President Roosevelt chose national labor leader Mr. Robert Fechner to be the director of the Emergency Conservation Work program. The program quickly gained popularity with America, and in less than four months, tens of thousands of those unemployed young men were working, putting money in their pockets, and sending money back home to desperate families barely scraping by.

One of the ways in which The Great Depression affected my grandfather was his being selected to work for the Pennsylvania Department of Forest and Waters as part of the Emergency Conservation Work program in President Roosevelt's New Deal. For my grandfather this meant full-time employment close to home at a desirable pay rate, given the economic plight gripping the country, affecting the general economy, his family, and himself.

His job was to be a foreman in an Emergency Conservation Work camp location, where these newly enrolled, young men would be performing conservation work in the forests.

His work started in 1933 and continued with this popular part of the New Deal through 1939. During this time period, he would be boss, teacher, and father-figure to these young men performing the many conservation service projects in the program that affectionately became known as the "Civilian Conservation Corps." This name eventually replaced the original "Emergency Conservation Work" name.

My grandfather, like so many others, commonly referred to the Civilian Conservation Corps as the three Cs, or just the Cs. Those young men who enrolled in the program were generally referred to as "enrollees," though I do not remember my grandfather talking about enrollees; he always referred to them respectfully as "boys," and in many cases he would refer to them most affectionately as "his boys."

Fortunately for myself and many folks who have become Civilian Conservation Corps enthusiasts who are now looking back in time at this piece of local history, my grandfather was a packrat and kept mostly everything that may have some sort of declared or undeclared value. This included a treasure trove of photographs and textural documents related to his time in the Civilian Conservation Corps camps.

When my grandfather passed, I was in the military. While home on leave for his funeral, my mother asked me if there might be anything in my grandfather's possessions I may want, I responded by saying, "Let me think about it." Later on, we were looking through remaining items in his shop, and we came upon a wooden chest and found it contained textural documents, drawings, photographs, and other miscellaneous items he had acquired during his time in the Corps. The documents in that wooden chest were what I asked my mother to hold onto for me.

Years later, after I was out of the service while visiting my parents, my mother reminded me of the documents that were retained from the wooden chest. I took a brief look through the numerous items and quickly realized there was quite a treasure of documents and photographs telling much more of the story of the Civilian Conservation Corps camp located in Poe Valley, Coburn, PA, than I or most had ever known. This cursory review put a spark of interest in me to want to learn more about this camp my grandfather was a part of.

Over the course of time, my interest in the Civilian Conservation Corps in Poe Valley grew. Then in 1983 I contacted others locally who had a part in the program and learned everyone knew who Sum was. With the help of my wife, my mother, and Corps veterans Sam Wise and Ray Hazel, we organized and held a reunion in June of 1983 for camp veterans. With help from these same folks and others, my wife and I would subsequently host thirteen more annual reunions.

Although the organized reunions came to an end in 1996, I continued to gather information and memorabilia about the Civilian Conservation Corps camp in Poe Valley. In 2012 a desire to commemorate the legacy of the Civilian Conservation Corps in Poe Valley again spurred me to organize, with the support of my wife, the local historical society, and the manager of Poe Valley State Park, a gathering of the very few remaining veterans and extended family members of veterans to keep the legacy of the Corps' spirit alive. This is again an annual event.

The information gained during those reunions, gatherings, and continued acquisition of knowledge about my "PaPa's Boys" is a story to be told. Armed with the many documents and information from the wooden chest and the memory of those times spent with my grandfather, information gained through shared stories, this book is my effort to tell the reader a few of the stories my grandfather told me about his time in the three Cs. Additionally, to tell the story of the creation of a recreation site deep in the Bald Eagle State Forest, known as Poe Valley State Park by my PaPa's Boys, having been performed under the guidance of a hastily developed, highly successful collaboration of federal, state, and local governmental agencies unlike no other time.

I was very young when my grandfather told these stories, and for me they were simply a part of being with my grandfather. While my memory of the details is limited, the opportunity to learn more and appreciate the benefits the Civilian Conservation Corps gave those young men, their families, and America, for me, will continue beyond memory and is to be shared herein.

Over the years while attending reunions and gatherings, I was advised by numerous attendees who are extended family members of a camp veteran, they had little knowledge about their relatives' involvement in the CCC. Others told me this was the first time they learned the story of the camp and the accomplishments that had been presented through oral and photographic means.

Within the pages of this book the reader will find numerous lists of enrollee names who served in the Poe Valley camp.

These lists are, however, known to not be a complete listing of all the enrollees who served in Poe Valley. These lists are in some cases accompanied by a date they were in camp, and some of these lists include the enrollee's respective hometown at the time they were in camp. Might a relative of yours served in a Civilian Conservation Corps camp? Might he have served in Poe Valley? You may just find his name or maybe even a photograph of him depicted herein.

CHAPTER 1

EMERGENCY CONSERVATION WORK

Under the direction of Robert Fechner, the Emergency Conservation Work program was organized and implemented in the springtime months of 1933. This implementation was organized through a cooperative effort of federal, state, and local governmental agencies for the singular goal of providing immediate employment opportunity for the growing mass of eighteen to twenty-five year old, unemployed, unmarried men in America of the time.

The unprecedented cooperative spirit of the departments of War, Labor, Agriculture, and Interior put more than 200,000 of these young men to work in camps performing forestry and land conservation projects all across America by the end of June 1933, and more than 550,000 young men were working in Emergency Conservation Work camps across America by mid-1935, indicative of the popularity of this part of President Roosevelt's New Deal.

The creation of an Emergency Conservation Work camp had the look of a military operation, as was the way of the US Army who had been given the task to mobilize and establish these new Emergency Conservation Work campsites. The War Department quickly developed mobilization strategies to move the enrollees throughout the country. Various operating military facilities were selected to be induction centers for new enrollees into Emergency Conservation Work. These initial enrollees, after signing on to the program, were sent to one of these centers. After their arrival for a period of approximately ten days, the enrollees were given general physical and dental examinations, fed well three times a day, issued surplus military clothing and footgear, perform limited physical strength training, learn the general way of living in an orderly military fashion, and given general information about what type of work they would be performing once they arrived at

7

their assigned camp location. Work projects in a camp were forest conservation and land management projects. Work projects were not performed on military facilities, nor would any works be performed in support of military needs or objectives.

For many enrollees, this was the first time they had eaten healthy three times a day and had more than one pair of pants and a good pair of shoes on their feet in many months. After approximately 160 of their fellow enrollees were ready to be mobilized to a camp location, these fresh, young men, along with two to four military officers, would typically embark by train on their way to their designated camp location.

As was the way of the army, the clothing and footgear issued to these young men may not have been tailor fitted, however, the clothing was not thread bare, and the boots would have new soles and a complete set of laces.

These young men would now depart the induction center on their way to camp locations unknown, certainly with trepidation about what this new adventure was to behold.

A bird's-eye look down onto an early first-stage Emergency Conservation Work camp would see rows of tents in straight lines and all sorts of equipment in an orderly fashion with a flag pole in a central position. This sight would lead you to think the Army had come to the area and set up camp, and rightly so as the US Army branch of the Department of War had been assigned the task of mobilizing and setting up temporary living quarters for 160 enrollees literally overnight.

Who better than the Army, as they had the operational know how, means, and experience to move significant numbers of personnel and equipment rapidly from point A to point B and set up a campsite immediately upon arrival. This was accomplished using World War One military surplus materials pulled out of storage facilities scattered all over America.

The accompanying military officers were in most cases reserve officers brought back to duty. In some cases, these reserve officers were also unemployed and glad for the opportunity for the employment opportunity.

Before embarking, these first groups were assigned a company number and a camp designation. The designations assigned to the first group on its way to Poe Valley, Coburn, Pennsylvania, were Emergency Conservation Work Company 1333, Camp S-63, Poe Valley.

The Emergency Conservation Work company had the look of the Army, had the feel of the Army, and had a daily operational structure like the Army.

Here, though, the training of young men to fight an enemy combatant was replaced with the learning of how to conduct forestry and land management conservation measures to improve and preserve America's depleted forests and lands and subsequently develop recreational sites for public use. The work project training of the enrollees, however, was carried out by other technical personnel at state and local levels without intrusion on the part of the military.

A bird's-eye look into a second-stage Emergency Conservation Work camp would typically show the tents had been replaced by wooden, barracks-style structures holding approximately forty enrollees in each barrack and other wooden structures of similar design serving as the Mess Hall, infirmary, headquarters, Officers' Quarters, forestry quarters, shower house, maintenance shops, and other miscellaneous structures, which would be required to support the work assigned to be performed in a particular camp. Other changes and improvements many times included an exercise yard, stone-lined walkways, wires on poles delivering electrical power throughout the camp from a generator building, and all things in a neat, orderly fashion, as was the way of the military. These campsites were typically positioned in remote, mountainous locations on leased lands or state and federal lands where forestry and land conservation work was to be performed.

The military's assignment was to use its organizational knowledge, capabilities, and experience to support the creation of Emergency Conservation Work camps. They provided organizational structure during development of the campsite, administration of the camp after the camp had been organized, and thereafter maintained the overall health and welfare of the enrollees.

They did this by assigning reserve officers called back to duty to these campsites. Once there, these officers ran the camp as if it were a military installation. There were, however, limitations to their command. These officers' principal mission was to provide organizational management for the needs in a camp like transportation, quartermaster, medical services, maintaining enrollee records, mess provisions, and ever-important paymaster.

In these camps, the command of strict Army policy and Army ways was relaxed. The enrollee was required to maintain their beds, personal hygiene, personal space, and all other areas, like the Recreation Hall and shower house, in the way of the Army, however, infractions were not resultant in the crushing, harsh, discipline-mannered ways of the Army. Here, if an enrollee did not want to conform to the life and way of the Emergency Conservation Work camps and decided to go home or "AWOL" (absent without leave), no one was sent after him to bring him back. The absent enrollee would simply and promptly be replaced by another enrollee most anxious to put money in his pocket and send money to family back home, simultaneously bolstering the self-esteem.

For most of the enrollees, this would be their first time away from home for any extended period of time, and for most the yearning to go home would be strong, yet the opportunity to have money in their pocket and a tingle of pride in being able to help their loved ones back home for the most part kept AWOL numbers low throughout the Emergency Conservation Work program. Enrollees choosing to go AWOL and not return received an unsatisfactory discharge certificate. This measure in many instances made an enrollee put a hold on going AWOL.

Conversely, enrollees who fulfilled their enrollment period were awarded a satisfactory discharge certificate, these certificates quickly became a highly prized possession.

Veteran Randall Boob remembered three enrollees had left camp not to return during his twelve months in camp. He stated when someone left camp, they were referred to as having "gone out over the knob." There are no records known to me available to provide an accurate accounting of how many may have chosen to leave.

We do know Poe Valley Camp S-63 was widely held in high regard throughout the district during its entire operational time and subsequently by veterans alike indicative of a camp with a very low AWOL statistic.

Many of these young enrollees had not graduated from high school, having dropped out of school in search of work to help out at home. And in many other cases they had left home and found a way of life on the street so as to not be a burden to their family, already struggling in desperation to survive the unprecedented economic hardships brought on by The Depression.

Director Robert Fechner realized providing opportunity for enrollees to further their education while in camp would be an easy fit and certainly help build up morale in these young men, many who felt themselves deemed to be burdensome to society in general.

While in camp, enrollees had the opportunity to take courses in various vocational arts, such as truck driving, truck mechanic, carpentry, typewriting, masonry, electricians, machine operators, and the like. With the acquisition of a skill and a satisfactory discharge certificate from the Emergency Conservation Work program, the likelihood of employment opportunity back home held promise.

There are other Emergency Conservation Work publications describing site-specific military commanders' actions, both positive and negative in respect to how they administered camp operations and camp discipline. In general, most of these reports and stories are positive in nature. The military is known for having a regulation and a manual to deal with most any circumstance and situation. Manuals for the operation of Emergency Conservation Work camps for officers was not available. This alone presented a new challenge for these officers, requiring them to develop a management style to gain the support and respect of the enrollees without the benefit of the Army's Uniform Code of Military Justice. They would also solicit the support of the superintendent, foremen, LEMs, and barracks leaders to help keep the peace and maintain order in camp.

On more than one occasion I heard discussions among veterans telling how they had an almost natural regard and respect of the military officers who wore their adorned uniform every day. These enrollees were young, impressionable individuals, who in most instances had limited exposure to the ways of the military, and for many this was their first exposure to anything military.

Veteran Sam Wise told me he "quickly learned the primary role of the military commanders was to provide for the overall health and welfare of the camp and had little or nothing to do with the work projects." Sam went on to say he was surprised at how easy it was to talk to the "Captain" (camp commander) about anything and, most specifically, "Captain Ayres went out of his way to help me get a job when I left the camp."

Camp documents and numerous articles in the *Poe Valley Ravin*, a camp-published newsletter, describe positive effects of camp commanders for the betterment of the camp and support of individual enrollee needs. There can be no question that all was not a wonderland, and many enrollees would not have such fond memories about encounters with the company commander. These commanders had overall control of the enrollees while in camp. They could dole out disciplinary actions against an enrollee for any determined infraction and had single authority regarding whether or not an enrollee received a satisfactory or unsatisfactory discharge.

CLEAN CUT

Neat and orderly is the way of the US Army. This was most certainly carried out by every company commander who was assigned to Poe Valley, which is evident in the records and in many photographs depicting camp life. The buildings were built in an orderly line. The barracks beds, bedding, and foot and wall lockers were kept in a neat, orderly fashion.

So was the way of life in this camp and every other camp in the country. Meals were served in the Mess Hall, where the tables, benches, and all equipment were maintained in the same fashion and cleanliness was a must. The enrollees were expected to keep and maintain prescribed order to all things. This neat and orderly fashion was kept mostly under the watchful eye of the enrollee barracks leaders and assistant leaders. These enrollee leaders were selected by the company commander to uphold the camp requirements on the part of the enrollees, and they were the Army's equivalent of corporals and sergeants, paid more for their service and expected to keep order and peace among the men in their barracks. Leaders received $15.00 a month more than enrollees, and assistant leaders received $6.00 a month more than enrollees.

Company commanders and their respective junior officers performed inspections on a routine basis in the way of the Army. Additionally, higher-ranking US Army officers from the regional and district command levels also performed inspections in the camp. Poe Valley received a generous share of inspections by the ranks of majors and colonels who were in those command positions.

Poe Valley was host to the highest-ranking officer in the US Army Third Corps area command structure. Major General James K. Parsons conducted a tour of the camp in August of 1940. An article in the camp newsletter tells of the visit and states, "General Parsons made an inspection of the camp which he found to be in good shape."

These inspections were made on the part of the Army to assure the camp commanders were meeting the obligations of the Army in fulfilling the goals of Emergency Conservation Work. The company commanders relied heavily on the support of their two-man support staff. This support staff was made up of two junior officers, typically, lieutenant in rank. These officers had multiple duties and would be required to multi-task as mess officer, supply officer, transportation officer, recreation officer, and any other assigned duties. Typically, the third junior officer was the camp surgeon, and this position also had additional assigned duties.

Among the documents found in my grandfather's wooden box was a memorandum issued by Company Commander Captain Malcom Coates, dated December 30, 1935. This particular memorandum was issued to the three other military officers under his command in Poe Valley. These officers were Lieutenant Ernest Brock, Lieutenant James Carroll, and Lieutenant Owen Dooley.

The memorandum is a two-page document indicating the requirements of these officers under his command. The memorandum included the following instructions:

> The work day for officers at Camp S-63, begins at 7:30 A.M. At that time all officers will have begun their duties.
>
> No officer will leave camp without consultation with the Camp Commander. When leaving he shall state the time of his return, also have some idea where he may be reached while absent.
>
> When the camp commander is absent, this information will be left with the officer of the day.
>
> From and after this date, all officers, including the medical officer, will take their turn at the duty of officer of the day. His duties are as outlined in the attached letter. The dates each officer serves will be by monthly duty roster which will appear on the bulletin board. The officers duty roster is to be arranged that each officer whose name comes up for duty on Saturday will also be on duty the following day, Sunday.
>
> Any officer may exchange duty dates with any other officer by mutual agreement and with the knowledge and consent of the Camp Commander. At all times, however, there will be two officers on duty at the camp.

The Commander further requests that no officer absent himself in excess of two nights each week. As many free evenings as possible should be devoted to various forms of morale building; encouraging the boys in their various activities, etc.

Until further notice there shall be an officers meeting daily except Sunday at the Officers' Quarters immediately after midday meal.

By order of Captain Coates

An addendum was issued by the camp commander with the same date as the memorandum. The addendum included the following:

Officers of the day will see to it that leaders and assistant leaders in charge take their required responsibility such as maintaining both order and heat in the Recreation Hall, maintaining order and comfort in the squad rooms, etc.

As a further addenda to duties of Officers of the Day, such officer will render in writing to the Commanding Officer any suggestions, improvements, or corrections which he thinks ought to be made.

He will fill out the daily barrack inspection sheet, and sign the same. Upon the visit of the inspecting officer from the Sub-District, each Junior Officer will follow around in order to hear the suggestions made.

By order of Captain Coates

As the way of the Army, paperwork was an endless duty, and to fulfill this need an enrollee would be selected to provide clerical support; typically, this duty was performed by an enrollee who may be familiar with a typewriter or was learning to type in the camp education program. Third Corps Area Command issued a list of reports to be rendered by the camp commanders. These reports covered virtually every aspect of camp operations. The total number of reports to be maintained was seventy-four. These reports had varying submission requirements: daily, weekly, monthly, first day of month, last day of month, and on day of occurrence. One can easily see the camp commander, junior officers, and clerk had a busy schedule to maintain these reports and their many other camp duties.

O. R. Dooley

ALPHABETICAL LIST OF REPORTS

Rendered by

THIRD CORPS AREA C.C.C. COMPANIES

NAME	Form No.	When	Sub-District	Dist.	Hdqrs. 3rd C.A.	Fin. Office	Acct. Office	QM Gen.	Misc.	File	
1. Accident Report	ECW-1	1st of Month	1 Orig. 1 Copy							1 Copy	
2. Accident, Investigating Off. Report	27	Within 24 hrs.		1 Copy		If claim involved extra	may be make 3 copies	1 Orig.		1 Copy	See "Accidents", Sec.X Con. Instr. for Details
3. Accident, Report of Drivers	26	At Scene of Accident				If claim involved extra	may be make 3 copies		To Company Com'dr.		Attach to Investigating Off.'s Report
4. Active Duty Report, Final		When Off. Reverts to Inactive Status	1 Orig. 1 Copy with 2 copies of S.O.								
5. Active Duty Report, Initial.		When New Officer Reports From Inactive Status	1 Orig. 1 Copy with 2 copies of S.O.								
6. Bill of Lading.	1058 1058-A 1059	When Supplies are Shipped at Govt. Expense							1059 to Carrier Orig. and 1 copy to customer	1 Copy Yellow	
7. CA 2-C CA 3-C		When Injury Occurs		(1 copy to WRGH if Patient goes there)					U.S.Compensation Bureau 1 Orig.	1 Copy	Form CA 3-C Upon Return To Duty
8. Death of Enrollee, Report		Immediately	Notify		Telegram of Facts			Written Report of Disposition of Remains AR 30-1820 Par. 12	Notify Nearest Relative		See Consolidated Instructions
DISCHARGE RECORDS											
9. Copy of Final Statements	870	Within 48 Hours of Discharge						CCC Central Records Office, Detail on Building Fort McHenry, Baltimore, Md.	1 Copy		If Member of Sub-District Detachment, Records go to CCC Central Records Office, through the Sub-District.
10. Special Order											
11. Check List											
12. Individual Records	CCC Form 1-A and 1 & Appli. Memo.										
13. Letter of Transmittal									1 Copy		
14. Copy of Notification to Relief Board									1 Copy		
15. Copy of Special Order		Within 48 Hours of Discharge									
16. Final Statement	WD 870						All				
17. Disch. Cert.	CCC 2										
18. Letter of Transmittal										1 Copy	
19. Notification to Relief Board									To Local R.B. Concerned	1 Copy	
20. Educational Reports	Form 6 and Mimeo Form Program	1st Day of Month	1 Copy thru channels		Direct to Ed Ad. Hq. 3CA 1 Orig. 1 Copy					1 Copy of each	
21. Efficiency Reports	AGO 67	Within 10 days of Change of Status	1 Orig. 2 for Medical Office							None	Rendered on all Officers on June 30

Schedule of reports required by military commanders (reports 1-21)

NAME	Form No.	When	Sub-District	Dist.	Hdqrs. 3rd C.A.	Fin. Office	Asst. Office	QM Gen.	Misc.	File
22. Fuel Consumption		Jan.1 & July 1 Each Year			1 Orig. 1 Copy				1 Copy	See Letter, Report of CCC Activities, dated 1B-13-34
23. Funds, return of and Statement of Balances	C of F 458	When Paid Vouchers or Funds are Returned				1 Orig. 2 copies				1 Copy	Leave form 45-0 Attached (blank)
24. Hearing, Record of		Within 24 Hours of Hearing	1 Orig.& incls.in Appeals or Dismis'ls							1 Copy	
25. Hospitalization	Corps Orders.	At once when Res. Officer is hospitalized.	Notify: Telephone and Letter		Notify by wire						
26. Hospitalization, 24 Hr. Report		Within 24 Hours following Entry	1 Copy Medical Officer		1 Orig.	(This report required whenever any civilian medical services are obtained.)				1 Copy	Mimeographed Forms Secured from Hq., 3 C.A.
27. Inventory and Inspection Report	WD IGD No.1	Approximately Monthly	1 Orig. 1 Copy							1 Copy Tissue	Notify Sub-District when Property is ready for Inspection.
28. Medical Department Rep.	51	Last Day of Month			1 Orig. (Surgeon)					1 Copy	
29. Medical Supplies Consumed, Expendable	By Shipping ticket	First of Month			1 Orig. 2 copies to Surgeon					1 Copy	
30. Memorandum Receipts	QMC 487	Debits for Sup. Received Credit for Sup. Disposed					1 Orig. 1 Copy			1 Copy	Debit: Issued to Credit: Turned in by
31. Mess, Monthly Account	469	Entered Daily	Will Inspect Weekly		(C.O. to inspect daily. To have all entries by noon for day preceding.)					1 Copy with Mess Papers for Audit	
32. Mess, Daily Bill of Fare	340	Each Day (Optional)	Will Inspect Weekly		(Costs, etc., entered in form 469 before noon of day following.)					All copies available for Audit	
33. Morale Reports		To Arrive by 2nd of month	1 Orig.							1 Copy	Use latest Forms
34. Morning Report	WD AGO 1	Daily	For Inspection When Audit of Co. Fund is Made							1 Orig.	C.O. Must Initial Daily and compute rations.
35. Motor Vehicle Inspection by C.O.	Certificate	Last of Month	1 Orig.							1 Copy	
36. Motor Vehicle Inventory	258 and 255	Before Jan. 5th Each Year			1 Orig. 2 copies of each 258 and 255		1 Copy of each			1 Copy of each	
37. Motor Vehicle Record Book, Abstract	QMC 222	Before Jan.10th Each Year			Orig.					1 Copy	Submit Form QMC 248 to Sub-District Commander for Inspection
38. Obligations, Report of, with breakdown		1st Day of Month			1 Orig.					1 Copy	Mimeographed Form sent out by Hdqs. 3d C.A.
39. Officers, Roster of	AGO 9	To Arrive by 2nd of month	1 Orig. 1 Copy							1 Copy	
40. Open Market Purchases, with breakdown	WD Form 8	1st Day of Month			1 Orig. 2 copies					1 Copy	

Schedule of reports required by military commanders (reports 22-40)

NAME	Form No.	When	Sub-District	Dist.	Hdqrs. 3rd C.A.	Fin. Office	Acct. Office	Q.M. Gen.	Misc.	File	
41. Orders, leave		At once	1 Copy	1 Copy	1 Copy	1 Copy with Pay Voucher			1 Copy to Officer	1 Orig.	
42. Orders, Special	Numbered Consecutively from beginning Each year	As Needed	(Disposition depending on circumstances)							1 Orig.	
43. Over, Short and Damaged Report	QM 445	When Shipments are Short, Over, or Damaged.	(See Par. 4, AR 35-6640 for various disposition depending on circumstances.)							1 Copy.	
44. Pay Rolls	366 366A	By 22nd of Month				1 Orig. 2 copies				1 Copy	Names typed on second copy to F.O.
45. Pay Roll for Personal Services	Standard Form 1013	By 20th of Month				1 Orig. 1 Copy				1 Copy	For Civilians and Ed. Adv.
46. Pay Vouchers, with Certificates	WD 336 336A	By 20th of Month				1 Orig. 1 Copy				1 Copy tissue	
47. Physical Condition, Certificate of		With Final Active Duty Report	1 Orig.								See Consolidated Instructions for Form
48. Physical Examination	63 AGO	With Initial Active Duty Report	1 Orig.								
49. Purchase Orders	QMC 308	When Purchases are Made.	File copies available for inspection		QM 1 Copy unsigned	2 copies 1 signed		1 copy unsigned	1 Orig. To dealer concerned (signed)	1 Copy	Purchase Orders and Blotter inspected weekly by Sub-District Commander
50. Report of Company Fund	Corps Mimeo. Form	Before 10th of each Month	1 Copy							1 Copy	Bulletin Board
51. Ration Return	460	By 7th of Month			QM 1 Orig.					1 Copy	
52. Ration Savings Account. Beginning of Month	373	By 7th of Month			QM 1 Orig.					1 Copy	Computed Ration for coming month
53. Ration Savings Account, End of Month	373 375A	By 7th of Month				1 Orig. 3 copies				1 Copy	Shows Money due for the past month
54. Receiving Reports	QMC 431	When Supplies are Received				1 Orig. 1 Copy	1 Copy			1 Copy	Except on Shipping Ticket
55. Religious Reports		Following last Sunday in Month	1 Orig.	(Include in Morale Report)						1 Copy	
56. Requisitions	QMC 400	As Supplies are needed. Anticipate Needs. Equipment Form 230				1 Orig. 3 copies	(See letter, Hq. 3 CA dated Jan.4,1935, subject: "CCC Requisitions for Quartermaster Corps Supplies" to see whether you send to 3d Corps or New Cumberland)		New Cumberland 1 Orig. 3 Copies	1 Copy	
57. Sanitary Report		1st Day of Month			1 Orig. Surgeon					1 Copy	Mimeograph form from Hq. 3d C.A.
58. Shipments, Report of	Standard 9	1st Day of Month						1 Orig.		1 Copy	
59. Shipping Tickets	QMC 434	When Goods Are Shipped					1 Copy		1 Orig. 2 Copies to consignee	1 Copy	Also to Drop Non-Expendable Property at end of month
60. Sick and Wounded Report	52	Last Day of Month			1 Orig. (Surgeon)					1 Copy	
61. Statistical Report, Medical	86 ab	Every Friday	1 Orig. Med. Off.							1 Copy	
62. Status, Change of Officer, other than Leave or Corps Orders		At once	Telephone		Telegraph						

Schedule of reports required by military commanders (reports 41-62)

office machines
'62A on rental basis   *long*

NAME	Form No.	When	Sub-District	Dist.	Hdqrs. 3rd C.A.	Fin. Office	Acct. Office	QM Gen.	Misc.	File	
63. Strength Return, Monthly		1st day of month			1 Orig.					1 Copy	Mimeograph Form from 3 CA (Use latest)
64. Survey, Report of	WDAGO 15	Property Damaged or Lost			1 Orig. 2 copies					1 Copy	
65. Transportation Cert. for Passenger Travel	QMC 20?	When Needed For Auth. Travel				2 Copies FO Washington,D.C.			1 Orig. To Traveler	1 Copy	
66. Transportation Requests	Standard 1028	When Needed For auth. Travel	Special Order to accompany all copies			1 Copy FO, USA Trans.Br. Wash.,DC.			1 Orig. To Traveler	1 Copy	Exercise care in preserving Transportation Requests
67. Transportation Requests, Report of	Form 2	1st Day of Month						1 Copy	Orig. to C.L.Hunter,Chairman,Trunk Line Asso. 143 Liberty St. New York	1 Copy	
68. Transportation Requests and B/L, Report of	QMC 200	1st Day of Month							Orig.to QM Supply Officer Wash.Gen. Depot, Washington, D.C.	1 Copy	
69. Traveling Library		On 20th of month	(See Par.12, Sec.III, Page 5c, Consolidated Instructions. Accountability at Hq., 3d CA)								
70. Weekly Work Report		Each Monday			1 Orig. 1 Copy					1 Copy	Mimeograph Form from 3rd C.A. (Use latest)
71. War Dept. Procurement Authorities	W.D. 23	By 10th of Month if Possible			Duplicate copy				Orig.		Send when FO has paid on Purchase Orders. Forms 23 sent companies monthly by Hdqrs., 3d C.A
72. Fire Drills	Letter	Last Day of Month	1 Copy							1 Copy	
73. Expendable Supplies consumed	Shipping Ticket	Last Day of Month				1 Copy	2 Copies			1 Copy	Attach 2 Credit Memo. Receipts
74. Fire Prevention	Special Order	Or.Order and when changed	1 Copy	1 Copy	1 Copy					1 Copy	

CHRONOLOGICAL CHECK
(Numbers refer to Alphabetical List.)

Daily	Each Monday	Each Friday	Each Saturday	1st of month	By 7th of mo.	By 10th of Mo.	No.3 mo
31 32 34	70	61		1 40, 29 57, 29 56, 33 63, 38 67, 39 68 (If possible send on 1st)	51 52 53	71	62A

On 20th of Mo.		Before 22nd of month	Last Day of month	About Monthly	Semi-Annually Jan.1 & July 1	End of Year
45 46 69		44	35 72, 60 73	27	22	36 37

SPECIAL CHECK
(Numbers refer to Alphabetical List.)

When Officers Reports from Inactive Status	When Officer Reverts to Inactive Status	If Officer Leaves for another Station	If Officer Enters Hospital	
5, 48, 62	4, 21, 47, 62	21, 62	25, 26, 62	

When Enrollee is discharged	If Enrollee Enters Hospital	If Motor Accident Occurs, Army or Technical, if under Army control.	
9 13 17, 10 14 18, 11 15 19, 12 16	26	2, 3	

Schedule of reports required by military commanders (reports 63-74 with 62A added at top)

During early reunions I had the pleasure of meeting two of the officers who had served in Poe Valley. Then Lieutenants Owen Dooley and William Kelly shared their remembrances. Both men described what they thought was a simplified command structure, allowing flexibility on their part to solve most issues when they would arise. Mr. Dooley remembered how matters of discipline were so drastically reduced in the Poe Valley camp versus his experiences on an Army post. Mr. Kelly told me he was most surprised that even petty crimes, such as minor theft and simple assault, were almost nonexistent.

He remembered one particular occurrence when a significant number of pairs of boots turned up missing from supply. This loss (thought to be theft) occurred during a period of time when the camp commander was away. After exhaustive investigation on his part without gaining any knowledge of the boots' whereabouts, he was prepared to give the captain the disappointing news as soon as he returned. When starting to tell the captain of the matter after his return, the captain let him know he had the boots collected and sent out for repair and had failed to let anyone know, as the boots had left camp in the trunk of the captain's car.

Mr. Dooley felt he had contributed much more to the program in the off hours when he replaced his officer's hat with a teacher's hat in the classroom environment supporting the Emergency Conservation Work education program. He also shared his feelings about the "boys," who he felt were there with a sense of purpose and were most respectful of the military officers. In addition, he told me he and his fellow officers thought their jobs were by far easier than the foremen, as the foremen were the ones who spent most of the day directing and "herding the boys" out in the field away from the confines of the camp.

Mr. Dooley described the typical day in camp to be as follows: Six A.M. wake-up call for all of the enrollees, giving them time to get dressed and get into formation for morning calisthenics. After calisthenics, they were to get dressed, prepare for the day's work assignments, and go to the Mess Hall for breakfast. After breakfast, they would then be turned over to the camp superintendent and foreman, ready to go to work at 8:00 A.M.

Depending upon work assignments, the enrollees were brought back to camp for lunch in the Mess Hall at 12:00 P.M. or ate lunch in the field.

After lunch, they returned back to their work assignments. When the work day ended, the enrollees returned to camp at 5:00, at which time they were released back to camp military command. The enrollees were then required to clean up and change into their dress uniform and report to the Mess Hall for the evening meal at 5:30.

After the evening meal, the enrollees were then on their own time until 10:00 P.M. when it was "lights out."

Enrollees at formation

CHAPTER 2

JUNE 1933 - DECEMBER 1933

CAMP S-63 DEVELOPS

After going through a simplified process of induction into Emergency Conservation Work, the initial group of enrollees to take up temporary residency in Poe Valley formed up Emergency Conservation Work Company 1333 in Fort Howard, Maryland, consisted of 182 enrollees, 4 enlisted men, regular Army, and 3 military officers—Lieutenant David Carter Jr., US Army, Lieutenant Commander Arthur Beddoe, US Navy, and Medical Officer and Captain Charles McNair, US Army, commanding, departed Fort Howard on June 20, 1933, and traveled by train to Lewistown, then they "creeped over tracks that apparently had not been used in many years as evidenced by the groaning of unused railroad ties into Milroy," as recalled by Captain McNair in a letter written several years later.

Upon arrival in Milroy, they detrained, loaded up into rented trucks, and motored over the Siglerville Pike, a narrow, rutted, dirt roadway into Poe Valley, situated deep in the mountains of Central Pennsylvania. This was a location where no one in the company had visited prior to this trip.

These anxious, young men, now under the watchful eyes of the military commanders, immediately went about the business of setting up their new temporary tent encampment home away from home.

For most, this was their first time away from home for any extended period of time; additionally, they found themselves in a remote, unknown, forested, mountainous territory. I can well imagine for many they must have found themselves thinking, *What have I signed up for, and I am giving serious thought to getting out of here, if I only knew where I was.*

This first group of enrollees were all from Pennsylvania with the majority from Columbia, Lancaster, Kane, and Clarion counties where employment opportunities were most scarce.

For many of these young men, this new mountain environment would be their first experience in the great outdoors. The territory was foreign to everyone, and one can understand their trepidation and fears of being lost or chased by bears and other unknown critters.

For these first timers, there was no one to give them any tips or what to expect or advice about how things go in this experience.

Any concern for their remote position would pass soon enough, as a cadre of foremen working for the State Forestry Service awaiting arrival of the enrollees quickly went about their task of putting these young hands to work, thus taking their minds off of where they were.

Their first work would be the erection of the tent city, which was to be their temporary homes.

Next, they assisted in the construction of permanent, wooden barrack structures replacing the temporary tent encampment. Simultaneously, they improved the existing rough trails and roads into, around, and out of Poe Valley.

The wooden structures initially consisting of barracks, Mess Hall, headquarters, infirmary, shower house, Officers' Quarters, Forestry Quarters, shops, and service structures were constructed

Initial tent encampment - new Mess Hall is seen behind small trees

largely in part by these new enrollees under the guidance of the foremen.

The enrollees arriving first in camp were provided with this excellent opportunity to learn basic carpentry skills, all the while building their living quarters. Subsequent to the initial erection of camp facilities, forestry work and improvement to and construction of trails and roads were performed and completed by enrollees under the guidance of the foremen.

The same narrow-rutted, dirt roadway they first traveled on into Poe Valley was significantly improved by this first group of enrollees using nothing more than picks, shovels, and digging bars, all the while walking several miles to the worksite and back to camp each day as trucks to transport the enrollees was not made available for nearly another two years.

The foremen providing the guidance were local men employed by the Pennsylvania Department of Forests and Waters through the US Department of Agriculture. Additionally, the foremen were supported by a smaller group of individuals who were commonly referred to as LEMs or Local Employed Men.

These foremen and LEMs were selected through varying interests for their skills and capabilities to meet the needs of the work anticipated to be performed in the camp. Most of these men had

Technical personnel in front of Forestry Quarters (Left to right: Robert Auman, Foreman; John C. Smith, Forester; Sumner Frankenberger, Senior Foreman; Amos Bennett, Engineer; William Throstle, Foreman; Luther Weaver, Superintendent; Miles Bressler, Foreman; Franklin Auman, Foreman)

backgrounds in the forestry services, lumbering, technical skills like carpentry, masonry and mechanics, and other related needed skills.

Foremen and LEMs were also hired to fulfill specific needs, as was the case in Poe Valley, where a blacksmith was required. The

TELEPHONES
REEDSVILLE EXCH.
20-21 · · · OFFICE
20-22 · · · RESIDENCE

THOS. C. HARBESON
DISTRICT FORESTER

PENNSYLVANIA
DEPARTMENT OF FORESTS AND WATERS
PENN FOREST DISTRICT

MILROY, PA.

FILE

June 22, 1933

Mr. Sumner Frankenberger,
Millheim, Penna.

Dear Sir:

    This is to notify you that you have been selected as a foreman in E. C. W. Camp number __63__ . This selection is contingent upon your being fully qualified to satisfactorily perform the work assigned by your Superintendent and by continuing to set a high example for your men in regards to moral conduct and temperate habits.

    You will report to your camp Superintendent at the above numbered camp in ___Poe Valley.___ , when notified. This may not be until July 1 or later.

Very truly yours,

T. C. Harbeson

L. L. Weaver will be Supt.

PREVENT FOREST FIRES---IT PAYS

Initial appointment letter for foreman Sumner Frankenberger

blacksmith was required not to make iron shoes for horses, but to pound out tools, shape wooden handles, and shape hardware items specifically required in the works of forestry services and the various construction projects to follow.

For this time period, it was more economical to have a "smithy" make specialty tools and hardware items on site than to purchase these items. More importantly, a smithy could fill an order for a needed tool or make modifications to improve performance of a tool the same day needed, keeping enrollees on the job additionally meeting project schedules.

These foremen were paid on a monthly basis. The pay scale varied apparently based on experience and skills. The foremen

Foreman Robert Auman (right) also served as camp blacksmith

were required to meet and maintain certain requirements and standards while in service. My grandfather remained in the position of foreman at the same pay rate for a period of twenty-nine months. He was then appointed to the position of senior foreman in December 1935 with a salary increase to $155.00 per month.

COMMONWEALTH OF PENNSYLVANIA
DEPARTMENT OF FORESTS AND WATERS
HARRISBURG

November 6, 1935

Mr. Sumner Frankenberger
C.C.C. Camp S-63
Coburn, Penna.

Dear Mr. Frankenberger:

I am glad to advise you of the final approval in Washington of your promotion to the position of Foreman, effective December 1, 1935 at a salary of $155 a month. This promotion is contingent on you being able to handle the work satisfactorily. At the end of a sixty day probationary period the District Forester will make a report and recommend you continuance or discontinuance in this position.

Very truly yours,

John W. Keller,
State Forester

PREVENT FOREST FIRES---IT PAYS

Promotion letter for Foreman Sumner Frankenberger

A camp engineer employed by the Pennsylvania Department of Forests and Waters through the US Department of Agriculture was also engaged to support the development of an Emergency Conservation Work camp. The engineer assisted with development, design, and engineering of the camp footprint. Initially, the engineer was charged with developing the campsite to include placement of all camp structures, roadways, pathways, and specific site needs. Additionally, the engineer needed to implement a water supply system, an electric power supply and distribution, a sewer system, and any other camp-specific utility needs. The remote location of Poe Valley did not allow for simple connection to any existing local utility service provider. The electric power supply was created via a gas-powered generator. A nearby freshwater spring was selected to provide the camps potable water, and a conventional, on-site, in-ground sewer system was developed. The camp engineer detailed the various design parameters for the camp, and subsequently the camp superintendent in turn directed the construction of these elements. The construction of the facilities and the utility systems was then performed by enrollees under the direct supervision of the camp foremen and the camp engineer. The first engineer in camp to support the work was Mr. L. E. Wilson.

A forester employed by the state Department of Forest and Waters was assigned to the camp. The forester was charged with establishing the forest conservation projects the enrollees had signed on to perform. These projects included timber surveys, timber conservation, fire protection, disease eradication, reforestation, and timber stand improvement. The forester was on site June 21, 1933, when the first enrollees arrived, coordinating and directing all conservation measures the enrollees were engaged in.

Pennsylvania, preceding The Depression era, was deemed to be progressive in forestry management, having an established Silviculture program. In 1923 the state Forestry Department became the Department of Forest and Waters, and the Bureau of State Parks was formed in 1929. These developments happened under the watchful guidance of the well-respected former leader of the US Forest Service—Gifford Pinchot. Gifford Pinchot, the state forester for Pennsylvania at that time, had a cadre of foresters in Pennsylvania's regional forests able to step in and fill many of the forester positions in the CCC camps. Subsequent to this service, Gifford Pinchot became a two-time governor for Pennsylvania.

When reviewing various documents related to personnel in Emergency Conservation Work one quickly finds interchangeable titles for the same position. In many instances the camp foremen, forester, superintendent, engineer, LEMs, and sometimes the education advisor would be referred to as "technical personnel" or "supervisory personnel" and in other locales "skilled personnel" and many times "camp administrators."

Salaries for these personnel also were not a fixed amount. Salary could and in most instances would vary between camps in the various districts and regions.

Form No. 3

EMERGENCY CONSERVATION WORK CAMPS

(Note.—This report to be filled on first visit to camp only, unless further request is made)

Camp No. S-63

State of Penna.

FORESTRY PERSONNEL

Fill in on this sheet, name of forest supervisors, not enrolled men, and amount of salary they receive.

NAME	OCCUPATION	SALARY
Auman, Edward R.	Blacksmith	$110.00
Auman, F. B.	J.F.C.M.	140.00
Bennett, Amos T.	J.C.E. *Resigned but on payroll.*	166.66
Lewis, Oscar S.	J.C.E. *On Leave without Pay.*	166.66
Bressler, Miles	J.F.C.M.	140.00
Frankenberger, Sumner	F.C.M.	155.00
Neese, Harry S.	Mechanic	120.00
Smith, John E.	J.F.	166.66
Throssel, W. J.	J.F.C.M.	140.00
Vonada, Paul W.	Skilled Worker Shovel Operator	150.00
Wert, Ralph L.	Squad Foreman	100.00
Weaver, L. L.	C.F.C.M.	216.66
Guisewite, H.S.	Machine Operator	120.00

U. S. GOVERNMENT PRINTING OFFICE: 1934   16—2457

Salaries of the camp technical personnel

Forestry Quarters where technical personnel resided

The foremen lived in the camp in the forestry quarters structure along with the assigned state forester. Additionally, the camp superintendent and camp engineer resided in this same structure.

In these quarters the occupants paid a variable rate fee for each meal and a fixed fee per month for accommodations. Receipts found in my grandfather's trunk reflected the cost for three meals a day ranged between thirty-five cents and forty-three cents per day, and accommodations in the forester quarters were five dollars per month.

Meal receipts for Foreman Sumner Frankenberger

```
ECW-S
Personnel
Pennsylvania


  Sumner Frankenberger
  Camp S-63
  Coburn, Pa.


  Dear Sir:

         You are advised that, effective _____ May 1st, _____ 1937,
  and until further notice, a payroll deduction of $ _5.00_____
  will be made each month from your salary while you have available
  for occupancy Government owned quarters described as _____

  _____ Class A _____.
```

R LYNN EMERICK
Procurement Officer

Quarters receipt for Foreman Sumner Frankenberger

I knew the financial effects of The Depression were the driving force for my grandfather choosing to become an Emergency Conservation Work camp foreman. Until recently, I did not know any of the specific financial conditions tipping my grandfather to make this life choice. Now, a most cherished anniversary present, my dear wife presented me with copies of my grandfather's US Department of Agriculture service records. In these records is a single-page resume of my grandfather's employment history leading up to the time he entered into the Corps. These records reflect his employment in the months and years before being selected to be a foreman in a Civilian Conservation Corps camp. Just prior to entering into the Corps, he was working as a carpenter at the rate of $0.35 per hour. These same records reflect he was working as a heavy machine operator at the rate of $0.60 per hour in 1929 before the now-infamous stock market crash of 1929 plunging America into The Great Depression.

To me, these records clearly indicate why he chose to sign on as a foreman in a Civilian Conservation Corps camp—the significant pay increase from $0.35 per hour as a carpenter to $0.88 per hour as a foreman in the camp in the summer of 1933.

These same records indicate how The Depression had harshly impacted my grandfather's family. For the period 1918 through 1931, my grandfather was the owner operator of a thrashing and sawmilling business. The acquired resume states the business was "sold due to depression."

Form P-8-ECW
ECW-S
Personnel
Pennsylvania

Date __July, 1, 1937.__

Camp No. __S-63__ __Coburn,__ __Pa.__

Name __Frankenberger__ , __Sumner__ , Title __Foreman__ Grade _____
       Surname   Given name Initial

Home Address _____ __Millheim__ __Centre__ __Penna.__
       Number & Street Post-Office County State

Age __37__ Color __White__ Married __Yes__ Single _____

No. of Children __One__ Other Dependents __None__ Health __Good__

Any Physical Handicap? __None__

EDUCATION:

Grammar School Attended __Yes__ Year Graduated __1915__

High School Attended _____ Year Graduated _____

College or University Attended _____ Year Graduated _____

Specialized in What Course _____ Degrees Rec'd _____

Trade Learned or Other Training __Carpentry, Extension course on Highway Engineering__
                           __and Machine Operating.__

Experience since Beginning Work: (Give employer's name and address, position held, duties, salary, period of employment and reason for leaving for each position held - use separate sheet if necessary)
__Farmers Thrashing Co..C. F. Stover Pres. Millheim, Penna__1915 - 1916 @ $ ###.50 per day. Year 1917 Operator @ $ 1.00 per day.

__Owner and Operator Thrashing and Saw-Milling 1918-1931 and sold due to depression.__

In springs of 1918 - 1929 worked for Penn Townshtp Road Supervisiors On road with Tractor,

Summer of 1929 for D. A. Kessler Road Contractor, Mount Carmel, Penna. Machine Operator @ $ .60 per hour.

Year 1931-1933 Carpentry Trade,Employer J. W. Bright, Millheim, Penna. @ $ .35 per hour.

Started June, 26, 1933. E. C. W. Camp S-63. as Jr. Foreman, was promoted to Foreman December 1935. Jr Foreman @ $ 140.00 per month. Foreman @ $ 155.00 per month.

Submit in quadruplicate-all copies signed in ink _____
                                        Signature

Resume of Foreman Sumner Frankenberger

The organizational charting of the Poe Valley camp was not complicated, as was the general way of the Emergency Conservation Work program. In some ways, the camp was often referred to as a "fly by the seat of your pants" outfit, generally meaning we will figure out how to do what we want to accomplish as we proceed.

The camp superintendent, independent to the military management team, was responsible for proposing camp-specific conservation projects to state forestry administration officials, who in turn directed the forester and superintendent on what conservation measures were to be performed.

The state forester and the camp engineer were also independent to the military management team in the camp. In camp, the forester and the engineer were responsible for further developing and coordinating work details to be implemented by the enrollees in accordance with recommended tasks assigned by the regional state forester with the camp superintendent.

The superintendent then issued directives to the foremen for execution of the conservation work selected to be performed.

A foreman would then guide twenty to thirty enrollees around camp or out into the forests, providing instruction on the work assignments for the day. This in-camp group of foremen also totally independent to the military management team, with the administration support of the Pennsylvania State Department of Forests and Waters, had the general responsibility of organization and execution of assigned conservation work projects during a typical enrollee eight-hour workday period.

The Army had a larger scale responsibility, as they were required to provide and maintain the overall general health and welfare of the enrollees. In camp, this was organized and accomplished generally through the effort of the three assigned US military officers. These military officers were similar to the enrollees in one respect: their assignment to camp was for a typical six-month hitch.

Immediately after disembarking from the train in Milroy, the Army and enrollee convoy moved into camp, prepared with tents, cots, mattresses, mess kits, enrollee issue kits covering toilet and showering needs, plus necessary equipment for a field kitchen mess. Additionally, the company arrived with enlisted noncommissioned Army officers, who performed and directed the field kitchen setup to include a seasoned mess sergeant and assistant plus two skilled truck drivers. The commissioned Army

US Military Officers - Camp Commanders (Left to right: Liuetenant Pennes, Lieutenant Fox, Lieutenant Price, and Education Advisor Mr. Dean)

officers and the noncommissioned Army officers immediately went about organization and direct set up of the encampment. These noncommissioned officers held the rank of sergeant, bringing with them the experience needed to take charge of the "totally green" enrollees in the early days of establishing the encampment. These sergeants had the knowledge and experience needed to direct the enrollees in erecting tents, set up of a field mess kitchen, erect potable water lister bags, establish a waste latrine plot, and all other necessary services to meet the initial needs of the first inhabitants of Camp S-63. One can well imagine how heavily these new enrollees had to rely on the skills of these sergeants. In the span of one afternoon and evening time period, on a summer day before darkness set in, tents needed to be erected for shelter, food required preparation and serving, a potable water source needed to be located, and field latrine established all by 160 enrollees who had absolutely no experience in these regards.

In advance, the Army made preparation for the acquisition of necessary staples to feed the company. These staples to include the necessary gear for preparation would come from the New Cumberland Army Depot and arrive simultaneously with the company in Poe Valley by truck.

Within twenty-four hours, the Army mess sergeant and the company commander negotiated with local merchants for fresh food supplies, such as milk, butter, bread, fruits, vegetables, and other perishables. Supply of needed fresh foods was contracted with local vendors throughout the life of the camp. Canned foods, boxed foods in bulk, and nonperishable food supplies came from the main Army Depot throughout the life of the camp.

Captain Charles H. McNair was the first commanding officer in Camp S-63. These military officers, along with the support of district and regional military commands, fulfilled the enrollees' day-to-day basic needs. This included all mess provisions, clothing, footgear, bunks and bedding, laundry, infirmary care, medical and dental needs, mail, canteen, physical exercise, recreation programs, and transportation. I believe for this part to say the Army was operating "on the fly" would in no way be a true assessment as the mobilization and providing for the needs of large numbers of men into unknown territory was standard order of business for the US military.

In the camp, these officers lived in separate quarters and took their meals in their quarters, as is the way of the US Army. An enrollee was selected to be a steward to the officers, taking care of quarters, mess, laundry duties, and keeping firewood ready at the fireplace. This fireplace was the only source of heat in the Officers' Quarters.

Fire was ever present on the minds of all in camp, and all-night fire-watch duty was assigned to the enrollees in the barracks on a rotational basis. Records available to me indicate no fire was ever recorded to have occurred in a barracks facility in Poe Valley.

Officers' Quarters (right foreground) standing prior to fire

All that remains of Officers' Quarters after fire in stone chimney and fireplace

Photos, however, suggest a fire watch apparently was not duty maintained in the Officers' Quarters, as the photos indicate the Officers' Quarters burned to the ground. The photograph chronology indicate the fire occurred in the winter period 1935. A new Officers' Quarters structure was subsequently constructed, salvaging the original masonry fireplace.

Photographs also depict fire was subject to a separate camp facility believed to be the supply room adjacent to the Mess Hall. The fire was retarded by camp enrollees saving the structure. The fire suppression system in camp consisted of fifty-five-gallon drums filled with water positioned outside of each camp structure.

Partially burned supply room

When Camp S-63 was established, there was one primary, rough, dirt roadway into Poe Valley. This roadway, known as the Millheim-Siglerville Pike, winds its way through the scenic seven mountains from Siglerville in the south into Poe Valley, and then winds its way northward to Millheim, passing through Coburn. From the north and west were a few rough trails barely passable by motor vehicle. Soon, these pathways became widened, straightened, and graded into roadways, through the efforts of Emergency Conservation Work, Camp S-63.

Initial camp establishment work projects equally important to the erection of the wooden barracks and related structures were the improvement of trails and building of roads providing access to and from Poe Valley. The task of road improvement and construction of new roads was made a part of the conservation work to be performed by the enrollees under the guidance of the foremen. This work commenced simultaneously with the conservation work activity. In the beginning, road construction activity was for the most part performed by these young enrollees using a pick and shovel, wheelbarrow, and "earthmover," commonly known as dynamite. My grandfather enjoyed using the term "earthmover" in lieu of dynamite and would tell of "earthmoving" days where the standard safety protocols were to simply "duck and take cover" behind trees and rocks while blasting tree stumps and huge rocks out of the way to clear the path for a new roadway. The program provided

Road building crew

Road building crew with crawler tractor supporting construction, enrollee Norman Wingard standing in front of tractor

written directives for the storage and transportation of dynamite in camp, however, they apparently relied on the foremen to provide instruction on the use and handling of dynamite and implementation of safety measures out in the field among the "boys."

I can remember thinking, *That sounds like a great job to have when I am older.* Then he would continue describing their tools of the trade and efforts while doing road-building work. These tools were two man crosscut saws, picks, shovels, steel pry bars, heavy sledge hammers, wheel barrows, and one powered tractor, and again, I can remember thinking this sounds like something fun to do. In my mind, the picture was one of being on a camping trip, no parents, no big brother, and no teachers telling me what to do, just spending all my time with my grandfather, who pretty much allowed me to do almost anything I asked and bought me a bottle of R C Cola almost every day. When he started telling these stories, I was eight to ten years old. Later, after becoming a teenager and on the operating end of a pick and shovel a few times, the desire to be one of my grandfather's "boys" had pretty much gone away.

In the beginning, the Poe Valley camp along with all other camps around the country were finding their way and would find the necessity for differing types of equipment to help with the operations of the camp and the work projects. Trucks of every sort were needed for numerous tasks. Enrollees needed to be transported out of camp and back and taken to project locations. Provisions needed to be picked up and brought into camp. And materials needed moved around, in addition to many other needs.

The Army provided two one-and-a-half-ton stake-body trucks to support the camp. The state was required to supply any additional trucks the camp would require. Additionally, as the camp work schedules and tasks were developed, the equipment needs to support them also needed to be supplied by the state. These vehicles were slow in coming in the beginning due to the mass development of more than seventy camps in the state needing the same or similar equipment.

The main mode of transport for the enrollees was dual-wheeled, one-and-a-half-ton stake-body-style trucks. These trucks carried the enrollees everywhere, as was necessary. In Poe Valley, for the first few months there would only be the two trucks available for use supplied by the Army. These vehicles were driven by enlisted military members who had been assigned to the camp by the Army. In Poe Valley, two military drivers were assigned. Locals well remember the vision of more than twenty enrollees standing up in the back of the trucks on the way to town. Wendell "Chappy" Musser of Coburn, PA, remembers thinking they reminded him of "cordwood stacked in the back as there were so many guys standing up in the back of the truck when they passed by."

For those first early months, each day, the foremen and the enrollees would "hoof it" from camp to their assigned work project locations. In many cases, three or more miles from camp. They then had to "hoof it" back to camp at the end of the day's work.

Eventually, more trucks were assigned to the camp by the state. These trucks, similar in size to the Army trucks, were then used to ferry the enrollees and the foremen to their project locations and haul materials needed in their work. The distinct difference between the state trucks and the Army trucks were the color of the truck. The Army vehicles were Army green. The color of state-supplied trucks was conventional black. State-supplied trucks bore license plates stamped "US CCC." Army truck plates were stamped "War Department."

In the early operational period, all in the Poe Valley camp shared one common experience—every thing, every day was a new experience. For these new enrollees, the challenges and

CCC truck driver and enrollee Kermit Wolfe

hardships being experienced back home, mostly the result of un-precedented economic loss, were, while in camp, replaced with the challenges of being away from home in unfamiliar surround-ings, learning to get along in an environment with all-new faces and an all-new way of living. They were now performing assigned, not chosen, work tasks eight hours a day.

In the beginning of the Emergency Conservation Work, the enrollee signed on for a six-month time period. By the end of their enrollment period, this first group of enrollees had established themselves a record of accomplishment and shared an experience like no other.

Collectively, they had fully cleared the lands and constructed the initial wooden structures as required for the establishment of Emergency Conservation Work Camp S-63 Poe Valley. This included creating pathways and roadways within the boundaries of the camp and state forest lands. Individually, the enrollees had acquired job skills, developed new friendships, and learned how to adjust into the regimental ways of the Army, all the while away from home, living deep in the forest of Central Pennsylvania, and most importantly providing support to loved ones back home.

A review of records available and commentary provided in camp documents describe the Poe Valley Emergency Conservation Work camp successful, receiving consistent, satisfactory, or superior ratings from state and federal inspectors. I believe the overall success at Poe Valley Camp S-63, Company 1333 was in part due to the general simplification of establishing those who would be in charge. The US Army had the responsibility to provide for the general welfare of the enrollee while in the camp area under guidance of the War Department. The technical personnel had the responsibility to organize and manage the enrollees in their work projects while out of the camp area under guidance of the agriculture department. This simplification was how most other camps in Pennsylvania operated.

Those early noncommissioned Army officers who accompanied the company from Ft. Howard and had directed the initial establishment of the camp were relieved of their Emergency Conservation Work duty and returned back to duty in the regular Army. These noncommissioned officers had been selected for their specialized skills in food preparation, field services, truck driving, and military organization. These noncommissioned officers while in camp were also charged with training selected enrollees to be their replacements.

Records indicate the noncommissioned officers departed the Poe Valley camp in early 1935. By this time the CCC program had evolved to include sending selected enrollees to military training centers for various occupations, particularly to cooks and bakers training. From this time forward the cooking and baking duties in the camp would mostly be performed by trained enrollees. Many enrollees took cooking and baking training received while in the CCC camps and advanced upon these skills, becoming cooks, bakers, restaurant managers, and owners in their future, lifelong occupations.

Emergency Conservation Work took place in all forty-eight states. The Army established nine separate Corps areas for implementation of the program. Each Corps area was subsequently divided into districts and subdistricts. Headquarters would be established in each of the Corps, district, and subdistrict locations where assigned Army officers coordinated the tasks assigned to the military. In 1936 the Poe Valley camp was a part of the Third Corps Area, District No. 1, Sub-District No. 4, having its headquarters located in the US post office building in Williamsport, PA. Reorganization and consolidation of camps occurred within the subdistricts, however, the camp would always remain in District No. 1, Third Corps Area.

The names of the military commanders in these positions change on a rotational basis. Active duty military commanders and reserve officers brought back on duty and assigned to these headquarter locations also served in these positions for a six-month period. Many of these military commanders remained in service to the program and reassigned to other Corps locations. One of the names, however, not changing in the military command structure would be the man to serve in the top Army command position, Army Chief of Staff General Douglas MacArthur. General MacArthur of World War Two fame was one of five military commanders to be awarded the 5-star rank of general of the Army.

Of concern to those responsible for enrollment at the local levels would be the "local men." These "local men" being men who worked the forest in their locality who were now also unemployed due to the economic downturn in lumbering. The concern was these local, unemployed lumbermen would perceive others were given jobs in their forests where they worked and made their living. The anticipated result leading to actions taken by these unemployed locals that were disruptive to camp development and safety.

To address this concern, administrators directed a course of action to make a special supplemental provision for enrollment of those unemployed lumbermen. Enrollment officials at the local levels were authorized to include enrollment of up to eight of these local unemployed lumbermen into the camps. This decision supported the program in two specific ways. One being to satisfy the concern regarding negative reactions of those local unemployed lumbermen. The other and maybe more important reason was these local men had the much-needed knowledge and experience of the forests where the camps were being set up. Their knowledge and experience could be used to support the technical needs associated with the forestry work to be performed by camp.

This small group of enrollees were enrolled as Local Experienced Men, more commonly known as LEMs. At no time when stories were shared with me was I made aware of any specific names of enrollees being enrolled as LEMs in the Poe Valley camp. There is no mention of LEMs in the documents I hold or those I was able to review during my research in preparation of this writing.

CHAPTER 3

INITIAL ACCOMPLISHMENT

In the beginning of the Emergency Conservation Work the first group of 186 enrollees had signed up for a six-month enrollment period. By the end of their enrollment period, this first group of enrollees had established for themselves a record of accomplishment. Collectively, they had fully cleared the lands and constructed the initial wooden structures as required for the site development of Emergency Conservation Work Camp S-63 Poe Valley. This included creating pathways and roadways within the boundaries of the camp and water, power, and sewer infrastructure.

The records indicate the Mess Hall was completed and dedicated on September 20, 1933, and before Christmas 1933 the first group of enrollees had completed construction of barrack structures, quarters for military personnel, infirmary, a shower house, found water, and walled up a reservoir. Individually, many of these enrollees had acquired their first full-time job and provided support to loved ones back home and maybe more importantly had developed a more positive sense of self-worth and character development.

Furthermore, this first group of enrollees would be discharged at the end of 1933. These enrollees now had a document in testament of their accomplishment as a certificate of discharge was issued upon completion of their enlistment period.

Also, this first class of fresh, young enrollees in Emergency Conservation Work at Camp S-63 had acquired basic technical skills in carpentry, masonry, and road building and would be departing Poe Valley to go back home where these newly acquired skills could hold promise of a brighter future. The small collection of successes in the first stage of work for Camp S-63 and more than seventy-five other camps throughout Pennsylvania held

Certificate of Discharge

from

Civilian Conservation Corps

TO ALL WHOM IT MAY CONCERN:

THIS IS TO CERTIFY THAT *ASS'T LEADER SAMUEL A. WISE , CC-310458 , A MEMBER OF THE

CIVILIAN CONSERVATION CORPS, WHO WAS ENROLLED ___October 11th, 1934___ AT
(Date)

___Poe Valley Camp S-63,Coburn,Penna.__IS HEREBY DISCHARGED THEREFROM, BY REASON

OF ** _____Expiration of term of enrollment._____

SAID Ass't Leader Samuel A. Wise___ WAS BORN IN ___Spring Mills,___

IN THE STATE OF ___Pennsylvania___ WHEN ENROLLED HE WAS ___Nineteen___ YEARS

OF AGE AND BY OCCUPATION A ___Laborer___ HE HAD Blue-grey___ EYES,

Light___ HAIR, ___Fair___ COMPLEXION, AND WAS ___Five___ FEET

___11½___ INCHES IN HEIGHT. HIS COLOR WAS ___White___

GIVEN UNDER MY HAND AT Camp S-63, Coburn, Penna. THIS ___Thirtieth___ DAY

OF ___September___, ONE THOUSAND NINE HUNDRED AND ___Thirty-six___

(Name)   (Title)

EDWARD R. AYRES, Capt. Cav-Res., Commanding.

C. C. C. Form No. 2
April 5, 1933

*Insert name, as "John J. Doe".
**Give reason for discharge.

3—10171

Enrollees' certificate of discharge (front side)

bright promise for the program. This group accepted the challenge of going into the unknown and accepted charge and direction from foremen they generally held in high regard, all the while living within the organizational structure of the US Army. I would indeed think this is certainly a measure in success.

Much more was yet to come. The next group of young faces was in route to replace the departing enrollees. They were being sent in

RECORD OF SERVICE IN CIVILIAN CONSERVATION CORPS

**Served:
a. From .10/11/34...... to .9/30/36........., under .Agriculture... Dept. at .Camp..S-63,Coburn,Pa.
          Roadbuilding &
Type of work .Dam.Project................ * Manner of performance ....Very..Satisfactory.......

b. From .... to ...., under .... Dept. at ....

Type of work .... * Manner of performance.................

c. From .... to ...., under .... Dept. at ....

Type of work .... * Manner of performance.................

d. From .... to ...., under .... Dept. at ....

Type of work .... * Manner of performance.................

e. From .... to ...., under .... Dept. at ....

Type of work .... * Manner of performance.................

Remarks:Honorably..discharged..September..30,.1936...Last..paid.to..include.Sept.30,.1936

.....The.Project..Sup't.Mr..L..L..Weaver,.Millheim,.Penna.,.makes.the.following

.....estimate.of.Ass't.Leader.Wise.as.a.workman.:..."1.Very..Satisfactory."

.....Immunization.completed:..10/29/34..Typhoid.&.para-typhoid:..10/22/34.
.....Smallpox:..10/15/34
.....Selecting.Agency.notified.of.discharge.

.....Enrollee.notified.of.ineligibility.for.reselection.for.a.period.of.one.
.....year.from.date.of.discharge.

.....Provisions.of.the.Federal.Compnesation.Act.have.been...read.to.this.man.

.....Due.U.S..for.C&E:..None..Due.Camp.Exchange,.1333rd.Company.Ys:.None.

Discharged:.September.30,.1936................. at .Camp..S-63,.Coburn,.Penna.

Transportation furnished from ...Camp.S-63,Coburn,Pa................. to ......Coburn,Penna,.by.truck.
                                                                          transportation.

(Name)   (Title)
*Use words "Excellent", "Satisfactory", or "Unsatisfactory".   EDWARD R. AYRES, Capt. Cav-Res., Commanding.
**To be taken from O. C. C. Form No. 1.

U. S. GOVERNMENT PRINTING OFFICE   8—10171

Enrollees' certificate of discharge (back side)

from various locations throughout the state, however, there had already been significant requests by enrollees to sign on again for another six-month hitch. The general approval rating of the program by the public and certainly by enrollees quickly had officials giving consideration to program rules so as to allow reenlistment.

These new enrollees had all shared in the excitement that came with their first payday. Payday came once a month. Enrollees were paid $30.00 per month for their service. The enrollee received $5.00 cash, and a $25.00 allotment was sent back home. For so many of the families back home, the allotment was a life saver, helping to pay for food and all other sorts of needs. These allotments helped to shine a beacon of hope on an economically dispirited nation.

During reunions, veterans shared, in many instances with emotion, the conditions and experiences ongoing back home of how desperate their families were and that these allotments did indeed put food on the table and coal in the bin.

In the initial years of the program at the end of an enrollee's "hitch" (enrollment period) or every six months, a new enrollee took the place of the outgoing enrollee. These replacements found themselves simply taking over where the others left off, taking on new challenges themselves.

Generally, during the first camp enrollee transition periods, foremen's names in the camp would remain the same, however, the names of enrollees and military personnel most certainly changed as their enlistment period had come to an end at the end of December 1933.

During the first two enrollment periods, additional structures continued to be erected between January 1934 and June 1935, thereby completing the initial camp layout plan developed by the camp engineer. This work included a generator building, headquarters building, incinerator, blacksmith shop, water reservoir, and a Recreation Hall.

Enrollees carrying their duffel bags after arriving in camp via truck

Headquarters

Officer Quarters

Forestry Quarters

Mess Hall

Mess Hall interior

Barracks building

Barracks building interior, set up and maintained in the Army way

Recreation Hall

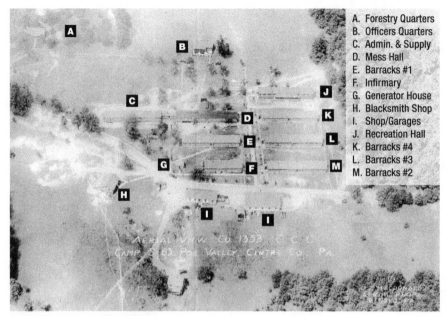

A. Forestry Quarters
B. Officers Quarters
C. Admin. & Supply
D. Mess Hall
E. Barracks #1
F. Infirmary
G. Generator House
H. Blacksmith Shop
I. Shop/Garages
J. Recreation Hall
K. Barracks #4
L. Barracks #3
M. Barracks #2

Aerial view of camp, circa 1936

All the while, work on road building and forestry improvement continued at a "hectic pace," Veteran Ray Hazel remembered, so as to beat the winter weather.

With the completion of the initial camp structures, the focus to commence forestry conservation and management services along with road-building work took a forefront in the daily work schedule. This work schedule included trail development, tree inventory, tree planting, eradication of unwanted harmful vegetation, and the many chores of forestry management as prescribed by the camp forester. During the winter periods, roadbuilding slowed due to weather factors. On those days when performing forestry management work and road building, this work was typically located several miles from camp. The men were loaded onto trucks and hauled out to the work site for the day, then picked up at the end of the work day. Foremen organized the day's schedule, making sure needed hand tools were in the trucks and providing instruction on what to do, in order to show these "city boys" how to properly swing an axe or push and pull a two-man crosscut saw.

My grandpa commented many times about how many of the enrollees had little or no experience on handling most of the tools

Enrollees with a two-man crosscut saw, tool of their trade

they were required to handle when they came into camp. He was proud of the way many of the enrollees, after being properly instructed on handling of these forestry and road-building tools, took the lead in demonstrating the proper "how to" way and wanted to take the lead in "showing off" their learned skills while training the new guys coming into camp. Let me make it clear here that I am referring to the handling of axes, digging shovels, digging picks, crosscut saws, and other callous-forming, muscle-building, and sweat-raising tools.

These young men were not handling the small tools for the trade of today where almost any tool is either powered by a gas or electric motor such as chain saws, powered trimmers, and powered loading equipment, such as motored track loaders and backhoes. In the Emergency Conservation Work camp, the trees were felled with two-man, crosscut saws and double-bit axes, and gravel for roadbeds was shovel loaded and shovel off-loaded by hand using one-and-a-half-ton, flatbed trucks before dump trucks eventually arrived.

When the enrollees were on work projects away from camp, their lunch was brought to them by mess stewards on service

Digging shale loose in shale pit with picks and loading trucks with shovels by hand

trucks. When lunchtime came around, the primary concern would be "is the lunch truck on time" today? Typically, the mess cooks prepared a nourishing, warm meal and had it sent out to these hungry, young men in insulated canisters to be served at the lunch break.

The foremen also ate whatever was being served alongside the men. The only difference was the foremen had to pay for this meal, while the enrollee did not. My grandfather took delight in an enrollee who expressed dissatisfaction in the cooks' choice that day by reminding the disgruntled enrollee that at least he did not have to pay for something he did not like.

Another learning process in the camp was to make sure the enrollee truck driver knew for sure where he was going, particularly if it was the chow truck. These young men were traveling on mostly unmarked mountain roads, in an unknown forest, without the benefit of a well-drafted map or compass. One can easily imagine how taking a wrong turn might occur, making the chow truck a bit late every once in a while. Foremen quickly learned a most important part of their daily scheduling was to be certain truck drivers either knew where they were going or had a "shotgun" driver who knew which turn to take.

Food aplenty was a significant selling point for potential recruitment, where the promise of three meals a day in many cases contributed heavily to the signing of a new enrollee.

Line up for chow at lunch truck out in the field

During reunions, food stories were plentiful with many describing a positive experience about meal quality and quantity, and conversely there were many a story about food troubles.

One of these food-trouble stories told by enrollee Randall Boob went something like this:

> I went to the Mess Hall for my first evening meal where each table was set up with tableware and food in bowls and on plates to accommodate 8, after waiting for the chow whistle to blow indicating commencement to eat I was shocked at how quickly all of the food sitting on the table was grabbed at and simply disappeared in front of my eyes by ill-mannered food thugs. I knew right then the mannered home style passing of foods was not the way it goes here.

However, this was not the way it went at each meal, as it was indeed a matter of how well-mannered the other seven guys were at the table at that time.

Others described how getting "seconds" at the table was many times unheard of, though mess stewards say the amount of food placed on the table before the whistle was blown was of sufficient quantity to allow for seconds. Apparently, not everyone getting seconds would mostly occur when the meal consisted of a menu everyone enjoyed, like roast beef, mashed potatoes, and apple pie.

Conversely, there would in many cases be sufficient quantity for thirds whenever the menu consisted of undesired items, something like Spanish pork pie and plum pudding.

To create an atmosphere of manners, cleanliness, and order, military commanders established dinner meal dress requirements. Enrollees were required to clean up at the end of the day's work period and change into their dress uniform, including a tie, before entering the Mess Hall.

NOURISHMENT

Young men enrolling into the Emergency Conservation Work came from diverse backgrounds and ethnicities, ranging from center city, rural farming regions, and small towns statewide. The harsh economic conditions of the time were shared by all of these young men. A most common economic plight experienced by most of these enrollees was the minimal supply of food on the table at home. For many, the prospect of three meals a day was reason enough to enroll in the program. Generally, once they arrived in camp, they were not disappointed in the menu selections and ample portions made available. The US Army understood well the nutritional needs of young men in their care. In the Emergency Conservation Workcamps, they maintained the same nutritional values provided to the regular US Army service members. The Mess Hall in camp was a facility most everyone looked forward to entering. Here, three meals were made available every day, food

Suppertime line waiting to get into the Mess Hall, enrollees wearing dress uniform, holding their issued mess kits

was plentiful, and included a main-course dish, fresh fruits, fresh baked goods, and rotational menus. Food was prepared in the camp kitchen under the direction of an experienced Army mess sergeant by enrollees learning the trade. Certainly not every meal would be to the liking of every enrollee, given their diverse backgrounds. Complaints about what the mess cooks had prepared was not uncommon. What was common, however, was the weight gain of most enrollees. Numerous reports prepared by the director of the program advise the average weight gain per enrollee in the Civilian Conservation Corps was twenty-eight pounds.

Detailed accounting of provisions in the camps was required by administrators. Accounting on a unit basis for meats, canned foods, fresh foods, fresh eggs, boxed foods, and all other ingredients were maintained. Inspection reports, including provision accounting for Poe Valley, show the average cost for provisions was $0.040 per enrollee per day in 1935. The reports show the cost per enrollee per day in 1938 was $0.428.

Inspection reports included menus posted by the camp commander. The menu board posted for August 5–7, 1935, is shown in the images below.

1333rd Company CCC
Poe Valley Camp S-63
Coburn, Pa.

August 16, 1935

August 5
Breakfast

Canned Prunes
Cream Beef
Fried Potatoes
Toast
Corn Flakes
Coffee
Milk
Sugar
Butter

Dinner

Boiled Franks
Sauer Kreut
Boiled Potatoes
Catsup
Vegetable Salad
Bread
Bread Pudding with Rainsins
Butter
Ice Tea

Supper

Baked Beef Hearts
Mashed Potatoes
Stewed Tomatoes
Gravy
Sliced Cucumbers
Plain Cake
Bread & Butter
Ice Punch

August 6
Breakfast

Canned Pears
Fried Bacon
French Toast
Sirup
Rice Krispies
Coffee
Bread & Butter
Sugar

Dinner

Roast Pork
Mashed Potatoes
Gravy
Stewed Spinach
Cole Slaw
Rice Pudding
Ice Tea
Bread & Butter
Sugar

Supper

Roast Lamb w/Dressing
Mashed Potatoes
Gravy
Creamed Lima Beans
Vegetable Salad
Coconut Pie
Ice Punch
Bread & Butter
Sugar

August 7, 1935
Breakfast

Bananas
Scrambled Eggs
Fried Potatoes
Wheat Flakes
Coffee
Bread & Butter
Sugar

Dinner

Baked Beans
Mashed Potatoes
Cheese Salad
Bread Pudding
Ice Tea
Bread & Butter
Sugar

Supper

Roast Beef
Mashed Potatoes
Gravy
Creamed Peas
Lettuce Salad
Jam
Bread & Butter
Ice Punch

EMERGENCY
AUG 20 1935
RECEIVED
CONSERVATION WORK

Federal inspectors menu report

	Number served ___				
TOTAL COST ___ $21.59	TOTAL COST ___ $12.84			TOTAL COST ___ $32.15	
FRIDAY:		**Camp Meal:**		Salmon	10	3.00

FRIDAY — TOTAL COST $21.59

Item	No.	Cost
Extract Vanilla	1	.78
Eggs	30 doz	4.96
Syrup	2	.58
Butter	3	.93
Jelley	1	.73
Hot cereal	7	.35
Milk Fresh	225	6.30
Milk Evap	8	.48
Bread	50	2.50
Pears	2	1.12

Camp Meal — TOTAL COST $12.84

Item	No.	Cost
Cheese	24	4.32
Macaroni	20	.80
Katsup	2	.22
Tomatoes	1	.37
Pickles	1	.44
Lima Beans	100	2.00
Pepper	1	.15
Bread	50	2.50
Butter	3	.93
Peanutbutter	3	1.01
Field Meal:		
Milk Evap	5	.30
Flour	100	1.98

TOTAL COST $32.15

Item	No.	Cost
Salmon	10	3.00
Sardines	102	3.86
Hash, Cor.Beef	2	1.00
Lard	50	4.10
Corn	4	1.22
Celery	1	3.85
Pickles	2	1.06
Pepper	1	.09
Butter	4	1.24
Jelley	6	1.48
Milk Evap	8	.48
Pineapple	25	4.00
Oranges	2	6.70
Lemons	1/2	2.70

SATURDAY — TOTAL COST $24.98

Item	No.	Cost
Corn	3	.81
Syrup	1	.29
Bacon	28	4.34
Bread	50	2.50
Butter	4	1.24
Cereal	200	3.32
Milk Evap	5	.30
Apricots	1	.12
Milk Fresh	225	6.30
Prunes	2	.76
Sugar	100	5.00

Camp Meal — TOTAL COST $15.04

Item	No.	Cost
Spaghetti	20	.81
Spaghetti Sauce	1	1.00
Corn	3	.99
Beans Lima	100	3.00
Tomatoes	9	.74
Katsup	2	.74
Bread	50	2.50
Butter	3	.93
Jam	1	.73
Milk Evap	1	.42
Field Meal:		
Peaches	5	1.90
Mixed Vegetables	1	.34

TOTAL COST $30.58

Item	No.	Cost
Onions	50	1.00
Spinach	3	.81
Milk Evap	12	.72
Corn	1	.33
Celery	1	3.80
Cabbage	50	1.25
Applebutter	2	.18
Jam	1	.73
Peanutbutter	1	.43
Bread	25	1.25
Butter	4	1.24
Mangerines	2	4.30

SUNDAY — TOTAL COST $21.44

Item	No.	Cost
Eggs	30 doz	5.70
Milk Fresh	200	5.60
Grapefruit	24	1.68
Milk Evap	7	.42
Coffee	50	5.00
Butter	4	1.24
Bacon	15	1.80

Camp Meal — TOTAL COST $14.79

Item	No.	Cost
Chicken	100	18.00
Pickles	2	.62
Corn	2	.66
Celery	1/2	1.06
Mayonnaise	1	.64
Butter	4	1.24
Jam	1	.73
Milk Evap	6	.42
Peaches	3	1.19
Ice Cream	6	6.00
Field Meal:		

TOTAL COST $16.45

Item	No.	Cost
Eggs	30 doz	5.70
Beans W.&B.	20	1.68
Jam	1	.73
Butter	5	1.55
Milk Evap	8	.48
Peaches	2	1.06
Sugar	100	5.00
Baking Powder	1	.25

TOTAL COST $21.44	TOTAL COST $30.58	TOTAL COST $16.45
TOTAL WEEK COST $128.59	TOTAL WEEK COST $30.24	TOTAL WEEK COST $71.84

GRAND TOTAL COST $430.67

Number of boarders in camp ___ 10

Federal inspectors menu report depicting food costs

Potable water service for the camp initially came from a nearby stream, where the stream water was collected in large containers and trucked to camp repeatedly on a daily basis. This water was tested and treated in accordance with military standards. Soon after the camp was established, a water spring capable of being able to supply the needs of the camp was discovered about 1,000 yards from the campsite. The spring outlet was walled, creating a reservoir with the construction work being performed by the enrollees under direction of the camp foremen. Water flowed from the reservoir via gravity into a 1,000-gallon holding tank and again tested and treated in accordance with military standards. Eventually, camp infrastructure included a pump to move water from the holding tank to the other camp facilities, much to the satisfaction of enrollees since it eliminated the bucket brigade detail work.

EDUCATION

Furthering the education of the enrollee was seen by Emergency Conservation Work administrators as a requisite to be added to the program. Administrators recognized a significant percentage of enrollees were high school dropouts. Director Fechner appointed an education program administrator to organize and execute an education program.

Education advisors were subsequently selected from the locale of the camp and assigned to the camps. Many times, these advisors were unemployed individuals who came into camp with backgrounds in the teaching profession. Paul Zigler, an education advisor in Poe Valley, took the position earning $0.80 per hour (equivalent to $14.83 by 2018 standards), the hourly earning value was learned from an entry in Mr. Harry Ziegler's diary, Paul's father, dated "1-5-35."

The educational advisor in camp was given the charge to organize and develop an education program in the camp, taking advantage of every local resource. For this reason alone, the educational program in one location could be considerably different from that in another camp location. Continuing their education was an enrollee's choice and was not any part of a mandate or obligation of enrollment. Continuing education was developed by the individual camp advisor following a recommended set of suggestions by the Emergency Conservation Work education office. In the beginning, advisors provided instruction in the basic, conventional three Rs of school: "reading, writing and arithmetic." Enrollees realized early on they had quite a bit of free time available to them to pursue any interests, as they generally had their evening time and weekend time free to themselves.

The development of the Emergency Conservation Work continuing education program grew rapidly throughout the country and certainly did so in Poe Valley. Instructional books for many of the trades, such as carpentry, masonry, electrical, mechanics, and others, were printed up and distributed throughout the camps where advisors sought assistance from local sources to teach a specific course.

Many times, as was the case in Poe Valley, the education advisors would convince the foremen and military officers to fulfill the part of instructor. The foremen had found themselves in a similar "time on their hands" scenario, just like the enrollees, with their evenings free to themselves. The foremen had also developed a sense of camaraderie and caring for these young men and wanted them to depart Poe Valley better equipped to take on the challenges of life when they arrived back home. Many veterans at reunions easily recalled a particular foreman's name and described what he had learned either in the foreman's classroom setting or on the job.

The forested environment, camp facility needs, and the work assignments in camp provided a natural OJT, "on job training," educational opportunity.

Enrollees quickly spread the word among their buddies that there was individual opportunity in the camp's education programs that would give them a "leg up," so to speak, when returning home and out applying for a job. This leg up was a letter of recommendation from an Emergency Conservation Work camp foreman, military officer, or education advisor in testament to an enrollee's character and learned skill. These letters, though not prolifically executed, were highly desired on the part of the enrollee and potential employer alike.

Throughout The Great Depression era of the 1930s, the job market opportunities for these young men were most difficult, however, a fresh-faced, well-nourished, young man armed with a discharge certificate and a letter of recommendation from an Emergency Conservation Work camp definitely provided a leg up.

In Poe Valley one of the principal educational resources local to the camp was the Pennsylvania State College located in nearby State College, Pennsylvania. Courses were developed to assist the enrollee in furthering their education towards the completion of their high school diploma, and other offerings allowed enrollees to acquire a few college credits. I do not have any specific course offering or any tabulations on how many enrollees may have taken advantage of this offering. I only have general information stating there were course offerings and these courses were administered in camp through the camp education advisors. These courses were some of the earlier correspondence courses engaged by the relatively young Pennsylvania State College. The Pennsylvania State College grew to become The Pennsylvania State University,

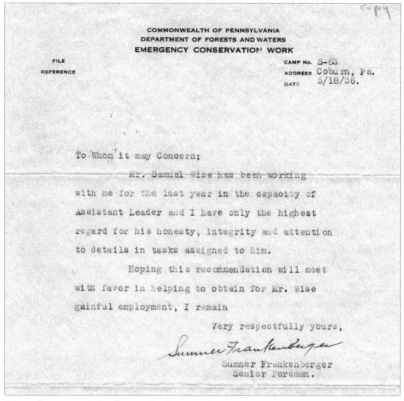

COMMONWEALTH OF PENNSYLVANIA
DEPARTMENT OF FORESTS AND WATERS
EMERGENCY CONSERVATION WORK

FILE
REFERENCE

CAMP No. S-65
ADDRESS Coburn, Pa.
DATE 5/18/36.

To Whom it may Concern:

Mr. Samuel Wise has been working with me for the last year in the capacity of Assistant Leader and I have only the highest regard for his honesty, integrity and attention to details in tasks assigned to him.

Hoping this recommendation will meet with favor in helping to obtain for Mr. Wise gainful employment, I remain

Very respectfully yours,

Sumner Frankenberger
Senior Foreman.

Letter of recommendation for enrollee Samuel Wise

now a top-ranked university well-known for its agriculture and engineering programs, among others.

Several of the veterans attending reunions told me their individual education background stories. They noted when looking back upon their experience that furthering their education, achieving credit towards a high school diploma, and being promoted in Emergency Conservation Work camps was a contributing factor when signing up and becoming an enrollee.

Several veterans stated that even though they did not fulfill all of the requirements for a high school diploma prior or while in camp, advancement while in camp spirited them on to complete those requirements after they completed their Emergency Conservation Work service.

Many other veterans told me their individual learning experiences in camp in the technical skills of masonry, carpentry, truck driving, and motor mechanics were the principal factors in their choosing to select these vocations as their lifelong occupations when they returned back home.

In the February 1937 issue of the *Poe Valley Ravin*, an article titled "Truck Driving Class" reads, "Plans are nearing completion for running a class for men interested in learning to drive truck. Each member of this class will study the Motor Vehicle Code of Penna. In addition to the lessons in truck driving." In my collection of documents, I have a truck driving course book prepared by the Department of the Interior for the Civilian Conservation Corps consisting of more than 120 pages, which was the most comprehensive study for truck driving training at the time.

An excerpt from the course book is below:

> One of the first prerequisites of a good truck driver is pride
> and care in the operation of his truck. If the driver does
> not recognize then he will never go far as a truck driver
> for continual expense for repair of damaged parts and for
> parts worn out through carelessness will soon cause him to
> be replaced no matter for whom he works. Those who can
> learn Truck Driving while in camp and go out with a good
> recommendation stand a good chance of securing employment
> in this field after leaving camp.

Many of these veterans also told me the opportunity to advance their education in the vocational arts was in many ways directly related to the positive influence of the camp foremen. One of the most common experiences shared with me by veterans was the relationships developed between enrollee and foreman. The foremen in many cases became father-like figures in their camp experience, since in most cases they were of age to be their fathers and so it was natural for them to be perceived as such.

The foremen managed much of the enrollees' daily time, directing the labor being performed and, in many instances, led by example. The foremen, in addition to other duties, made sure the enrollees were properly dressed for the job, had the right equipment or best available, kept track of their charges, and most important had the crew back in camp on time for chow.

Most foremen were held in high regard by the enrollees, as the foremen so much of the time, in so many ways, mentored these young men as if they were indeed family. One of the direct responsibilities of the foremen as a part of their continued employment was their capability to example good moral conduct and temperament.

During reunions on many occasions I was told my grandfather was easily remembered for his sense of humor, willingness to guide and train his charges on how to do things better, offered a less-backbreaking way, and made them feel that their tasks were always accomplished with a sense of purpose.

The education programs in the Emergency Conservation Work program like so many other aspects would develop and grow and change rapidly during the life of the program.

Early on, the six-month hitch would typically not allow an enrollee opportunity to fulfill all the requirements for a high school diploma. As the Emergency Conservation Work program grew in later years, enrollees were provided opportunity to "reenlist" for another six-month term, thereby making their time in camp a period of one year. I learned several veterans of Poe Valley did indeed fulfill all of the requirements to achieve a high school diploma while in camp. I do not have any records or tabulations as to the numbers of enrollees who signed on for continuing education programs and/or how many may have attained a high school diploma while in the Poe Valley camp.

Director Fechner realized the importance of including opportunity for education advancement of enrollees while in camp during their enrollment period. The placement of an education advisor in each camp was a key element in the success of the Emergency Conservation Work education programs. The capability of education advisors to properly assess the desires and needs of enrollees in their charge and assist them in the pursuit of their individual goals certainly varied from camp to camp. Records and enrollee achievements suggest the Poe Valley education advisors were able to meet the challenges and demands of their positions.

Many veterans spoke only in kind regard to the capability of the camp's education advisors to help them and other enrollees further their education resume while in camp. I do not have any specific information on the Poe Valley camp education advisors attesting to their individual backgrounds and experiences, however, I do know these men were well respected by their peers and remained in camp for extended periods of time, suggesting they were capable of fulfilling their mission.

Mr. N. H. Grieb was the first education advisor in Poe Valley arriving April 10, 1934. Mr. Grieb split his duties between the Poe Valley camp and Camp S-66 Loganton, PA.

Education Advisor Mr. Holcomb (left) and military commanders (names unknown)

The names of the education advisors were posted in the camp newsletters. The newsletters reflect there were two additional advisors assigned to the Poe Valley camp. The first two issues of the *Poe Valley Ravin* newsletter do not have an issue date, however, it is believed these first issues were created sometime in the middle part of the year 1935. These first issues list Mr. Newton Holcomb as education advisor. Subsequent issues of the camp newsletter list Mr. Holcomb in this position through May 1938.

From June 1938 to July 1941, the newsletter lists Mr. Homer Dean as education advisor.

Other individuals supporting the education advisor are also listed in the newsletters. The names and service periods are as follows:

Mr. Jason Wolfe W.P.A. Academic Instructor
May 1936 – December 1936

Mr. Paul Ziegler W.P.A. Recreational Teacher
May 1936 – May 1937

Mr. Harry Kreamer W.P.A. Vocational Teacher
May 1936 – May 1941

Each enrollee had a record of their enrollment. These records followed the enrollee throughout their entire enrollment period. There is a section in the enrollee's record titled "education activities." This section is where all education activities of the enrollee were noted. There are two separate subsections: General & Vocational Education and Job Training Activities.

In each of these two subsections would be a listing for recording each subject or type of job taken, date taken, and rating of the enrollee.

The education column in the March 1937 *Poe Valley Ravin* noted education certificates to be awarded.

"The following men who are leaving or have recently left camp have been awarded certificates for their completion of various educational courses and other accomplishments during their stay in camp."

Leader Anthony Malesic, First Aid, Typing, Shorthand
Instructor, Associate Editor Poe Valley Ravin.
Ass't Leader Donnely, First Aid, Typing Instructor, Editor Poe
Valley Ravin.
Charles Zapalsky, Typing, First Aid.
John Polinsky, Typing.
Rolland Stark, First Aid, Algebra.
Peter Zopchak, Typing, First Aid, Woodwork.
Henry Zelesnikar, Woodwork.
Paul Wilchinski, Typing, English, Spelling.
Thomas McCrossin, Typing, Spelling.
Joseph Okonieski, English, Arithmetic, Spelling.
Archie Lafferty, Arithmetic, Typing, First Aid.
Jacob P. Mike, Arithmetic.
Leonard W. Powell, Woodwork, Arithmetic.

As the Emergency Conservation Work program matured, the education programs became more structured with course offerings ever changing. The courses offered in one camp would not necessarily match those in another camp for varying reasons. The documents available to me indicate the vocational arts were the first course offerings in Poe Valley, which included carpentry, masonry, truck driving, and truck mechanics, as noted previously. These course offerings changed with time.

A more significant change to the education program came in the summer of 1937. By congressional mandate, any new enrollee was required to have a minimum ten hours per week of course education made part of their agreement when they enrolled in the Civilian Conservation Corps.

Classes and schedules were prepared by the education advisor. The classes were taught by the education advisor, foremen, LEMs, and military commanders. In Poe Valley, the education program became more organized with the classroom atmosphere under the direction of Mr. Homer Dean. Additionally, the focus on education was heightened in the later years of camp operations as new enrollees were required to take classes as a part of the enlistment agreement they signed before and after a regular workday.

The education program got its most significant boost in early 1938 when approval came for the erection of a new structure dedicated solely to education program functions. The May 1938 edition of the *Poe Valley Ravin* tells the following story:

> "New Ed. Building"
>
> Under the direction of Mr. Harry Kramer and with the assistance of the members of his Carpentry Class our Education Building is rapidly nearing completion.
>
> When completed it will be the Mecca of scores of enrollees wishing to increase their knowledge of current affairs and also seeking training in a good trade.
>
> The building will consist of several classrooms, a workshop, educational office, typing room and a supreme library.
>
> If the boys keep working as earnestly as they are now it will not be long until the Education Department moves into their new quarters.

New education building under construction can be seen at top center of this photo

EDUCATION

CLASS SCHEDULE FOR THE PERIOD
October 23 to December 31, 1939

MONDAY	5:30–6:30 PM	
Blacksmithing	E. R. Auman	Blacksmith Shop
Blue Print Reading	C. H. Hutt	Library
Saw Filing	F. B. Auman	Blacksmith Shop
Auto Mechanics	H. S. Neese	Reading Room
Forestry	H. C. Steel	Ed. Class Room

	5:30–7:30 PM	
Typing	R. Smull	Ed. Office

	5:30 - 8:30 PM	
Woodwork	H. Kramer	Wood Shop

TUESDAY	5:30–6:30 PM	
First Aid	Dr. Pennes	Ed. Room
Art	H. Kramer	Art Room

	6:30–7:30 PM	
Foreman Training	C.H.Hutt	Ed. Room

	6:30 PM	
Recreation Trips		
Basketball Practice		

WEDNESDAY	5:30–6:30 PM	
Truck Driving	Miller & Wert	Art Room
Tree Identification	B. McPherson	Ed. Room
Mapping and Survey	E. F. Hoyt	Ed. Office
Road Construction	P. Bradford	Library

	6:30–7:30 PM	
Typing	R. Smull	Ed. Office
Business Arithmetic	H. Dean	Ed. Room

	5:30–8:30 PM	
Woodwork	Harry Kramer	Woodshop

THURSDAY	5:30–6:30 PM	
English	A. J. Price	Library
Mechanical Drawing	L. Fox	Art Room
Poultry Keeping	H. Dean	Ed. Room
Journalism	R. Robson	Ed. Office

	6:30–7:00 PM	
Health	L. Fox	Rec. Hall

	7:00–7:30 PM	
Company Meeting	L. Fox	Rec. Hall

	7:30 PM	
Feature Motion Picture		

FRIDAY	6:00 PM	

Basketball Practice

Leadership training will be held every other Monday night in the Library at 6:30 P.M., first class will be held Monday evening October 9

CLASS SCHEDULE FOR THE PERIOD
November 1 to November 31, 1940

MONDAY	7:00–8:00 AM	
Blacksmithing	E. R. Auman	Blacksmith Shop
Dynamiting	L. L. Weaver	Educational Building
Blue Print Reading	C. H. Hutt	Library
Saw Filing	F. B. Auman	Blacksmith Shop
Auto Mechanics	L. E. Sherwood	Forestry Garage
Forestry	B. D. McPherson	Ed. Class Room
	5:30–6:30 PM	
Group Guidance	William Kelly	Ed. Class Room
Woodwork	Harry Kramer	Woodshop
TUESDAY	**7:45–8:30 AM**	
Safety	Ralph Wert	Recreation Hall
	6:30–7:30 PM	
Foreman Training	C. H. Hutt	Ed. Room
	4:15–4:50 PM	
Foremanship Training	C. H. Hutt	Forestry Office
	5:30–6:30 PM	
Health & Hygeine	Fox, Kelly, Dean, & Hutt	Ed. Class Room
Art	Harry Kramer	Art Room
WEDNESDAY	**7:00–8:00 AM**	
Truck Driving	Miller & Wert	Reading Room
Surveying	E. F. Hoyt	Educational Office
Road Construction	P. E. Bradford	Ed. Class Room
	5:30–6:30 PM	
First Aid	B. D. McPherson	Ed. Class Room
Woodwork	Harry Kramer	Woodshop
	7:30–8:30 PM	
Social Courtesy	Lee Fox	Recreation Hall
Motion Picture	Jones	Recreation Hall
THURSDAY	**5:30–6:30 PM**	
First Aid	Dr. Thissel	Library
Government	Homer A. Dean	Ed. Class Room
Woodwork	Harry Kramer	Woodshop
	6:30–7:00 PM	
Leadership Training	Foxx & Hutt	Ed. Class Room
FRIDAY	**4:15–4:45 PM**	
Teachers Training	Homer A. Dean	Ed. Class Room
	5:30–6:30 PM	
Poultry Keeping	Homer A. Dean	Ed. Class Room

RELIGION IN CAMP

In addition to the other duties assigned to the Army in support of the Emergency Conservation Work program, they would support the spiritual guidance and needs of the camps utilizing the Army's established Chaplain Corps. Chaplains were assigned to each of the Army's district and subdistrict commands staff. From here the chaplains conducted scheduled camp visits.

While these chaplains served well, there were simply not enough chaplains to fulfill the needs of more than 4,000 Emergency Conservation Work camps throughout the country. Support came when civilian clergy took a leave from their congregations for limited time periods and become chaplains to serve the camps. In some locations, local ministers and priests volunteered, receiving a limited stipend to support the needs of camps in their local areas.

The mission for the clergy in these camps was to provide nonsectarian messages to bolster the enrollees' spirits and general morale character without the "fire and brimstone" stumping some faiths were known to represent.

In Poe Valley the chaplains serving the camp were the assigned Military Chaplains from the district and subdistrict command. Limited information is available to describe the messages presented by the chaplains in Poe Valley.

Little is known about chaplain services in Poe Valley before the fall of 1937. There are no written references made to this important part of the program prior to this time. In the fall of 1937, several references appear in the camp newsletter regarding chaplain services, wherein a Captain W. T. Brundick, chaplain, appears in camp.

A chaplains' page, however, commencing in 1938 is many times included in the *Poe Valley Ravin* newsletters. These pages provide written word to support the moral character building and suggest a bimonthly schedule for visitation to the camp by the chaplain was maintained.

An article appearing in the March 1939 issue of the *Poe Valley Ravin* suggests the chaplain had found a way to get his message across in the form of a competition among the men. The article reads as follows:

"Chaplain M.C.'s Quiz Contest Lawless and Bodek capture honors"

March 10 – Chaplain Estes conducted a quiz contest on one of his bi-monthly visits to Poe Valley. Sixteen enrollees competed for the two-dollar first prize and one-dollar runner up award.

A large assortment of general questions was fired at the competitors. Upon failure to answer, the question was given to the audience. The one giving the correct reply was given ten cents. The winners were Joseph Lawless, first prize and Albert Bodek, second prize.

An additional article appears in the January 1940 issue of the *Poe Valley Ravin*:

"Chaplain Estes Greets Rookies"

On one of his bimonthly visits to this camp, William B. Estes, chaplain, subdistrict "A," greeted the enrollees who had entered the company during the past two weeks. His talk centered on "Living a Useful and Full Life." As usual it was one of those gripping, pulsating talks for which he is known.

After speaking to the entire company, Chaplain Estes greeted each of the rookies individually in the education building. He distributed to each of the new men either a prayer book or new testament.

The following is an article as it appeared in the May 1939 newsletter under the heading "Chaplain Night Again Observed."

Once again Lt. Estes, popular chaplain of the Sub-District "A", invaded this camp armed with his usual bit of philosophy in relation to the bible.

After the short services were over, the chaplain conducted a spelling contest. Fourteen men participated for the awards. Harold Unger captured the top honors to win the two dollar first prize. John Sabo won second prize of one dollar.

Number two barrack picked a convenient time to win their first softball game since early last season. As a result of their 9 to 2 victory over number three barrack, the entire team was treated by Chaplain Estes.

In addition to Chaplains Estes and Brundick two other Chaplains are referenced in the newsletters, First Lieutenant George E. West, sub-district Chaplain and Lt. McGuire Sub-District Chaplain who would serve the needs of the enrollees in the Poe Valley camp.

CROSSWORD PUZZLE CONTEST

In the early years of the Civilian Conservation Corps the education advisors assigned to the camps were challenged with administering a limited, organized education program and needed to take advantage of opportunities in the camps and outlying regions for the overall development and betterment of their own program.

In the March 1936 edition of the *Poe Valley Ravin* the education program advisor Mr. Edward Newcolm used one of the best-known ways to get the attention of those he was trying to further educate in the form of a cash offering for the solution to a crossword puzzle he posted in the same edition of the newsletter. He offered the princely sum of $1.00 to anyone providing the "correct solution of the puzzle." He did, however, additionally require the solution must also be "accompanied by an item of news, poetry, etc. for the 'Ravin.'"

I wish I were herein providing the reader with the name or names of those who may have been able to solve the puzzle and fulfill the supplemental requirements, but unfortunately no more information was made known in the latter issues of the camp newsletter.

For those crossword puzzle enthusiasts reading this book, please enjoy solving the same crossword puzzle put in play by the camp education advisor in Poe Valley in 1936 (page 70).

COMMANDERS CONTESTS

The military had long established operating procedures for military installations and simply adopted most of these procedures into the management of the camps. Swift and many times harsh disciplinary measures were the long-standing means used by the military to maintain order and control, however, these measures were not adopted into the conservation camps. Well-known for its ranking order and chain-of-command policy, the Army adopted a similar way for the camps. In the camps, the Army's equivalent ranks for privates, corporals, and sergeants would be replaced

THE FOREMAN'S BOYS

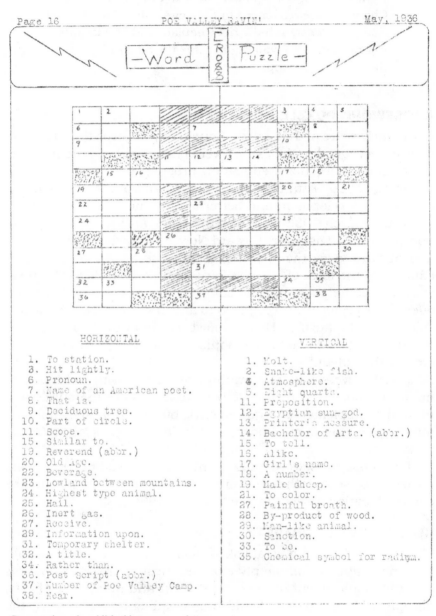

HORIZONTAL

1. To station.
3. Hit lightly.
6. Pronoun.
7. Name of an American poet.
8. That is.
9. Deciduous tree.
10. Part of circle.
11. Scope.
15. Similar to.
19. Reverend (abbr.)
20. Old Age.
22. Beverage.
23. Lowland between mountains.
24. Highest type animal.
25. Hail.
26. Inert gas.
27. Receive.
29. Information upon.
31. Temporary shelter.
32. A title.
34. Rather than.
36. Post Script (abbr.)
37. Number of Poe Valley Camp.
38. Near.

VERTICAL

1. Molt.
2. Snake-like fish.
4. Atmosphere.
5. Eight quarts.
11. Preposition.
12. Egyptian sun-god.
13. Printer's measure.
14. Bachelor of Arts. (abbr.)
15. To tell.
16. Alike.
17. Girl's name.
18. A number.
19. Male sheep.
21. To color.
27. Painful breath.
28. By-product of wood.
29. Man-like animal.
30. Sanction.
33. To be.
35. Chemical symbol for radium.

Crossword puzzle published in camp newsletter

with enrollee, assistant barrack leader, and barrack leaders. It was the responsibility of the barrack leaders and their assistants to direct and monitor the enrollees in maintaining the operational procedures and policies developed by program officials.

Enrollees were required to follow general rules mostly pertaining to daily schedules, personal hygiene, order in the barracks and company areas, and light-duty assignments. The barrack leaders were the first in line to hand out disciplinary measures when needed. These measures typically included things like additional duty to "clean the barrack floors" or "clean the shower room" or "clean grease traps" in the kitchen and maybe another night added on for "fire watch" that month, minor discipline for minor infractions. When an enrollee had conducted themselves in an egregious, unsatisfactory manner, the barrack leader would turn the enrollee over to camp commanders for determination of disciplinary measures.

The military also had a long-standing record of handing out individual and group rewards whenever inspections and ratings of performance were found to be well above standard in the superior and excellent classes. They instituted these same policies in the Emergency Conservation Work camps.

Camp commanders established monthly and quarterly contests that included the entire company's performance by having a "Best Barracks" performance contest. Each of the four barracks would be rated on barrack cleanliness, neatness of enrollees' bunks and individual space, and overall compliance with established policy. A winner was selected, and some measure of reward was provided by the company commander for each member of the barrack.

Similar contests were conducted at the district and regional levels of the Third Corps area. Senior military commanders from these offices conducted inspections of the camps on a scheduled basis. They would compile their findings regarding the individual camp performances related to established policy and would in turn reward a selected camp with a "Superior" or "Excellent" rating banner. For the most part, the reward was more about "bragging rights" than something tangible being issued.

It is unknown to me if any of these "bragging rights" banners were ever awarded to Camp S-63, Company 1333. We do know Poe Valley received superior ratings on more than one occasion, however, I do not know how many superior ratings were required to be awarded a regional or district banner.

THIS TOWN, POE VALLEY CAMP

During the span of eight and a half years, approximately 2,600 men lived in the Poe Valley Emergency Conservation Work campsite. This campsite took on the persona of small-town America with the exception of having its own post office. The closest post office was in the nearby town of Coburn.

A unique description of Poe Valley was provided in an editorial in the August 1936 edition of the *Poe Valley Ravin* newsletter:

"This Town, Poe Valley Camp"

Say, fellows, do you realize that you are living in a typical country town in Central Pennsylvania? Yes, indeed, it has all the earmarks of a country village. A quiet, peaceful, little resort, yet ensuing the advantage, and in some cases surpassing the standards of other towns of larger size.

Its situation is an artist's dreamland, Nature in all its glory affords the colorful background and camp site. The noise and whirl of a city environment is replaced by a quiescence that is characteristic of Mother Nature. It spells rest-a happy repose for fatigued mortals.

Yes, our camp town has its main street, connected by minor avenues of travel, and even boasts walks bordered with beds of flowers, and evergreens for beautification. And erected thruout the area are homes, hotels in one sense, improving the comforts of an average home life.

No town would be complete without a store (our canteen and supply room) and a place where these tired bodies of ours may secure nourishment. Outside they call them restaurants: here we designate it as our Mess Hall.

Then too, you have only a short distance to walk until you come into the shadows of a hospital. Not many country towns can pride of such a possession. Equipped for minor operations and general medical practice, the camp town has the services of a competent doctor and experienced male nurses. That even is not the end of comparison. A blacksmith shop, our own electric system of lighting for every building, an adequate water supply piped into the various structures; a garage, and you dare not forget the public baths, all these are assets paralleling out side centers of habitation.

Incidentally, your recreational opportunities are enhanced by the various facilities provided by your "Civic Council" the Company Officers in charge. They are vitally interested in your welfare, even to the end whereby they afford leisure time pleasures. If not inclined to participate in group recreation, the public camp library beckons you enter its portals, there to delve into the writings of Shakespeare, the current periodicals or the contents of practical courses of school-nature.

In addition to this, you are given the opportunity to enroll in the camp public school, and secure advanced instruction or work for a high school diploma. Do you appreciate the comprehensiveness and the opportunities inherent in this typical country town?

The Mayor you surely have one in the person of Captain Ayres, and his judiciary council composed of Lt. Carroll and Lt. Brock, with the assistance of Mr. Holcomb, Education Advisor. It's all real, no fake, and they form the judge and jury when legal advice is to be forthcoming, but in the true sense, they are the backbone of the town, working daily for its welfare and the good that may be accomplished. All they ask of each "Citizen" is-pull with us, and the heaviest burden and the strongest obstacle will fade in the distance. So it behoves each enrollee, as a citizen of Poe Valley Town to use, keep, preserve and respects unique rendezvous of Centre County.

CHAPTER 4

TRAGEDY STRIKES

The first issue of the camp newsletter coincidentally shared the same timeline with the tragic accidental death of a Poe Valley camp enrollee.

Enrollee Bernard Oyler from Kane, Pennsylvania, was killed by a falling tree. During early reunions several accounts were shared regarding Mr. Oyler's death by several veterans all explaining the tree that fell on Mr. Oyler and resulted in his death was unfortunately a tree he was helping cut down as part of the day's work detail. Another story to be shared regarding his death indicated he was indeed helping to fell a tree when the chow truck arrived and Bernard headed toward the chow line believing the tree was in no danger of falling, when indeed it started to fall. He started to run away from the tree, but the tree struck him, killing him instantly.

As part of the research into the development of this writing, I learned records of accidents resulting in the death of an enrollee were available at the National Archives. Able to acquire a copy of the accident report, I also learned Enrollee Bernard Oyler's death was indeed the result of a falling tree striking him, resultant in his death. An accident report prepared by the district Forester provides a detailed account of the incident.

Subsequent to Mr. Oyler's tragic death the camp Recreation Hall was renamed Oyler Hall to honor his memory. His name was framed into the wood railing on the front porch of the building.

This tragic loss of life was not to be forgotten. A stone marker commemorating Mr. Oyler was erected by the enrollees on the campsite in front of barracks number two and remains in place to this day.

A young enrollee and first-time editor of the very first edition of the camp newsletter wrote an article about the death of enrollee

E.C.W.Camp # S-63   Coburn, Pa.

January 31, 1935

S. M. Lauderdale Safety Engineer

Emergency Conservation Works

Office of the Director

Washington, D.C.

Dear Sir:

In reply to your letter of January 28,1935 will give you details of Bernard Oyler's death.

While cutting timber on Little Flat on the Forest Stand Inprovement Cutting project, a tree was notched by an assistant leader. Mr. Oyler, another assistant leader helped to saw the tree down. And after being told at this very tree, by the Foreman and the other assistant leader not to saw it off. The orders were ignored and the tree fell at right angles to where it was notched for.

The boy got excited and instead of making one step to a side he started to run in the direction in which the tree fell. He consequently was hit on the head by a limb about five (5) inches in diameter and was almost immediately killed. It was thirty-five (35) feet from the stump to the spot where he was hit.

The boys were all given numerous talks on safety in all lines of work. My foreman are all woodsmen by experience of years of work along that line and will say that they are all instructed to teach all men along the line of safety as they are going along with the work.

It is with great regret that such a thing as this should occur but after all the orders were disregarded we could do no more.

Very Truly Yours,

L. L. Weaver   Camp Sup't.

Enrollee Bernard Oylers accident report

Bernard Oyler in a manner befitting any seasoned editor's writing skills. I have read this article many times over and find the words this young man put to paper were what I believe to be a visionary look into the future of what was to become the legacy of the Civilian Conservation Corps.

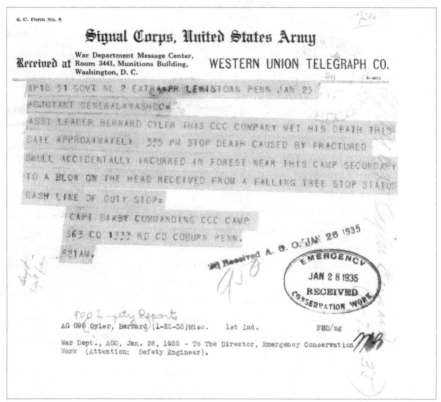

Incident telegram sent to War Department

Recreation Hall named in honor of Bernard Oyler, see name set into the front porch

Stone monument erected by enrollees honoring Bernard Oyler in front of Barracks No. 1

The following is what the editor wrote:

> The first major accident in this camp occurred recently in the death of Bernard Oyler.
>
> With his passing a feeling of sorrow pervaded the Camp that could not be dispelled. We all mourned his death, and his friends of whom he had many, especially so. A well liked fellow, quiet and unassuming, who did his work and did it well, he had just been made an Assistant Leader. Death, at any time is awesome, but when it strikes a young man it makes us pause and think.
>
> Let us remember that he died in the line of duty, a way that we would all like to go to the unknown. Perhaps someday, somehow, the work Bernard Oyler took part in, the work of conserving the great forests of this country, will benefit countless scores of people, however humble his work now seems to us. His part in this task will go on. With that thought let us remember him—a part of a great venture to help his family and his country.

While other accidents would occur during the Poe Valley camp era, the only accident resulting in the loss of a life was that of enrollee Mr. Bernard Oyler.

TRANSITION TO CIVILIAN CONSERVATION CORPS

About two years after implementing this New Deal program, the origin name Emergency Conservation Work started to disappear from newspapers reports, radio, and reference by the general public. The more preferred name of Civilian Conservation Corps, which took the name from the term used by President Roosevelt during his inauguration speech, was to replace Emergency Conservation Work. The Civilian Conservation Corps program name introduced by the president had by this time accumulated a significant favor of acceptance by the American public.

I was not familiar with the origin name Emergency Conservation Work until after my grandfather's passing, while reviewing the documents he had held onto all those years. During discussions he always used one of two separate reference names, being either the "three Cs" or the "CCC" in any conversation. I do not ever remember him saying "Emergency Conservation Work."

I did remember hearing the more common reference name, the Civilian Conservation Corps, while in high school when doing a brief study of The Great Depression and the New Deal program instituted at the time by President Franklin Roosevelt. Had I been more wanting to excel in my high school studies, I could have taken my grandpa to school and provided a living history presentation on the successful Civilian Conservation Corps piece of the New Deal program. Looking back, I'm sure that day would have provided for me a desperately needed A or A+ grade so as to maintain my C+ average.

Records and day-to-day correspondence had the heading "Emergency Conservation Work" through mid-year 1936. The official name change occurred in June 1936 when Congress approved funding and the change in name, continuing the popular program.

HOLIDAYS

Typically, no leave was given by military commanders for the Thanksgiving holiday, though, they were given the Thursday off. The Friday following, however, was a work day, and enrollees were required to be back on the job. Certainly, the enrollees missed being at home to celebrate this holiday with family and friends, so the mess stewards attempted to fill the void of homesickness with a grand feast. This feast included the traditional turkey meal with

DINNER

———

ROAST TURKEY

SAGE STUFFING GIBLET GRAVY

PARSLEY POTATOES CANDIED SWEETS

CRANBERRY SAUCE

BUTTERED CORN CREAMED PEAS

HEARTS OF CELERY

PLUM PUDDING WHITE RUM SAUCE

MINCE PIE

PUMPKIN PIE ICE CREAM

FRUITS IN SEASON

CIGARS CIGARETTES

BREAD BUTTER

FRENCH DRIP COFFEE

Thanksgiving menu posted inside of the camp Thanksgiving holiday card

all the trimmings and much more as indicated by the menu items listed on the camp Thanksgiving holiday card.

Among the numerous articles found in my grandfather's wooden chest were two Christmas greeting cards for the years 1935 and 1936. These cards had a decorative front cover and consisted of four pages. The first page listed the menu of foods to be prepared and served by the camp mess stewards for the Christmas meal. The 1935 menu listed many classic dishes, including oyster stew, sweet mixed pickles, half chicken, mashed potatoes, candied sweet potatoes, creamed corn, cranberry sauce, giblet gravy, mince and pumpkin pie, as well as other desserts, cigars, and fruit.

I learned from enrollees, the opportunity to go home and celebrate the Christmas holiday with family was allowed by camp administrators, however, the cost and means of transportation was the responsibility of the enrollee. This job held by an enrollee in the Civilian Conservation Corps was similar to any other job, wherein the employer typically provided time off for the holiday,

Christmas holiday card

however, within a few days you would be required to be back on the job. Subsequently, many enrollees did not get home to spend time with family, principally due to lack of funds for travel and time limitations.

The above menu suggests that while many enrollees would not be at home with family celebrating the holiday meal, they were with new friends sharing a most fabulous spread given the limitations imposed due to the economic hardships of the times. These treats helped to reduce some of the sadness these young men felt, not being able to be back home with family and friends seated around the table for the traditional holiday meal.

Holiday leave time periods were determined by the camp commanders. Each commander had varying needs and schedules, and thus, leave periods varied. Additionally, the day of the week upon which the holiday fell affected leave schedules.

An article in the June 1939 issue of the *Poe Valley Ravin* newsletter describes Christmas leave:

The Christmas leave of the enrollees of this camp will begin on December 22. They will be permitted to go home on the night of the twenty first. They are due back on the morning of December 27.

Those who are going on leave for the News Year's holiday will go home on the night of December 28 for five days and are due back in camp for work on the morning of January 3.

ACHIEVEMENTS

The first contingent of enrollees making up Civilian Conservation Corps, Company 1333, Camp S-63 spent most of their six-month enrollment period in camp, making camp. This first group of CCC boys to arrive in Poe Valley were busy building the structures needed for the camp and creating the camps roads, walkways, and utilities infrastructure. After completion of these facilities and as the winter season of 1933 came upon them, they set out to work on the first of many road construction and forestry management projects that would become the legacy of the Civilian Conservation Corps.

After the first six months of camp occupation, the first contingent of enrollees would be replaced by a new group of enrollees, and these new "boys" continued with the road construction and forestry management projects under the guidance of a now-seasoned group of foremen and state and military administrative personnel.

Continuing through the early winter period of 1935, every six months saw a new contingent of enrollees taking over for the preceding group of enrollees who would welcome these new faces and then hand off their well-honed, smooth-handled axes, picks, shovels, and grub hoes.

After completion of the camp facilities, the next five six-month enrollment periods had the enrollees constructing new roads, reshaping and improving old roads, and working the forests on multiple improvement projects, all the while cutting in new trails and improving old trails alike.

An article written by the camp superintendent, Mr. Luther Weaver, in the June 1936 issue of the *Poe Valley Ravin* provides the following resume of achievements of the camp:

Milage third class truck trails constructed 34
Milage second class truck trails constructed and maintained 24
Milage of fire lanes constructed and maintained 50
Milage of boundary lines repaired 30
Bridges built 10
Acres forest stand improvement 2,100
Acres 5% stock survey 14,000
Forest culture, acres, disease control 3,500
Forest culture, acres, forest stand planting 75
Poe Paddy Park acres 35

Amid cold and rain of the fall, men worked at top speed to get quarters and administration buildings ready for occupancy. All the while road construction was carried on apace. First, Siglerville-Millheim Pike, then Poe Valley Road. Next, the roads to Poe Mountain Tower and Mountain Church were constructed, the boys walking to and from work, as there were no trucks to haul them. Two and one-half miles were but fun for these young men who were eager for an opportunity to do honest toil and help the helpless at home. Nor was the grade of work lowered because of hardship.

During 1934 and 1935 there was no slackening in road construction and fire lane construction. Little Poe Road was pushed forward to the top of High Mountain. Pine Swamp road was partly relocated and built to connect with Big Poe Road.

These roads offer easy access to valuable forest stands, particularly Pine Swamp Road, which borders several hundred acres of white and scotch pine plantings and is an important link to what has been pronounced one of the most picturesque drives in Pennsylvania forests—Poe Paddy Skyline Drive (a dirt path). Little Flat Road follows an old lumberman's path, which led to the famous "slide" of Slide Mountain. Here the keen eyes of those in authority spotted Penns View, whose dizzy height and precipitous declivities have a sheer drop of hundreds of feet. What a scene!

Before the end of 1934 Redder Hollow, Synagogue Gap, and Panther Hollow roads were realities. The Reider Hollow road not only makes a link to the chain of scenic drives, but opens up valuable privately owned forests through which it passes. The Narrows Road was the last to be built in 1935.

The resume of achievements would be most impressive for any well-managed construction company using skilled workers and a full complement of mechanized equipment and tools. Maybe, more impressive in this resume of achievement, is that it was accomplished by a new company, using unskilled labor without the benefit of adequate mechanized equipment, wherein for the most part, the work was performed using hand tools and materials selected from the surrounding areas. All by a bunch of "kids," as they were most commonly called by many locals and the public at large.

Many conversations overheard during the reunions held over the years between veterans of the camp were of the days when the "kids" were making small rocks out of big rocks for road bed material by swinging ten- and twelve-pound sledge hammers all day long.

There are no known day-to-day logs or other records available to describe the specific means and methods of how work tasks were performed on a day-to-day basis. Instead, shared stories by all and photographs tell the story of the work. These stories and photographs depict road building, trail building, tree felling, and other sorts of forest-service tasks where the work was performed by hand, using pick and shovel, axes, two-man saws, sledge hammers, and a few small trucks. This work was not easy for most. For many this work was their first work experience where a full eight hours of toil would be followed by the same toil the very next day. For some, this work was similar to what they knew back home, and for others it was a shocking experience where the swinging of an axe or sledge hammer was the work performed

Foreman's crew holding brush hooks, tool of the trade to chop out unwanted vegetation

Enrollees John Shinskie and "Tex" believed to be Elwood Ward felling a tree.

all day long. The work assignments changed, and opportunity to learn other skills was provided. One of the common themes among veterans telling of their time in camp would be that work some days was "back breaking hard but we never felt we were forced to do something we could not do."

WHO IS BAILEY AUMAN?

My grandfather had many friends in the community. Having been born in the region and being in the farm implement business where farming was the mainstay of the region put him in touch with almost everyone in the area. The region was settled early on by German immigrants. Common surnames to the region included Auman, Bailey, Boob, Boop, Bressler, Hosterman, Kerstetter, Mensch, Musser, Myer, Weaver and Stover. In this short list of names are names included in the roster of foreman's names who served in Poe Valley where my grandfather was the senior foreman—their boss. At no time when my grandfather told stories of his time in the CCC camp, he never said or inferred he was the boss of his foremen pals. He spoke of their trials and tribulations and their antics to entertain themselves and the accomplishments these men would achieve while in service in the camp.

In almost every CCC story he told, another foreman would be included as part of it. In particular, one of his pals was Foreman

Frank B. Auman, who he always referred to as Bailey Auman. As a youngster, when a CCC story was taking shape, I would remember hearing Bailey Auman, and my grandfather did this or jointly Bailey and I had figured out how to do that. From my very beginning, I was taught to always address any elder as Mr. So and So or Mrs. So and So, never did my parents or grandparents allow my brother or myself to address anyone without the proper prefix. If we would happen to make a slip, corrective admonishment came quick and apologies were required to be made. My older brother and I were mostly well-mannered, and I am proud to say it was a good lesson to be passed on when I later became a parent.

Now, back to being a youngster and how confusing growing up can be at times. Just who was Bailey Auman? I knew several families having the surname Bailey and several families having the surname Auman, and in my young mind I thought maybe my grandfather was talking about two men at the same time. Then confusion beset confusion when my grandfather referred to some of his other pals, who had names like Meyer Hosterman or Stover Rossman. I can remember thinking to myself, *If I ever meet any of these friends of my grandfathers with multiple surnames, how am I supposed to properly address them. Would it be Mr. Bailey or Mr. Auman?* Eventually, I would seek clarity from a higher authority, my big brother George, seven years my senior. He would set me straight by telling me, "Ask Mom." So I did ask Mom, and she taught me it was common practice in the region for the family of a newborn boy to be given the middle name of his mother's maiden surname in respect to the family.

Eventually, when conducting research for this book, I learned my grandfather's pal Bailey Aumans's given name was Frank B. Auman.

The records tell us Frank B. Auman was the only foreman in camp who was there to meet the first group of enrollees on day one and remain in service in the camp until the last day the camp was in operation.

THE SNOW STORY

The camp was isolated from the general public, yet only a few miles from the nearby town of Coburn. The post office and the railroad station serving the Poe Valley camp were located in Coburn. In addition to moderate economic gain, the townspeople would gain support from the camp in time of need. One of these times would come in the winter of 1935 when record snow storms dumped on the area. One of these storms would end with snow reported to be more than two feet deep. This made movement in and out of the camp impassable by motor vehicle. The camp commander, Captain Coates, directed equipment and all enrollee labor be redirected to move snow and make the roads passable.

The shared story goes something like this: Two years after the camp was underway, an R4 bulldozer was assigned to the camp to assist in the construction of roadways and the dam project. A skilled machine operator was hired as part of the Forestry Department to operate the acquired bulldozer. This new operator, Mr. Harold Guisewite, was a local from the nearby town of Coburn. Mr. Guisewite had demonstrated his capable skills in the operation of the machine as work on the dam was progressing and starting to take shape with the support of the much-needed machine. Once the snow storm passed, Mr. Guisewite was directed by the company commander to take the R4 bulldozer and clear a path to Coburn six miles away. Mr. Guisewite was more than eager to perform this work since Coburn was his hometown. It would be two days before Mr. Guisewite returned back to camp after clearing the road of snow. Mr. Guisewite reported the locals needed roads cleared of snow and he had the machine to do the job, and subsequently did so. He also reported that the state roadmaster asked him to clear snow from the road leading to nearby Millheim.

Deep snow in winter of 1935

The camp commander was very pleased with the service Mr. Guisewite had provided to these local towns during this emergency period. He was, however, concerned the locals would anticipate this same service would be made available the next time a snow storm occurred.

A NEW WORK ASSIGNMENT

For two years after the initial works to construct camp facilities and development of the needed infrastructure for camp operations was completed, daily work schedules for the enrollees was focused on forestry management tasks and much-needed road improvement construction. During this same time period, discussions among officials developing project assignments for the camps were starting to look at recreation development to additionally serve the public. The works of the "boys" in the Civilian Conservation Corps camps was now quickly expanding Pennsylvania's state park system.

Discussions among state officials at regional meetings, camp administration, and technical personnel at this time started to focus on what new project assignments might be considered for their future. Indeed, a most significant project was about to take shape in Poe Valley.

This project would require more man hours, more equipment, more materials, more engineering, and more effort, making it the largest single project to be undertaken by the enrollees and administrators of Poe Valley Camp S-63 during its existence.

The Poe Valley camp had been selected to take on the construction of an earthen masonry dam, creating a twenty-seven-acre, manmade lake and recreation site to serve the public, encouraging visitation of Poe Valley in the scenic mountainous region of Central Pennsylvania.

This was not the first earthen dam proposal in Pennsylvania's Civilian Conservation Corps program; however, it was one of the largest earthen dam structures proposed to date.

A letter dated October 1, 1935, from the US Department of Agriculture, Forest Service sent to State Forester John W. Keller authorizes the construction of the dam.

Company 1333 and its management team was now assigned their largest and most significant challenge to date, to construct the proposed earthen masonry dam, therein creating Poe Valley Lake.

CHAPTER 5

BUILDING THE DAM,
OCTOBER 10, 1935 – DECEMBER 19, 1937

In the early part of 1934, camp engineer Bennett and others sitting in on a regional superintendents meeting proposed an earthen dam be considered for construction in Poe Valley. The idea apparently was already under consideration, as subsequently, the camp engineer was instructed to review various suggested locations and to explore Big Poe Valley from the junction west to the already situated site of Camp S-63. Mr. Bennett, known for being most thorough when performing any assigned task, explored all of the topography in the outlined area and, subsequently, provided a suggested placement for an earthen dam creating a recreational lake using the flowing water of Little Poe Creek. The location Mr. Bennett proposed was located approximately two miles east of the S-63 campsite.

Additional review and input by state and federal officials led to the eventual recommendation to move forward with the dam construction that the camp engineer, Bennett, had put on the table. Engineering and design development, modifications to design proposals, and funding delays slowed movement on the project through late-summer 1935.

Federal and state officials granted final approval for the project and subsequently authorized the construction of the earthen masonry dam in a letter dated October 1, 1935.

This letter, along with ten pages attached to it, were found among the documents my grandfather held onto.

The letter addressed to Mr. John Keller, State Forester, came from the United States Department of Agriculture signed by Regional Inspector G. T. Backus. The letter directed that the

Cover letter authorizing dam construction

work could proceed, allocating approximately 5,100 man days for skilled labor, and all other costs shall not exceed $15,000.00 (excepting enrollee labor man day costs—estimated to be 28,864 man days).

ECW Dams   Date Prepared Sept. 11, 1935

Form E. C. W. D-1

Name of dam.   Poe Valley

   Preliminary report of dam proposed for construction by E. C. W.

1. Location. (a) State Penn'a. (b) County Centre (c) Penn State

   Forest. (d) Name of drainage. Susquehanna

2. Work to be done by CCC Camp 63 and 64 under supervision of State

   Forest Service.

3. Purpose of dam. Recreational

4. Description of site. (To include depth and characteristics of

   various strata of soil to bedrock and description of bedrock.

   State number of test pits or bore holes.) _____11_____

   Earthen dam with masonry spillway.

   Base to rest on clay strata.

5. Description of dam. (a) Type. Earth (b) Height. 32 feet (c)

   Length 660 feet. (d) Volume (Cu. yds.) 31,302.

6. Description of spillway. (a) Location. Right side (b) Type.

   masonry. (c) Width 60 feet. (d) Flood capacity 4000 CFS. (e)

   Freeboard above flood capacity. 2 feet.

7. Description of watershed and reservoir.

   (a) Area of watershed. 4.94 square miles.

   (b) Area of reservoir. 23 acres.

   (c) Maximum depth of stored water 20 feet.

   (d) Average annual precipitation 40 inches.

   (e) Average slope of watershed is moderate.

   (f) Watershed is barren, sparsely, moderately, heavily

       timbered.

   (g) Timber stand on reservoir area heavy. Miscellaneous.

       hardwood--no value appro. 12 acres.

Form E.C.W. D-1 (page 1)

Attached to the authorization letter is Form E.C.W. D-1. This two-page form is signed by A. A. Doppel, Assistant Regional Inspector. This form provides a general description of the project,

8. Plans and specifications

   (a) Completed. Yes.

   (b) Attached hereto. Yes.

9. Estimated cost.

   (a) Materials and supplies. $4365.85.

  *(b) Equipment. $11,250.00, if purchased.

   (c) Labor (Other than enrolled men) $2418.75.

   (d) Enrolled men 28,864 man days.

Note. Rent equipment costing over $500 each. AAD

Project approved Oct. 1, 1935 A. A. Doppel, Inspector
                      Asst. Reg.

*Heavy equipment purchased can be used on other ECW Dam projects.

Form E.C.W. D-1 (page 2)

including location, purpose, type of dam, and a four-item cost estimate.

Poe Valley Dam Estimate

Hand Labor	Man Hours

	Hand Labor	Man Hours
1. Clearing	12 Acres @ 200 hrs.	2,400
2. Soil Stripping	2425 Cu. yds. 4 hours	9,700
3. Embankment	31 02 Cu. yds. @ 6 hours	190,812
4. Excavation (Core and base preparation)	5000 Cu. yds. @ 4 hours	20,000
5. Concrete	290 Cu. yds. @ 5½ hours	1,595
6. Masonry	425 Cu. yds. @ 6½ hours	2,763
7. Gathering stone	2000 Cu. yds. @ 4 hours	8,000
8. Dry Riprap	1725 Cu. yds. @ 5 hours	8,625
9. Stream Control		500
10. Placing logs	512 feet @ 3 hours	1,563
11. Seeding and Sodding	30,000 sq. ft., 20 sq.ft.per.hr.	1,500
12. Gathering logs	512 feet @ 5 hours	2,560
13. Gravel placing	680 Cu. yds. @ 4 hours	2,720
	Total Man Hours	2 0,913
	Man days	28, 64

Materials		
Cement	925 Bbls. @ $2.65	$2,451.25
Sand	448 Tons @ 2.00	896.00
Stone	325 Tons @ 1.00	325.00
Trash Gate	436 lbs. @ .05	21.80
Bars and misc. steel		270.00
4" tile	12 ft. @ .15	1. 0
Sluice Gate		400.00
	Total	$4,36 .85

Dam construction cost estimates (page 1)

Attached to Form D-1 were two pages titled "Poe Valley dam estimate." The estimate itemized thirteen cost lines describing man days allocated in each of the cost lines. The total man days

POE VALLEY DAM

ESTIMATE

BASIS USING HEAVY EQUIPMENT

1. Skilled labor (Masonry)		$ 318.75
2. Skilled labor (Shovel-Roller)		2,100.00
3. One ½ yard gas shovel		2,688.00
4. One 10-ton gas roller		1,250.00
5. One ½ yard gas mixer		262.00
6. One 3-inch gas pump		120.00
7. Material		4,365.85
	Total	$11,104.60

Man days   5,100

Dam construction cost estimates (page 2)

for enrollee labor is estimated to be 28,864. A second estimate page having seven line items estimates the costs for supplemental skilled labor, equipment rental, and materials to be $11,104.60.

COMMONWEALTH OF PENNSYLVANIA
DEPARTMENT OF FORESTS AND WATERS
WATER AND POWER RESOURCES BOARD

SPECIFICATIONS FOR ECW DAMS

CLEARING

Clearing as applied to recreational dams shall mean the removal of all trees and brush in the flooded area to an elevation at least 2 feet above the flow line. In order to improve boating and wading advantages along the shore, in some locations where the flooded area is limited, it is advisable to remove all stumps to an elevation of 4 feet below the flow line. Where the project is for swimming only, all stumps should be removed from the flooded area.

SOIL STRIPPING

Wherever this item is indicated on the plans or drawings, it shall mean the removal of grass, roots, and soils containing living or dead vegetable growths, or soils which are too pervious, or soils which are deficient in satisfactory bearing qualities, or otherwise unfavorable in the opinion of the engineer. In estimating the quantity of this item, an average depth of one foot is taken.

EXCAVATION

This item may mean excavation to facilitate stream control, excavation to secure satisfactory foundations, or excavation for the replacement of one class of material with another, and for embankments. Wherever the item applies to stream control or replacements, the excavated material shall be placed, generally, within 500 feet of the taken point. Excavations for foundations of embankments, masonry, riprap, crib-work, etc., shall be carried to depths, or to materials the bearing or consistency of which are

Dam construction project specifications (page 1)

Six additional pages were attached to the authorization letter providing the general specifications for the work. These pages satisfactory to the engineer.

EMBANKMENT

Embankment materials shall be taken from pits selected by the engineer, or, when satisfactory, from the excavation items and wheeled, hauled by truck or other means, or all, and placed in locations as indicated by this item on the plans or drawings. Impervious material, so called, shall be placed in layers and compacted in a manner satisfactory to the engineer. The matter of layer thickness will depend on the method of compacting. If done by hand tamping, the layers shall be 3 inches thick; if by truck trafficing, the layers may be placed 6 inches thick. If a 10-ton roller is used, the dirt layers may be placed 8 inches thick. Adequate moisture control, as directed by the engineer, shall apply in the construction of earthen embankments.

MASONRY

Masonry items as applied to dams generally mean a masonry as nearly watertight as possible. Only tough, durable, clean stones of known weathering qualities shall be used, and these in all cases should be embedded and completely surrounded, except on exposed faces, with mortar so as to produce a masory which shall be dense, sound and practically impervious.

RIPRAP HAND PLACED

Three classes of hand placed riprap or pavement may appear as items in ECW dams.

1st. Twelve inches deep, in which three-fourths of the stones shall be the full depth of 12 inches, and stones under 9 inches in depth shall not be used except as spalls.

2nd. Eighteen inches deep, in which three-fourths of the stones shall be the full depth of 18 inches, and stones under 12 inches in depth shall not be used except as spalls

Dam construction project specifications (page 2)

describe the materials to be used and specifications for how the work was to be performed.

3rd. Three feet deep, in which three-fourths of the stones
shall be the full depth of 3 feet, and stones under 18 inches shall
not be used except as spalls.

All stone selected for this work shall be tough and durable
in quality and shall be placed on edge, if necessary, to meet the
specifications of depth, in the positions of this work as shown on
the drawings. Stones shall be laid in close contact, and projections
above the desired elevation napped off to grade. Voids shall be
filled with spalls, tightly driven in place. As a general requirement all classes of riprap shall be laid on a bed of gravel or
broken stones, the thickness of which shall be at least 6 inches.

GROUTED STONE PAVEMENT

Wherever this item applies, it shall mean a class of work
similar to Hand Placed Riprap with the exception that the surface
void spaces shall not be filled with spalls, but shall receive suc-
cessive slush applications of 1 - 3 mortar, liquid enough to be
broomed and flow into the spaces between the stones.

LOGS AND CRIB WORK

Logs used in the upper 6 feet of crib structure shall measure not less than 8 inches in diameter at the small end; all other
logs shall measure at least 10 inches at the small end. Logs
shall be stripped of bark, be sound and free from rot, and reasonably straight. Notchings at crossings may be necessary and desirable in order to provide better bearings and to keep the crib work
approximately level. Filler strips or blocks shall not be placed
between crib logs. Logs shall be pinned together at all crossings
with three-fourth inch iron pins. To facilitate the driving of
these pins and in order to prevent splitting at log ends, starting or guide holes, of diameter no larger than the pin itself and
4 to 8 inches in depth, may be bored into the logs before entering

(3)

Dam construction project specifications (page 3)

the iron pins.

As a primary consideration in the building and life of a log crib-rock fill dam, it is essential that the plank cutoffs, the planking on the crib, and the upstream embankment be constructed in a careful and conscientious manner so that seepage through, around, or under the structure be reduced to a minimum. Wherever the crib is laid on a yielding base, the bottom logs should be embedded or trenched for at least three-fourths their diameters into the base. If the base is rock or existing timbers, the crib logs should be securely fastened thereto. In all cases the first or bottom layer of logs should be laid normal or at right angles to the stream flow. The stone fill in the crib should be hand placed, not dumped, with the idea of placing the maximum amount of stone in the cribs in order to apply as much weight as possible to the structure. The crest of the spillway portion of the dam should be so constructed that it will maintain its position at a level grade, and produce a water cover over the entire spillway even under conditions of low stream flow. This will very much increase the life of the structure.

STONE

In nearly all locations where ECW dams are proposed for construction, there is a supply of field or surface stone which is tough, durable and sound, and when clean is satisfactory for masonry riprap, pavement, and crib fills. Care should be taken to prevent the use of any rotten, soft stones, or stones of a shaley or porous nature.

CONCRETE

Wherever this item appears on plans or drawings, principal locations being the lining of gate towers, intake wells, and surrounding blow-offs conduits, it shall mean concrete of one part cement,

(4)

Dam construction project specifications (page 4)

two parts sand, and four parts stone by volume, or any reproportion-
ing of the cement and aggregate as the engineer may direct in order
to obtain maximum strength or density. A mechanical two-minute mix
is preferred, otherwise it may be done by hand to conform to the
same standard. A total water content of six gallons per bag of
cement shall not be exceeded, and where possible less water shall
be used depending on the desired strength and conditions of placing. All concrete shall be deposited in layers not deeper than
8 inches, and layers shall be maintained reasonably level as the
work progresses. Sufficient spading, tamping, booting, etc., shall
be applied to the mass while being placed so that it will conform
neatly, and with the desired density, to the finished lines and
grades of the particular work as shown on plans or drawings. No
concrete shall be placed in water unless the procedure and conditions of placing are approved by the engineer. During and after
placing, concrete shall be properly protected against weather and
temperature changes. Covering, wetting and curing of the finished
work shall be done in a manner and for such periods of time as
directed by the engineer.

SAND

Sand which is too, fine, or sand containing an excess of silt,
loam or clay, shall not be used in mortar or concrete. Some local
bank sands in State Forest areas are satisfactory to use if mixed
with coarse cleaner sands. Only sands approved by the engineer should
be used in masonry or concrete items.

MORTAR

All mortar used in masonry work and slush applications of
stone pavement shall be mixed in the proportion of one part cement
and three parts sand by volume. Where used for pointing, the mix-
ture shall be one part cement and two parts sand by volume.

Dam construction project specifications (page 5)

SLOPE PROTECTION

Slopes of embankments, or slopes in cuts or excavations, shall be protected against erosion. This may be done by stone riprap, hand placed or loose, or by seeding, sodding, or the planting of vines. The type of protection or cover for a particular slope shall be determined by the District Forester and the Engineer.

(6)

Dam construction project specifications (page 6)

The camp engineer and camp superintendent were now, in turn, responsible to manage the dam construction project in accordance with these few pages of printed instruction. Initial design acceptance called for a 660-foot-long earthen dam to be 32 feet high and 130 feet wide at its base, with a 33-foot-wide masonry spillway at the south end of the dam breast.

The engineer's log for the construction of the dam has the following posts:

> October 9, 1935 — *"Mr. Hodges visited location of dam and went over the various preliminary phases and giving instructions for procedure in the work to be done."*
>
> October 10, 1935 — *"Bailey Auman began cutting and clearing area for dam."*
>
> (The construction of Poe Valley Dam officially commenced on this date.)

By late October 1935 most of the overgrowth where the twenty-seven-acre lake was to be developed had been cleared. All of this clearing process was through the labor of the CCC boys under guidance of the foremen using axes, grub hoes, two-man crosscut saws, and monumental bonfires. In the beginning, mechanical equipment supporting the ground-clearing work included one crawler diesel tractor, several stake body trucks, and two dump trucks.

The heavy equipment received in camp was not new, and required constant maintenance effort according to my grandfather, and these unfavorable equipment operating conditions are supported in daily activity logs.

According to my grandfather they had about as much time in the "fixing" of motor equipment as they had in the operating time of the equipment.

During the period between mid-October through early December 1935, the land areas where construction activities for dam construction were to commence were prepared for the work. This included ditching for the blow-off pipe to control water flow, surface stripping for the dam breast, and a low-grade construction access roadway. During this same time period, weather had not been very favorable to the project; nonseasonal heavy rains slowed progress, as did early winter periods of snow and cold temperatures.

Work did proceed as excavation, installation of piping, form-work for concrete placement, and concrete placement would take place. I remind us all that this period foreshadowed the development of concrete delivery trucks. All concrete to be used on the project was mixed on the job in a small one-third yard mixer with all ingredients put into the mixer by hand. This means CCC boys were shoveling sand, stone, and cement into the motorized mixer, adding water initially carried in buckets from a nearby stream, and then delivering the concrete to placement locations with wheelbarrows. Remember that these were the days when wheelbarrows had flat-rim, steel wheels. Pneumatic tires for small equipment use was not commonplace. Pushing a heavy load of concrete on steel wheels on bumpy, stony dirt paths is not an easy task.

By mid-December the work pace slowed. Unseasonal, cold weather, rains, and snow one cause, and project administrators and inspectors were not in agreement on issues slowing the work. Combining these two factors, work on the dam project was halted on December 11, 1935, and did not resume until February 1936.

At the end of February, inspection of work previously performed found concrete work protected from the rigors of winter were satisfactory as to be expected allowing work to resume.

Plan revisions would now be issued with extensive changes. One of the most significant changes was relocation of the spillway. The spillway was now to be constructed on the north side of the dam breast, rather than the south side as previously detailed, and would be sixty feet wide. Partial excavation work for the spillway had already been performed on the south side of the dam breast. Work immediately commenced to have the spillway constructed on the north side as instructed by inspectors. Inspectors also advised other changes were forthcoming and revised plans would be issued. Again, work on the construction of the dam was halted from April 11, 1936, through May 4, 1936, awaiting the revised plans. Limited work resumed on May 4 at the direction of inspectors still awaiting the revised plans.

Throughout the early part of the construction year 1936, the general progress of the work was not going smoothly; weather, design document revisions, conflicting instructions between state and federal inspectors, and equipment issues were most problematic. The various documents I have and the engineer's log repeatedly reference proper equipment was not available to perform the work.

Proper equipment in this case meant having a second crawler tractor, bulldozer, a power shovel, air compressor, and operable water pumps. The log indicates repeated promises by state-level management personnel to have equipment brought into the camp were not fulfilled. When some equipment finally did arrive, it was found to be in condition requiring constant repair to keep it operable, and many daily log entries indicate the equipment was "down for repair." The following is one such log entry, dated 6-17-36.

"Note tractor failure—R5 tractor came to us in bad condition. Front cylinder busted. Trailbuilder hanger bolts sheared off requiring machine shop work increasing the size from 3/4" to 7/8". Generator was shorted and had to be rewound. Front wheel bushing shot."

Numerous log entries indicate mechanics were required to perform repairs, yet mechanics were not available. As was the way of the Civilian Conservation Corps and Poe Valley camp they would figure it out as they went, and so in Poe Valley they would call on the equipment operator and foremen to roll up their sleeves and take on the role of a machine mechanic. Apparently, my grandfather was a fair mechanic, as numerous entries in the daily log indicate he and equipment operator Guisewite were performing equipment repair duties and successfully keeping the equipment on hand operable. This equipment included diesel crawler tractor, bulldozers, air compressors, dump trucks, and various pieces of equipment with small engines like water pumps and a cement mixer.

Later, while listening in on discussions between veterans at reunions, I learned enrollees had rolled up their sleeves as well and worked hand in hand with the mechanics of the day and learned a trade at the same time, all the while keeping the dam construction equipment in operation. This OJT (on job training), through necessity, eventually became actual Civilian Conservation Corps administered education course programs.

On May 9, 1936, a "top dog" federal inspector visited the camp and reviewed work activities. He found concrete placed at the blow-off pipe area was potentially not up to standards, suggesting the sand mix was not quality material. This same federal

Page 11

These statements and conclusions are obviously in error.

A fire pump and 700 feet of hose was ordered, same to be used for sprinkling clay on fill. This was reported favorably by Mr. Fisher. Mr. Fisher said he would not send a third tractor until Mr. Mulford indicated that we probably could use it. (Note conversations Weaver-Mulford.

Mr. Weaver went for four Reo dump trucks. Our Chevy trucks were given in exchange for them.

THURSDAY June 11th, 1936

Continued work as previously reported. Continued grading spillway. No additional tractor came today. Work is being retarded for lack of heavy machinery. Weaver went to Milroy again to request that this machinery be given us as per statement of Messrs Betts, Hodges and Fisher.

FRIDAY June 12th

Continued work as previously reported. Tower up to height of 19' 6". Poured concrete in this section. Received plasticity mould. Tractor came from Coudersport this evening at 6 P. M. Size 5-R.

Continued to grade spillway. Tractor was used in hauling large stone for tower wall. This has been done frequently and thus delays grading work. Need the oft requested dirt remover. All trees around spillway were cleaned to proper width.

SATURDAY June 13th

Rained intermittently all day. No work. No additional information for dirt remover. Mr. Weaver again made request forsame as per promise of Mr. Betts.

MONDAY June 15th

Continued masonry on tower. Continued to haul stones for Rip-Rap of west side of fill. Continued to grade spillway. Continued to clear stumps and trash west side of dam. Geisweite worked on R-5 Tractor getting same ready for efficient work.

TUESDAY June 16th

Continued masonry on tower. Continued grading spillway. Continued to haul stones for Rip-Rap west side of fill. Continued to clear stumps and trash on west end ofdam working down toward centre. Both tractors worked on spillway. Used Compressor to drill in shale rock which is very hard. Messrs. Mulford and H Hutt came in today and brought metric scales forclay testing, 1/10 gram to 100grams.

No Plasticity needle received as yet.

WEDNESDAY June 17th

Continued to grade spillway. Small grader broke down at Noon. Big grader used one (1) day. Small grader use one-half($\frac{1}{2}$) day.

Continued to haul stones for Rip-Rap West side of Dam breast.

Continued masonry on blow off tower.

Poured concrete in six (6) feet section.

Continued to clear stumps and trash on West central section of dam.

N O T E:—T R A C T O R   F A I L U R E.

R-5 Tractor came to us in bad condition. Front cylinder busted. Trailbuilder hanger bolts sheared off requiring machine shop work increasing size of bolts from $\frac{3}{4}$" to 7/8". Generator was shorted and had to be rewound. Front wheel bushing shot!

Engineers daily log (page 1)

THURSDAY June 18, 1936

Continued grading spillway. One grader working.
NOTE:--AIR COMPRESSOR NOT WORKING DUE TO A DEFECTIVE VALVE SYSTEM.
Continued masonry. Ready to pour concrete.
Hauled stones for Rip-Rap. Cleared central part of Dam from stumps and refuge.
Mr. Swope came into Camp prepared for work at 10:00 A. M. Will work with Engineers on Dam inspecting and so forth.

FRIDAY June 19

Continued grading spillway. Got R-5 tractor ready and worked both graders in P.M.
Continued masonry on Blow Off tower. Poured Section of concrete.
Continued to haul stone for Rip-Rap, West side of Dam breast.
Compressor did not work due to lack of repairs.
Mr. Hutt came to camp and requested that estimate be made for all purchaseable material. Same to be put out for bids. Estimate was made by Mr. Swope and myself(A. T. Bennett).
Copies of same are on file:
Fire pump & Hose not to be sent us. Mr. Hutt reported that Mr. Hodges would not come for inspection until Tuesday, June 30. Last visit Tuesday, June 2nd.

SATURDAY June 20

Note: Contention with Mr. Weaver as to line of excavating along road for up streamside of spillway. I asked that the line of cut be a sustained straight line for entire length of spillway. Mr. Weaver' said it should be curved and so ordered the operator.
The objection to this curvature is two fold. 1st: the distance between south side of road and north side of cut is not sufficient to allow curvature. 2nd: the road way of old location would be cut down and furnish an approach to north side of spillway for storing sand and crushed rock.
Mr. Weaver referred this matter to "r. Swope who also agreed that the line of excavation should be sustained straight line.
The decision was against us both.

MONDAY June 22nd

Continued to grade spillway. Both tractors working.
Got compressor started again. Compressor had top valve on valve cap and stems out. Received new valve and made x stems.
Finished masonry on tower and poured concrete in last section. Placed 4" concrete coping on top of wall.
Wing walls to tower not finished as yet. Will continue on wing walls tomorrow June 23, 1936.
Started placing stone for Rip-Rap, East side of Dam breast. Same to have back slope one (1) on two (2) and one (1) on one (1) front.

TUESDAY June 23rd

Continued to grade spillway. Began to dig clay core. R5 tractor was used to push out some of the clay. The tractor was run over the blow off pipe. I protested to Mr. Weaver who said it would not hurt the pipe as the ground was about level. Also that if the blow off was not strong enough to hold the tractor

Engineers daily log (page 2)

it was very poor. This action of tractor on top of the blow off pipe could cause the concrete to crack.

Men were set to work with pick and shovel to dig and slope the core trench. This trench as shown on revised plans is 16 feet wide instead of 21 feet as shown on original plans.

Continued to build south wing wall of blow off tower.

Continued to haul stone for rip rap east toe of dam breast. L5 tractor broke down today at 1:30 P. M. and was not ready for work at quitting time.

WEDNESDAY June 24, 1936

Continued to excavate spillway. Got R5 tractor repaired at 10:30 A.M. Used both tractors on spillway rest of day.

Started doubleshifting tractors on spillway excavation today.

Continued to haul stone for rip-rap East toe of dam breast.

Finished mas nry on wing walls for blow off tower. 3 P. M.

Continued to dig core trench.

Shot 50 holes in hard shale at east end of spillway. These holes averaged about 7 feet depth.

THURSDAY June 25th

Continued to grade spillway both tractors working doubleshifts.

Shot holes on west end of spillway in hard shale. Continued to drill hard shale on northside of spillway.

Continued to haul stones for rip rap wall along east toe of dam breast.

Continued to dig core trench south side of blow off trench. Checked levels for excavation for spillway. Swope instrument man.

FRIDAY June 26th

Continued to grade spillway. Both tractors working double shifts. Hard blue shale covering nearly half of area from north to south. Continued to drill holes into this shale. Continued to dig core trench.

Continued to haul stones for rip rap south side of blow off along east toe of fill.

Had Mr. Swope to make an experiment with clay to be used for fill.

Took ½ yd of sifted clay (3 openings per lineal inch or 9 orifices per square inch) puddling it to an unknown assumed plasticity and shaping it to a mound 15 inc es in height. Into this mound an opening 10 inches deep and 10 inches diameter was made. Into this orifice we poured 2 ½ gallons of water. This was left set for 24 hours. At the end of 24 hours the water showed a subsidence of ¾ inch.

SATURDAY June 27th

Restaked spillway. This showed that the change of line for excavation narrowed the cut for spillway to the extent that we will have to shift the north end about 5 degrees to get room for wall and slope at this point. The original plans showed the spillway set to an angle with the breast of the dam.

Estimate of Concrete and Masonry in Blow Off tower:

Concrete	28 cu. yds.
Masonry	270.5 cu. yds.

Estimate as of June 27th.

MONDAY June 29th

Continued to grade spillway. Both tractors working 2 shifts. Also continued to drill hard shale.

Engineers daily log (page 3)

inspector, Mr. Bechtol, additionally stated unless construction of Poe Valley dam was "not in full swing by first of July he would recommend the discontinuance of it."

It seems to me after reading through the engineer's log, the left-hand group of inspectors had not informed the right-hand group of inspectors about issues, and conflicting instructions issued were definitively slowing the progress of the work.

Then more rains set in during the early part of the month of May, further hampering getting construction activity "underway in full swing." Finally, all was ready to go, weather was now cooperating, and in the latter part of May construction activity was again "underway in full swing."

Work proceeded at a moderate pace during the latter part of spring and early summer of the year, however, records indicate the used heavy equipment was subject to more than its fair share of breakdowns.

Records also indicate the camp engineer and superintendent repeatedly advised officials of the breakdown conditions and subsequent need for replacement equipment and were met with nonresponse for extended periods of time, leaving the men of Camp S-63 to maintain the equipment as best they could, while attempting to maintain a construction schedule.

INTERRUPTED BY FLOOD WATERS

Yet another interruption halted the work on the dam during this period when one of the most damaging floods on record occurred in June 1936. The flooding was the result of combined melt water from record winter snow falls and excessive rains all through the spring months, saturating ground levels, and record-setting rains in early June caused streams and rivers to overflow, causing widespread damage throughout Central and Eastern Pennsylvania.

The mighty Susquehanna River flowing through these regions overflowed many a small town and cities along its route. The boys of the numerous CCC camps throughout the region were called upon to help with flood-relief efforts. The boys of Poe Valley mobilized promptly to Lock Haven, PA, assisting with flood cleanup.

A letter addressed to the camp commander of Company 1333, dated 7-30-1936, expressing the thanks of the citizens of Lock Haven and the American Legion Post 131 was received by and subsequently copied into the August 1936 issue of the *Poe Valley Ravin.*

William Marshall Crawford Post No. 131.

AMERICAN LEGION
LOCK HAVEN, PA.

July 30, 1936.

Commanding Officer
1333rd Company
Camp S-63
Coburn, Pa.

Dear Sir:-

In behalf of the Members of the William Marshall Crawford Post, American Legion, and the Citizens of   Lock
Haven, I wish to extend to you, and through you to the
men of your Company, this expression of our appreciation
of the splendid services rendered by you and your Company to the city of Lock Haven following the disastrous
flood of March 17-19, 1936.

Your response to our distress call was prompt and generous. The efficiency and orderly manner in which you met
the situation merited the respect and admiration of all.
The confidence and courage which your presence inspired
during those dark days will never be forgotten. It will
make an interesting story for future historians of our
city.

Sincerely yours,

CHALMER EDWARDS
Post Commander

Letter of appreciation from commander of the American Legion Post, Lock Haven,
Pennsylvania

The earlier negative sentiment previously expressed by Mr.
Bechtol, however, did not sway the CCC boys and the camp
administration from moving forward. Revised plans and a new
R7 Caterpillar bulldozer arrived in camp in addition to other
needed equipment, and the work pace apparently picked up in

a satisfactory manner, as not another entry in the daily log included a comment by federal inspector Mr. Bechtol.

Mr. Matthew Townsend shared the following story:

> His father Albert Townsend had been visiting with his uncle, camp engineer Amos Bennett in the summer of 1936. The young Mr. Townsend, then being about 14 years old, was taken to the train station in Coburn awaiting scheduled delivery of a new bulldozer to arrive by train. Camp project administration not wanting to lose an on-site operator for a whole day in camp would have the young Mr. Townsend, after having been shown the how to's of driving a bulldozer, drive the bulldozer from the train station back to camp. The trip, taking all day and most of the evening, was successful. Mr. Townsend shared his only concern regarding the trip was would something still be available to eat when he showed up with the bulldozer as he knew the evening mess hours had passed. Yes, dinner was there when he arrived, his reward for a job well done.

While the arrival of a new bulldozer was a big help, the bigger help came July 18, 1936, when a steam shovel arrived in camp. This single piece of equipment had a significant impact on the construction of the dam. It was used for so many differing tasks, and it had the capability to dig out large stumps quickly, load dump trucks with two scoops, and dig trenches at a rate no group of enrollees with picks and shovels could match, as long as they could keep that "blessed thing running." My grandfather talked much about the after-hours maintenance work being performed by himself and the operator Mr. Paul Vonada, on the "used" steam shovel sent to them.

Throughout the mid-summer and fall periods of 1936, work on the dam construction was in full swing. Work was being conducted two shifts a day so as to take advantage of the available daylight during this time. The overall length of the dam breast, spillway, and blow-off tower was becoming apparent. Much of the work was dedicated to finding adequate clay material for fill. The fill was then to be trucked, dumped, and spread out to be layered and rolled in the breast area of the dam. The clay material was generally available within the confines of the cleared thirty-acre area adjacent to the dam breast location; however, desired-quality

Steam shovel operating in camp, operator is Paul Vonada

clay materials would quickly run out in a chosen area, requiring relocation of the steam shovel being used to dig out the clay.

Each move of the shovel took a considerable amount of time, as a dry-level pathway was required. Apparently, a heavy rainstorm could halt the ability of the steam shovel to move under its own power on the slightest incline, as is described in project documents. I remember my grandfather telling me the laborious work involved to move the steam shovel during wet, rainy periods in the summer and fall and snowy periods in the winter. He told of the laborious work by the "boys" to place heavy, wooden timbers down onto the ground by hand in front of the moving shovel, creating a temporary wooden roadway for the steam shovel to have traction.

He explained they did not have a sufficient quantity of these heavy, wooden timbers to provide more than a few feet of planking in front of the shovel as it moved, thereby causing the boys to immediately pick up the timbers from the back of the shovel as soon as it passed over them and immediately bring the timbers to the front of the shovel pathway, allowing continued movement of the shovel.

He also told me of the same need for the heavy timber pathway they would have from time to time to allow movement of their heavy crawler tractor equipment during periods of inclement weather.

I remember him telling me how frustrating it was to have progress slowed simply for not having a sufficient quantity of these heavy timbers at the site where they were surrounded by forests, all the while awaiting purchase requisitions for heavy timbers to be approved by the Department of Forest and Waters. Please remember, my grandfather's resume included being the former owner of a sawmill business. Imagine the irony and compounded frustration he must have dealt with being able to mill the needed timbers himself, if he had the mill available, and the inability to get the Department of Forest and Waters to fulfill a request for timbers from their own forests in a timely fashion.

By this time the labors of the CCC boys, supervisory staff, and equipment operators was becoming ever more apparent to any- one who stopped by for a look. Visitors to the site were, however, few and far between.

Although contrary to what one might have thought, visitation to the camp and dam project area by the public was very minimal. It was not until a much later time when I realized just how remote Poe Valley was to the folks living within close proximity to the camp.

Traveling into Poe Valley by motor car was over course, dirt roadways still being developed through the labors of the CCC boys. Sunday drives of the time were mostly taken on smooth highways, miles away from Poe Valley, if taken at all.

Full curiosity had not yet set in to the folks of the region. The idea of a recreational park being the result of the labors of the CCC boys was not yet well-known, nor had it yet formed in their minds there was more going on in Poe Valley than forest conservation measures being performed by a bunch of kids from the city.

Work on the dam project again slowed as winter set in. Documents indicate unseasonably wet weather all through the month of November slowing the progress of placing fill material, and when wet weather was not problematic, colder temperatures would become problematic, allowing freeze action to occur and adding to slowing the progress of fill placement and masonry work. Subsequently, work was halted on dam construction activi- ties in the early part of December and did not resume until the later part of March 1937.

The CCC boys and foremen who were assigned to the dam construction project were reassigned back to road building and various forest stand improvement projects.

During the period between late March through May 6, 1937, work was not in full swing on dam construction. Numerous inspections were required to be performed by state and federal officials to verify dam construction work previously halted and sitting through the winter period had not suffered any damage as a result of the harsh weather. These inspections were subsequently performed during the latter part of the month of March 1937, and all work was found to have weathered the winter months in a satisfactory manner. Approval to resume construction was granted in early April.

During this same period, a new contingent of enrollees were turned out for work and promptly withdrawn so as to get adequate clothing and gear for their work activities, again slowing the progress. Records show clothing requisitions were repeatedly being delayed at district headquarters. Then more rains set in during the early part of the month of May, further hampering getting construction activity underway.

Finally, all was ready to go again, weather was cooperating, and dam construction activity was scheduled to get underway in full swing by mid-May.

To meet established construction schedules, double shifts were employed to take advantage of the long daylight periods of late spring, summer, and early fall.

All did not go swimmingly; the engineer's log shows the weather would not support keeping construction on schedule. Between May 14, 1937, through June 24, 1937, it rained thirteen of twenty-seven scheduled working days. The clay being used as dam-fill material could not have excessive moisture content. Digging of clay and rolling in clay could not be performed during rainy periods.

During the double-shift time period, a second engineer Mr. Smith would come to Poe Valley from the Joyce Kilmer Camp No. 148 to assist with dam construction on second shift. Mr. Smith remained in this position until September 13 when the double shift work schedule came to an end.

On June 1 Mr. Herb Smull, a local skilled mason, came to camp to lead the stone masonry work on spillway construction. The side walls of the spillway were constructed of heavy, locally acquired sandstone. The rough-shaped stones were collected by the enrollees and brought to the work area by truck and wheelbarrow. Here they were shipped and set by hand. Most of these stones were too heavy to be handled and set by hand. A jib-pole-style crane was erected to support placement of the stones. In 1936 most jib pole cranes were nonmotorized on construction sites as being the case in Poe Valley. Rope cables attached to large diameter hand crank wheels were used to hoist the stones into position. Excavation for the footings and placement of concrete footings was performed by hand. The only motorized equipment to support this part of the work would be the concrete mixer. Work on the dam proceeded near its planned schedule through July 23. During this period, clay fill was hauled in and rolled in place any day weather permitted. The construction schedule would, however, fall off as two issues contributing to the delay collided at the same time in late July. The first "truck trouble" as noted in the engineer's log explains "spindles" on the Reo dump trucks were experiencing excessive breakage, requiring repair at a time when repair parts were not readily available. Numerous inspections and load modifications would be made in an effort to determine the cause. These trucks were taken out of service and replaced using Chevrolet dump trucks. The Chevrolet trucks could not be loaded with as much material as the Reo models, which contributed to delay. Eventually, the Reo dump trucks were brought back into service.

Another matter without explanation is noted in the engineer's log for the period of July 23 through August 13. The logs reveal the work progress was impeded due to "shortage of men." It tells the enrollee count made available to the work project from actual company strength was restricted for reasons known only by Army commanders. Through all of the challenges experienced, work proceeded and was determined to be no more than ten days behind schedule on September 8.

For the next thirty days, work commenced at expected pace with the exception of a few minor issues. Several of these issues were experienced on any construction project then and now, material shortages, and equipment breakdowns.

One of these issues, however, was experienced only in a construction camp environment. The engineer's log dated September 17 tells the following:

> Men were sent out late this morning because the cooks failed
> to get up and have breakfast on time. 1 hour and 20 minutes
> were lost. When Mr. Weaver told the Company Sergeant that

the men would be held late so as to make up the lost time the sergeant became impudent and nasty. This indicates that they are not trying to cooperate with us so as to make progress with the work.

For the period May 1 through October 15, the lion's share of work required to construct the dam would include placement of clay fill for the dam breast, spillway masonry and rip rap, stone walls at spillway, concrete weir at spillway, and stone facing on the dam breast. These components now mostly all fitted together showed the dam at substantial completion (near 95 percent) on October 30, 1937.

In early November three principle works remained to be completed on the dam. Placing shale atop of the clay fill on top of the dam breast to protect the clay surface from erosion, level and clean the twenty-seven-acre reservoir bed, and the installation of the gate valve in the control tower. For the most part, this work proceeded as expected except for the gate valve.

There are numerous entries in the engineer's log starting in early August regarding acquisition of the required gate valve. Through early November the ordering of and arrival date of the needed valve is still uncertain to camp supervision. Once installed and closed, this valve will allow for the filling of the reservoir by the channeled Little Poe Creek.

The gate valve finally arrives November 18. However, it is missing its valve stem. For the next few days, cleaning and leveling of the reservoir bed continues.

Engineer's log:

November 19: Mr. Hodges visited camp today. Examined valve, tapped it to see if it was sound. Pronounced it O.K. Instructed us to have a fish commissioner present when creek was closed so as to take care of the fish below dam.

The valve stem arrived on November 24, the day before Thanksgiving.

Excitement was building throughout the entire company as the dam construction project all had been a part of neared completion and was ready to be filled with water. All wanted to see the water rise and flow over the spillway for the very first time.

Veteran James Murphy shared the following story at a reunion that went something like this:

> Around Thanksgiving time all of us were getting excited as we realized the dam project would soon be a lake. I remember we were betting on the day water would run over the spillway. Everyone wanted to talk to Bennett the engineer and get him to help out to determine the day and time. Some of us were betting monetary sums of up to a quarter while the most of us were betting differing quantities of cigarettes. He remembered he did not win nor could he remember if anyone actually won big.

The following excerpts taken from the engineer's log take us through the time period when excitement in camp was building, awaiting the date and time when water would run over the spillway for the very first time.

Engineer's log:

November 26: "Friday after Thanksgiving put in gate valve today. Everything fitted nicely and Mr. Frankenberger did the job in 1-1/2 hours. The water was not entirely shut off".

December 2: "Closed valve at 2:12 pm, Lt. Curtain, Mr. Holcomb and Chaplain Butterbach were present. Mr. Weaver turned the valve rod closing the valve"

December 4 & 5: We inspected the impounding water on both days and find it to be filling at the rate of 15 inches per day. Everything seems O.K.

December 6: The water rose 15 inches in the dam today. Everything is satisfactory.

December 7: Dam filled 13 inches today. Water is spreading out over a larger area and will continue to spread so that the fill height will be retarded.

December 14: Inspected breast of dam and find no signs of water through fill. Water raised 6 inches in dam today. It is within 16 inches from top of the wing walls on the tower.

December 15: Snowed and rained all day. No work done around dam. Water continued to rise.

December 18: Rained today. No work. Dam filled to within three feet of flow line. Inspected the breast on east side and find no gullies as a result of rain or thaw.

December 19: Water went over spillway at 4:15 A.M. Dam was then full for the first time. Engineer Bennett watched the spillway get its baptism. Water attained full flow at 5:45 A.M.

After this date there are only eleven more entry dates in the engineer's log. They describe daily activities and other works. Included is a short sentence noting minor erosion experienced on the east end of the spillway requiring attention and additional placement of stone to retard this erosion.

Opening of the valve was required to lower the water level to perform the erosion control work. The log tells the work was promptly completed and the valve was again closed, and water went over the spillway for the second time on December 30.

During the period between September 1 through November, indecision about park development was noted numerous times in the engineer's log. State officials were not in agreement on development of beach areas, bath houses, and a floating dock proposed to be placed on the south side of the lake.

Finally, Engineer Bennett was directed to locate and stake the areas on the south side of the lake, as was indicated on a new hand-drawn sketch issued by Park Board officials during a camp visit on November 11.

The new sketch required beach sand placed where previously directed by officials to be relocated to the new position shown on the sketch. Work on beach sand relocation and beach area development again proceeded on November 12. This work was slow in its progress due to inclement weather conditions and continued indecision about park development by officials. On December 22, officials visited camp to again review proposed plans for park development work. These officials would direct ongoing park development work to be halted until final plans have been further reviewed and approved by the Park Board.

These same officials directed Engineer Bennett to stake new roadway to the south side of the reservoir connecting to Poe Valley Road, as per previously approved plans.

The direction to stake a new roadway would be the last entry in the engineer's log.

Photos shown on pages 116–120 provide a limited chronology of work being performed during the construction of the dam

The initial completion of Poe Valley Dam, circa 1941

Poe Valley Dam, circa 2018

The engineer's log provided the information, allowing the opportunity for me to share so many of the details described above. Certainly, those who were part of the construction of the dam would tell their remembrances of the many tasks and ways on how work was performed for the proper construction of the dam. In addition, comments and updates on construction progress would be told by enrollees reporting in the camp newsletter.

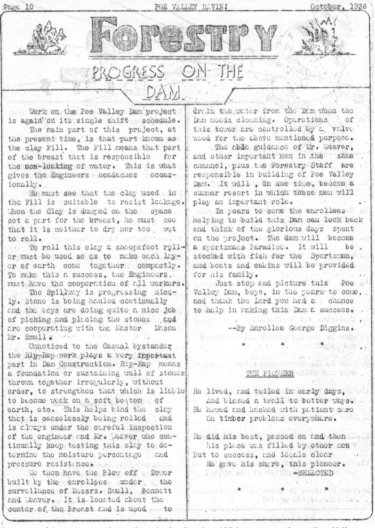

Progress of dam construction written in the October 1936 camp newsletter *Poe Valley Ravin*

THE OTHER DAM STORY

My brother George always enjoyed telling the following story our grandfather shared about Poe Valley's indigenous dam constructors:

Camp superintendent Mr. Luther Weaver holding one of the critters that were holding up the work

> The small creek feeding what would be the lake created by the construction of the dam was also selected by a family of beavers to be the site of construction for their own dam. The beavers went about their work and promptly completed construction of a dam. The beavers must have certainly felt the prompt completion of their dam, showing how easy it was to outwork a bunch of boys, would show their dam was more important than the monstrosity being built before their eyes. Water now channeled in undesired directions was not satisfactory to project administrators. Foreman directed the boys to go down and tear out the beaver's dam only to find it all but rebuilt by the following morning. After a few rebuilds our grandfather directed the boys to use the one tool to do the job once and for all, dynamite. Kaboom, and the beavers moved out.

Certainly, today the removal of beavers would be performed using alternate means so as to not cause harm or loss to a family of beavers. In the 1930s, however, there were many uses for a beaver's pelt not allowed today.

INSPECTORS AND THE DOG ROBBER

My grandfather lamented about the many previously mentioned state-level and federal-level inspectors who came to camp to perform multiple inspections and how these men in most instances either held up the progress of the work or requested multiple changes be made in the work, particularly during the construction of the dam project. These inspections included regional-, state-, and federal-level inspectors. Many times, according to what my grandfather mentioned, and as is noted in the engineer's daily log, these inspectors would many times contradict directions given by another inspector, and subsequently time would be lost while awaiting a final decision on a particular issue.

At the time, I was not of an age to fully understand what he was saying, but now, after working in the construction industry with various governmental agencies, I understand what levels of frustration he was talking about.

My grandfather, somewhat of a practical jokester, and his foremen buddies invented ways in which to amuse themselves, mostly at the expense of the unsuspecting inspector "guest," who happened to make unfavorable comment or hold up the progress of the work, either warranted or not. When these inspectors came to visit the camp, they would typically be invited to join the superintendent, engineer, and foremen at meal time in the foremen's quarters. Here the food was brought to them by the mess runners and served family style.

My grandfather told me with a little laugh in his voice of the escapades brought onto the unsuspecting individual. They would set up the table in advance of the meal and assign chairs for the "guest," and at this position a flower-decorated water glass was placed. This was a special glass, although looking like the other glasses, it was known as a "drip" glass. There was a very small hole in the glass hidden in the flower, and when the unsuspecting person would drink from the glass, a small dribble would weep out, drip onto the unsuspecting guest's chin, and fall down onto the table, making it look like the person drinking from the glass had a problem. Of course, the foremen would act as if nothing had happened and make sure the mess runner was refilling the glass all through the meal.

If the chosen guest had fully irritated the foremen, more practical "jokestering" was to take place. In a case such as this, the "drip" glass was only half of the setup. The tables were covered with a waterproof fabric called oilcloth, this fabric hung down over the edge of the table, and the foremen would position themselves around the table so as to hold up the cloth, creating a gutter profile in the cloth around the table and innocently, without being caught in the act, pour a small amount of water into the gutter. When the guest took a drink of water, the drip glass dribble was supplemented with the water in the gutter being dumped unsuspecting onto their lap. One can well imagine the self-control required of these practical jokesters to keep from snickering and giving into the joke played.

When the foremen thought an inspector had been unduly harsh when making a noncomplimentary remark about the progress of the work or had criticized the quality of the work unjustly, other practical jokes would come out of the bag.

My grandfather told me in one of these instances the "dog robber" was sent out in advance of the inspector's departure to reposition a directional road sign, most of the inspectors not being all that familiar with the roadways in and out of the camp would end up with an innocent long-way-about tour of the Bald Eagle Forest. This particular practical joke was learned by one of the unsuspecting inspectors who returned to the camp after having been lost for quite a period of time only to find out the "dog robber" had already repositioned the sign back to its proper direction. This learned outcome then shared between the inspectors resulted in inspectors during subsequent visits requesting an enrollee in a separate vehicle lead the way out of camp.

Now, about the "dog robber." This was a term given to an enrollee who had been assigned to run messages between the camp administration building and the forestry quarters building and serve as mess steward, ferrying meals between the Mess Hall and the forestry quarters building that housed the foremen.

The forestry quarters building was where the foremen also eat their meals. The dog robber performed other miscellaneous assigned duties to include being the set-up man for practical joke operations. The dog robber term came from the old line about scraps from the table that would go to the family dog, except in the CCC camp the runner would eat their meals with the foremen, and thus rob the dog of any leftover scraps.

CHAPTER 6

THE *POE VALLEY RAVIN*

As referenced previously, one of the most common education programs throughout the Civilian Conservation Corps all across the country was the development and continuing production of a camp newsletter. Camp newsletters were generally the follow-up to a nationally published Civilian Conservation Corps newsletter called *Happy Days*. The national newsletter was published and distributed to all Civilian Conservation Corps camps. The national published newsletter provided enrollees with the general news about the current state of the Civilian Conservation Corps program and included all sorts of articles about happenings in camps throughout the country. Like most newspapers, it also included classified advertisements. In the classified section, everything from jewelry items to new homes were offered for sale.

Poe Valley Camp S-63 like so many other camps started a camp newsletter. The camp published its first edition of their newsletter early in 1935.

The February 1937 issue of the *Poe Valley Ravin* page 9, titled "Education," provides insight into the development and official naming of the newsletter:

> The first issues were born in the company supply room and nursed by editor S. T Whelan a former supply sergeant and named by John D. Hannum a former enrollee company clerk.
>
> That first edition was created in the supply room on stencils donated by Lt. Carroll with only a paper clip as a stylus and mimeographed at Camp S-69 Livonia, PA.
>
> The first issues were published irregularly, without a definite schedule. It was decided that in order to publish the paper regularly it would be necessary to purchase more

Cover page of the CCC national newsletter *Happy Days*

equipment including a mimeograph machine. Former Ass't Leader Thomas Graham came across with the suggestion of getting advertisements and agreed to be advertising manager. This position he filled most capably, getting his quota of advertisements each month until this practice was discontinued for all camps in the corps area. By this means the present mimeograph and additional equipment for stenciling were purchased and partly paid for. Then the paper was published monthly in the Education Office. When advertising was discontinued, the balance was paid from the 'other Funds of the Company,' but during the time advertising was secured for the paper, it was entirely self-supporting.

The newsletter was so named to pay tribute to the famed author Edgar Allen Poe and his widely known poem "The Raven."

Poe Valley was so named after the Poe family who had settled in the region in the earlier part of the nineteenth century.

Local legend has it the famed poem was penned after a visit by Edgar to Poe Valley researching family history, however, verification of fact has yet to be found to confirm the famed author ever trekked through Poe Valley.

Once the newsletter was started, the publication was produced monthly through June 1941. It was produced as part of the camp education program under the guidance of the camp education director. The publication was produced typically by a staff that generally included an editor-in-chief, press room manager, advertising manager, and reporters. All of the staff members were enrollees. For many of the newsletter staff, this was the first time they ever sat down at a desk holding a typewriter. These enrollees subsequently learned writing skills and typing skills supporting an opportunity to seek gainful employment after discharge back home. Here was another example of the education opportunities offered to enrollees.

After the newsletter was completed each month, it was then cranked out on a mimeograph machine and distributed to all of the camp members, including all administration personnel. Among the numerous documents found in my grandfather's foot locker were copies of numerous newsletters. I was most fortunate to acquire additional copies of the newsletter at auctions and several were gifted to me. I learned via the Internet there is a most significant repository of camp newsletters at the University of Chicago. Through additional good fortune, I was also gifted copies of the *Poe Valley Ravin* from the University of Chicago repository through the kindness of Pennsylvania State University professor John Shingler.

More than sixty *Ravin* newsletters were published in the Poe Valley camp. The start date of publication is unknown, as initial newsletters were published without having a date printed on the newsletter. The last newsletter is believed to have been published in June 1941.

The newsletters provide a most insightful look at the life and times of Civilian Conservation Corps Company 1333, Camp S-63 Poe Valley. These monthly publications shared the happenings in the camp. Editorials were presented on every topic pertinent to the times and as could be conjured up in the minds of young men who had been witness to economic plight like no other time previous, and subsequently became part of a program like no other previous in America's history. These editorials told of a time where opportunity, hope, and prosperity were replacing the despondent hopelessness felt by the these very young men. The newsletter provided an outlet to express the satisfaction or dissatisfaction of being a CCC boy.

An editor and a production staff is the way of most any newsletter or newspaper. A full production staff developed the *Poe Valley*

Camp newsletter, *Poe Valley Ravin,* August 1936

Ravin on a monthly basis with the support of the camp education advisor. I was fortunate enough to meet and spend time with veteran enrollee Joseph McCreery at several of the early reunions I hosted, subsequently learning Mr. McCreery, during his time in camp, had been a contributor, a cartoon editor, and editor-in-chief of the *Poe Valley Ravin*. He told of many experiences about his time in camp and the satisfaction he enjoyed from being a part of the newsletter production. In particular, he told me how on several occasions when it would become deadline to print, he would be excused from his daily work assignment on dam construction to complete the month's production of the newsletter.

Joe, as he preferred to be known, told me his personal story about how he came to be in the Poe Valley Civilian Conservation Corps camp. He, like so many his age, was a young, unemployed

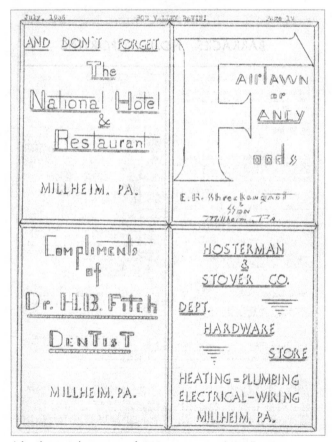

Advertisements in camp newsletter

youth roaming the streets in his home city, Philadelphia, PA, "running with the wrong crowd" and got nabbed by the police after committing a petty crime. He was presented before the judge and told me he was "given a choice between 60 days in lockup or 6 months in a Civilian Conservation Corps camp." Joe told me he had vaguely heard of the Civilian Conservation Corps program before this moment in his life, yet chose to give it a try, as he saw it would be a way to get out of a city where he had found no opportunity existed for a young guy like himself.

Joe's life successes started in the Civilian Conservation Corps. While in camp, he became a barrack leader and editor of the *Poe Valley Ravin*. As a Civilian Conservation Corps enrollee, he took root and success followed him out of Poe Valley as he went on to college and received a degree in accounting. Joe went on to

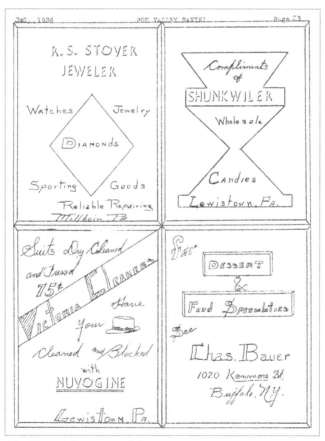

Advertisements in camp newsletter

become a certified public accountant, eventually owning his own successful accounting firm, settling in El Paso, Texas.

Federal program officials after receiving multiple complaints from vendors throughout the country, for what was reported as undisclosed reasons, would end allowing camps to seek out local advertisers and mandate all camp newsletters be advertiser free at the end of 1936. However, there were local vendors who supported the early development of the *Ravin*.

Original copies of some of the *Ravin*'s newsletters, many other documents found in my grandfather's wooden chest, and acquisition of the remaining monthly newsletters through the gift of Professor Shingler provide me with a wealth of information, which has been shared in this book. Additionally, I was fortunate to acquire a few copies of the newsletters at auctions, as gifts, and when antiquing.

Over the years my interests in Civilian Conservation Corps activities have led me to the acquisition of a large personal collection of memorabilia. Much of the period items of the time have gone by the wayside. Most being lost to limited interest, and limited distribution of the newsletters. Limited acquisition of keepsakes by enrollees due to the lack of funds to purchase and the mobility of the enrollees after discharge. Many of the pieces in my collection came from the wooden chest found in my grandfather's shop.

The advent of the Internet allows one to seek out items and see items we may not realize exists. This method is so much more fruitful than the hope of getting lucky at a flea market or antique shop.

One of those times when searching for Civilian Conservation Corps items online, I saw an interesting item: a Civilian Conservation Corps enrollee footlocker. The footlocker is a wooden chest fabricated to hold the personal possessions of an enrollee or foreman while in camp. Slowly, the memory became clearer. The wooden chest in my grandfather's shop that held all those documents he saved was indeed a CCC footlocker, and I did not have my mother hold onto it.

RECREATION ACTIVITIES

The camp facilities included a Recreation Hall where the enrollees could hang out during their off times. This facility was host to a pool table, dart board, and tables and chairs where card games, "a lot of poker," and board games were played. Additionally, this facility included a small library where many a donated book and magazine would be well-worn by the repeated use of enrollees.

Maybe more importantly, the camp exchange, also called the canteen, was located in the Recreation Hall. This was where cigarettes, candies, chewing gum, soda, and miscellaneous sundry items were made available, provided the enrollees had the few pennies, nickels, or dimes to shell out for these small luxuries.

Remember, most enrollees were obligated to send $25.00 or the lion's share of their monthly pay back home, leaving only $5.00 in their pocket for the month to spend on whatever they wanted.

Very few enrollees were not obligated to send an allotment back home. These few were held in high regard and admiration as being "wealthy," as was remembered by veteran Chester Slatwich.

Veteran Randall Boob remembered his first payday when he felt he had been shorted. He asked the officer in charge where the rest of his pay was, to be reminded "the folks back home need money too." He remembered this was all that was said, and he agreed his folks were in need, only then remembering the agreement he signed when he enrolled, authorizing the allotment be sent home.

In Poe Valley, one of the favorite recreational activities would be "movie night." In the early years of the camp, administrators reached an agreement with the movie theater manager Mr. Drew Kolb in nearby Millheim to bring a projector into the camp and show movies.

The camp newsletters provided us with some of the movie titles and stars of the time. Some of the movies shown were *When's your Birthday* starring Joe E. Brown; *Sea Devils* starring Victor McLagen, Preston Foster, and Ida Lupine; and *The Plainsman* starring Gary Cooper and Jean Arthur. As time went on, a movie projector was acquired and maintained in the camp.

August 10, 1937, the camp was treated to the showing of *Anything Goes* staring Bing Crosby, Ethel Merman, and Charles Ruggles by Mr. McCrork representing Films, Incorporated. Films, Incorporated would go on to rent the projector to the camp and supply four films a month for showing. Educational films could now be shown anytime to meet camp needs and schedules.

This acquisition of the rented projector allowed movie night to be scheduled and rescheduled as would suit the needs of camp operations and activities.

The camp published newsletters indicated four movies a month would be scheduled, and movie night was usually scheduled for Monday evenings. Recreation activities were scheduled by the camp education advisor and the company commander. Documents indicate activity scheduling generally remained constant from the initiating commander through the next command period.

The organizational structure of the US military included recreational activities for idle hours, and these activities were immediately put into play in the CCC camps. Mostly these activities would be team events like baseball, basketball, football, mushball, and volleyball. Many games were played in an inter-barrack league basis. Other games were sandlot style with teams comprised of members from one signup sheet playing a team from another signup sheet placed in the Recreation Hall. Other games were inter-camp in nature played between other local CCC camps in the district. Camp newsletters provide the box scores of these games and provided the story of wins and losses with short justifications written by the sports editor for each of these wins and losses, mostly telling the standout pitching or excellent shooting skills of the winning team. The sports page in the October 1936 camp newsletter told of the differing sports happening in the Poe Valley camp.

The sports section of the August 1936 issue of the camp newsletter notes "Badminton a new comer to the sport realm of Poe Valley is holding its own." That same issue reported that on August 22 the Poe Valley baseball team met the team from the Lancaster Valley Camp 113 and defeated them 16-2. The *Ravin* reads, "The score was one sided but much spirit was displayed by the defeated team." It continues, "The boys from Poe Valley were out for scalps because winning this game would bring them a notch closer to the top."

Baseball, the great American pastime, was held in high regard in the CCC camps, and many stories were shared by reunion goers telling of the poor quality of gear made available to the camps and the skills needed to repair gear so as to be able to play the game. The veterans enjoyed telling about the games won, especially when their respective barracks team, the underdog, had come out on top beating a more heralded team in inner camp play. Even more satisfaction was derived when the CCC boys would beat the

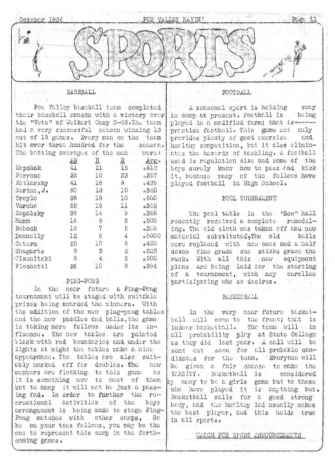

Sports page, *Poe Valley Ravin*, October 1936

local town teams after suffering from the many snide comments so often made about the boys from "back in the mountain."

Rain, a well-known reason for the cancellation of the game of baseball, would not be the only reason to halt the game, as was described in the sports page of the July 1936 camp newsletter. "On Sunday, July 19, the Poe Valley team journeyed over the mountains to Treaster Valley Camp S-64. They did not play for when they arrived, they discovered that Camp S-64 was quarantined with measles."

Baseball, by all accounts, was a popular team sport in camp, as box scores showed up in each of the spring through early fall *Poe Valley Ravin* newsletters published in the years 1935 through the last issue of 1941.

SPORTS

May 21.

SABO STOPS REBERSBURG
Pitching five hit ball, Sabo, of the "Poe Valley Ravens", set back the strong Rebersburg nine by a score of 7-2. Highlights of the game were--A triple play by little Tony Campana and "Big Red Robson"

The Lineup

RAVENS	REBERSBURG
Bosak cf	Hockman 2b
Yanick lf	Stover 3b
Ulick ss	Gentzel cf
Robson 1b	Hazel p
Dunsmore c	Boone 1b
Racan rf	Hoover ss
Demshak 2b	Cummings lf
Hramotnik 3b	Manz rf
Magent rf	Hock c
Sabo p	
Karpinski c	
Campana 2b	

Ravens------0-3-2-0-0-2-0-0
Rebersburg--0-1-0-1-0-0-0-0
Two base hits-Hramotnik, Yanick
Three base hits-Sabo
Struck out by Sabo-13 by Hazel 3

SOFT BALL
May 26
MILLHEIM TROUNCES CAMP 17-14
Millheim beats the camps-pick up team-in the last inning. Errors played a big part in helping the camp loose.

INTER-BARRACK
Those interested in starting a inter-barrack, soft ball league, turn their names into Bob Snull. From this inter-barrack league can be picked a team good enough to compete with outside games.

Barrack No 5 being to small to have a team, would like to combine with the Overhead. What do you think?

ROOKIE SHUTS OUT REBERSBURG

AL BOSAK PICKS RAVENS TO 1-0 VICTORY OVER REBERSBURG

The Poe Valley Ravens visited Robersburg May 27, to win their second game of the year. Bosak, who entered camp in April, should be an asset to the team. Alowing only one man to reach further than 2nd base, "Al handled the situation very nicely. This should make the team pretty tough, since Sabo was the only pitcher up till now

RAVENS	REBERSBURG
Karpinski lf	Hockman 1b
Yanick cf	Bohn c
Ulick ss	Gentzel cf
Ciesienski 3b	Tyson p
Sabo 1b-p	Cummings rf
Magent 2b	Stover 3b
Demshak rf	Hoover ss
Dunsmore c	Brogall 2b
Bosak p-1b	Mangelman lf

Ravens--0-1-0-0-0-0-0-0-
Rebersburg--0-0-0-0-0-0-0-0
Struck out by Bosak, 5 by Tyson 5.
Hits off Tyson 3, off Bosak 7
Two base hits--Tyson, Dunsmore, Yanick.
Errors- Ulick, Dunsmore, Sabo.
Sabo relieved Bosak in 7th inning.

LEAGUE GAMES
The games scheduled for the 25th and 26th were called off because of rain. They will be played at a future time. (Possibly May 30th and July 4th)

Baseball box scores

Mushball may be a runner up in popularity, as mentioned in many of the camp newsletters. The June 1936 issue provides the following report:

Mushball maintaining its popularity of last year at this camp has succeeded in attracting many of those players not so interested in its near kin, baseball. This year the camp is Captained by that peppy star from Dubois, Archie Watson.

The various camp mushball teams in this vicinity evidently remembering the defeats they suffered from the Poe Valley team of last year, have failed to accept any invitations to tangle with them this year. This being the case several games have been booked with various teams in Lewistown.

The first series of these games was with the Brought's Service Station team. The Poe Valley team got off to a good start by winning on their own diamond by the score of 7-2. Then in the return engagement they outdated the Lewistown boys by the score of 5-3.

The next series was with the high-powered Superior Ice Co. team. They came to Poe Valley with the reputation of being one of the best teams in Lewistown and left the camp with that reputation still intact. The final score was 8-3. The camp team was unable to get revenge in the return game and went down to defeat to the tune of 12-3.

But on Sunday June 28, they reversed their form, and when the Dry Cleaners from Lewistown came to camp, it was a different story. They returned to Lewistown cleaned in a double header by the scores of 6-0 and 7-3. The batteries for the first game were Davis and Hagan for Lewistown; Watson and Mandry for Poe Valley. The same battery performed Lewistown in the second game with Miller and Watson doing duty for the camp team.

The game of baseball before, during, and certainly after The Great Depression would be America's favorite pastime. Baseball being ever present in the Civilian Conservation Corps camps quickly became competitive between their respective camps. Many company commanders were known to promote special interest in the competitive spirit. The Poe Valley baseball team under the coaching supervision of Captain Bixby in 1934 took the team all the way to the sub-district level championship game being held in Mill Hall, PA. The winner between the Poe Valley camp and Shingle Branch camp held "bragging rights" and a silver trophy. The game was played October 15, 1934, with the Shingle Branch club coming out on top, and reported in the *Renovo Daily Record*.

I had not previously ever heard of the game mushball. Wanting to know more about this game, I was able to look it up on the Internet to find it is similar to and played in accordance with softball. A mushball is described as a fourteen-inch diameter soft, sponge-like ball. I decided seeing a mushball would help further

October 14-1934 · RENOVO DAILY RECORD

SHINGLE-BRANCH WINS SUB-DIST. BASEBALL CHAMPIONSHIP

The Shingl:branch baseball club, under the management of Vic Carlson came thru with the baseball championship of sub-district No. 6 by downing the Poe Valley Camp for the second straight playoff game at Mill Hall Saturday by the score of 4 to 2.

The game was a real pitchers battle between Hughes of Shinglebranch and Peters of Poe Valley with Hughes holding the edge. Poe Valley scored one run in the first inning. Shingle-branch came back in their half of the first to score two runs. Poe Valley scored again in the fourth to deadlock the count at two all. For the next four innings both pitchers showed their stuff and neither team scored. In the eighth, Shinglebranch scored twice on hits by Ribik, Parucha, and Turba. Both teams fielded well.

Saturday's game marked the close of a very successful season for the Shinglebranch baseball team. The team was well-managed by Vic Carlson and captained by Parucha. Lt. Mullins coached. A silver trophy will be presented to the team by Chaplain McGuire, the sponsor of the elimination.

SHINGLEBRANCH	AB	R	H
Ribik, lf	4	1	2
Ammeter, 2b	4	1	1
Parucha, ss	4	2	2
Turba, 1b	4	0	3
Arnold, 3b	4	0	1
Rulein, rf	2	0	0
Bodley, rf	1	0	1
Sychak, cf	3	0	0
Dempsey, c	3	0	0
Hughes, p	3	0	0
	32	4	10

POE VALLEY	AB	R	H
Evans, ss	5	0	0
Robins, cf	3	1	0
Mciris, lf	5	0	3
Croyle, 1b	4	1	2
Knappick, 3b	4	0	1
Cheverko, rf	3	0	0
Keic, 2b	4	0	0
Calahan, c	4	0	1
Peters, p	4	0	1
	36	2	8

Two-base hits—Ribik, Ammeter, Parucha, Turba, Croyle, Knappick.

Struck-out—By Huges 6, by Peters 5.

Base on balls—Off Hughes 3, off Peters 1.

Umpires—Boracki and Latone.

Baseball story in *Renovo Daily Record*

138

Shingle Branch, CCC District Champs, 1934

my knowledge of the game, so I went to a local large-scale, sporting-goods store, and when I asked the young man at the service desk if the store carried "mushballs," he looked at me as if I may have mush for brains. The young store attendant quickly recovered and realized I did not have a third eye and stated he would be glad to look up possible suppliers. After spending quite a bit of time on an Internet search, he came back to tell me all of the suppliers his store uses did not have a mushball available. As of this writing, I am continuing my search for the elusive mushball.

MUSIC AND DANCING

For most, music played a big part in recreational activity time. When enrollees had expressed interest in the music arts, the first step toward learning to play an instrument was the piano. There was simple reasoning for selecting the piano in Poe Valley, as this was the only musical instrument in camp for the first few years. The camp received its first piano via donation through the efforts of the education advisor, Mr. Holcomb.

Documents indicate learning to play other musical instruments was conducted outside of camp in nearby Lewistown.

I have no further information on what enrollees did to further their desires on learning how to play or what instruments they may have selected until the early summer period of 1937.

In the May 1937 issue of the camp newsletter an article appears describing a plan to form a camp orchestra. It goes on to explain that camp medical officer Lt. Silverstein traveled to New York City and acquired the needed equipment for the formation of an orchestra. It would seem Lt. Silverstein had heard the sounds of an orchestra put together with enrollees, combined from two nearby camps, Camp S-68 Weikert and Camp S-148 Mifflinburg, and felt he could do equally well with the boys in Poe Valley. Under the direction of Lt. Silverstein, the boys did go on to assemble an orchestra. The new orchestra provided the music for the Coburn festival in July 1938.

Continuing under the direction of Lt. Silverstein, the Poe Valley orchestra continued to develop and earn a cash prize for their fine play at the West End Fair held in Laurelton, as reported in the September issue of the 1938 camp newsletter.

Dated 12-27-1935, Harry Zeigler's diary, who is the father of camp education advisor Paul Zeigler, reads, "To the 5th annual high school alumni banquet in the I.O.O.F. hall - Poe Valley CCC camp orchestra furnished music for the evening."

I have been asked on several occasions if a radio was provided in the camp. The June 1936 issue of the *Poe Valley Ravin* advises a radio was the main attraction in the Recreation Hall after installation of new furniture. Oddly, knowing television was not yet available, I do not remember any of the veterans discussing listening to a radio as a pastime during any of the reunions or later gatherings.

Music played a significant part in one of the other well-documented recreation activities—camp dances. The camp dance was an activity enjoyed by the enrollees and the dames in the nearby towns of Millheim and Lewistown, who had become quite interested in wanting to learn more about those boys back in Poe Valley's woods.

Dances were selected to be part of camp celebrations and any reason was grounds for celebration. Some of those reasons were any type of a camp anniversary, such as the camp startup, second and third year anniversary dates, arrival of new enrollees,

Christmas, open house, spring and fall times of the year, and just about any other legitimate-sounding reason they could initiate.

The camp newsletters describe these dance activities. The dances were held in the "decorated for the reason" Recreation Hall or in the Mess Hall, and refreshments would be served. To make the dances a success, girls from nearby towns were invited through the efforts of the camp commander and the education advisor; subsequently, these girls were brought into camp for the event and returned back to their respective hometown by bus. The articles published in the camp newsletters describe each load of girls on the buses included chaperones. In one instance, a camp newsletter article notes the camp commander's wife was in charge of chaperoning the girls. The article did not include any information as to how many fathers of the girls were additional chaperones.

The August 1936 newsletter includes a reprint of a letter submitted by former camp commander Capt. Malcolm V. Coates describing the efforts and results regarding the very first dance held at Poe Valley Camp S-63 on November 15, 1935.

The music at these dances was in most instances provided by a small orchestra. Information acquired from issues of the *Poe Valley Ravin* indicate there were two separate orchestras from the nearby town of Lewistown who provided most of the music for the camp-sponsored dances. The first mention of an orchestra's name was Jimmy Loudens Orchestra, followed by Punch Harmon and his orchestra.

An article written in the March 1939 newsletter provides the following story:

> "Farewell Dance Mammoth Success"
>
> Punch Harmon leads good bye jive-fest. March 25 a farewell dance was held in the recreation hall last night in honor of the boys forced to leave camp by the time limit. Various critics have expressed their opinion that "Punch" Harmon and his orchestra are the best rhythmakers in Lewistown and as a result of last night's swing party, the enrollees and their guests are inclined to agree with them.
>
> Punch and all members of his band sing, and it would have been a treat to just sit and listen. It is easy to understand any one turns to "jitterbugging" when such an exponent of the pastime as these "Rhythm Modernaires" go to town.

Two busses supplied many of Lewistown's fairer sex the opportunity to attend the festivities.

Take it from one who spends all his spare time listening to orchestras that Punch Harmon is better than a lot of swingsters who depend solely on their musical efforts for a living.

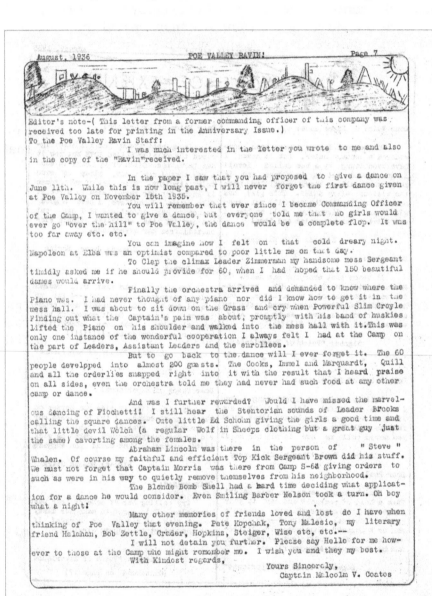

August, 1936   POE VALLEY RAVIN!   Page 7

Editor's note-(This letter from a former commanding officer of this company was received too late for printing in the Anniversary Issue.)

To the Poe Valley Ravin Staff:

I was much interested in the letter you wrote to me and also in the copy of the "Ravin"received.

In the paper I saw that you had proposed to give a dance on June 11th. While this is now long past, I will never forget the first dance given at Poe Valley on November 15th 1935.

You will remember that ever since I became Commanding Officer of the Camp, I wanted to give a dance, but everyone told me that no girls would ever go "over the hill" to Poe Valley, the dance would be a complete flop. It was too far away etc. etc.

You can imagine how I felt on that cold dreary night. Napoleon at Elba was an optimist compared to poor little me on that day.

To Clap the climax Leader Zimmerman my handsome mess Sergeant timidly asked me if he should provide for 60, when I had hoped that 150 beautiful dames would arrive.

Finally the orchestra arrived and demanded to know where the Piano was. I had never thought of any piano nor did I know how to get it in the mess hall. I was about to sit down on the Grass and cry when Powerful Slim Croyle Finding out what the Captain's pain was about; promptly with his band of huskies lifted the Piano on his shoulder and walked into the mess hall with it. This was only one instance of the wonderful cooperation I always felt I had at the Camp on the part of Leaders, Assistant Leaders and the enrollees.

But to go back to the dance will I ever forget it. The 60 people develpped into almost 200 guests. The Cooks, Immel and Marquardt, Quill and all the orderlies snapped right into it with the result that I heard praise on all sides, even the orchestra told me they had never had such food at any other camp or dance.

And was I further rewarded? Would I have missed the marvelous dancing of Fiochetti! I still hear the Stentorian sounds of Leader Brooks calling the square dances. Cute little Ed Scholn giving the girls a good time and that little devil Welch (a regular Wolf in Sheeps clothing but a great guy just the same) cavorting among the females.

Abraham Lincoln was there in the person of "Steve " Whalen. Of course my faithful and efficient Top Kick Sergeant Brown did his stuff. We must not forget that Captain Morris was there from Camp S-64 giving orders to such as were in his way to quietly remove themselves from his neighborhood.

The Blonde Bomb Shell had a hard time deciding what application for a dance he would consider. Even Smiling Barber Nelson took a turn. Oh boy what a night!

Many other memories of friends loved and lost do I have when thinking of Poe Valley that evening. Pete Kopchak, Tony Malesic, my literary friend Halahan, Bob Zettle, Crader, Hopkins, Steiger, Wise etc, etc.--

I will not detain you further. Please say Hello for me however to those at the Camp who might remember me. I wish you and they my best.

With Kindest regards,

Yours Sincerely,
Captain Malcolm V. Coates

Copy of letter published in the camp newsletter by former Camp Commander Captain Malcolm V. Coates

> All the enrollees feel that this occasion was the crowning point to their stays in Poe Valley. It is fitting that their departure should be recognized in such a manner.

Funding for these dance functions in most instances came from profits raised through sales of candy, soda, gum, and other available items sold in the camp exchange canteen and a recreation fund managed by the camp commander.

A farewell dance was held on September 22, 1939, honoring departing enrollees as reported in the September 1939 issue of the newsletter. The music for this affair was provided by Punch Harmon and his orchestra, reputed to be Lewistown's best band.

The evening's festivities were climaxed by a dancing contest to choose the best couples at a waltz and a fox-trot. John Sabo and his partner were chosen the best waltzers, while Karbinas and his partner were best at the fox-trot. Refreshments were served in the Mess Hall at midnight.

I learned during conversations with veterans at reunions that when additional funds would be required to support camp morale and various recreation activities, camp officers and camp foremen many times contributed personal funds to support the effort. Funds made available through the sales in the camp exchange also supported the purchase of a new piano for the Recreation Hall in September of 1937.

Other forms of entertainment made available to the camps were provided by local and regional based performers who would be invited into the camps to perform for the enrollees. Other performances were made available for the enrollees through another part of the president's New Deal package—the Federal Theatre Project. The March 1937 edition of the *Poe Valley Ravin* headlines a "Federal Show" and highlights the following:

> On Friday night, March 1937 we had the pleasure of witnessing one of the best shows ever seen in the Rec Hall. The show "The CCC Murder Mystery" was real enjoyment to all those who saw it. Even though it was a murder mystery, there were many laughs involved, and much fun was had by all present.
>
> The show was presented by the Federal Theatre Project who came with a cast of 10 people including 7 men and 3 women.

In supporting roles were thirteen men from the camp, most of the fellows played the parts of witnesses, but a few of the boys, including Marzucco, McCreery, Mandry and Wisnesky had important parts in the play.

The May 1938 issue of the *Poe Valley Ravin* headlined another show in camp, "Troupers To Appear" and reads, "On Wednesday evening June 1, 1938 a traveling vaudeville troupe that hails from 'Old Wyoming' will stage a show in the 'Rec Hall.' This troupe is unique in the fact that they carry a trained rooster and a trained dog which do many fancy tricks."

HUNTING SEASON

Pennsylvania citizens enjoy the benefits of the four distinct annual seasons, and for many the fall seasonal period brings in hunting season, a time for so many to get out into the woods and try their hand at bagging their game of choice. The forests in Pennsylvania afford hunters opportunity to bag small game and big game alike. Hunting for the elusive large-rack white tail deer, well-known as the "big buck," always put a large number of hunters in the woods. These hunters were in the woods around the area where the Civilian Conservation Corps camp was located. The camp was positioned on a leased parcel of land totally surrounded by a combination of private grounds and state game lands. In order to provide a measure of safety for the CCC boys, various measures were implemented. The October 1938 issue of the camp newsletter announced, "hunting season opens," two-thirds of a page provided instruction on the safety measures to be taken by enrollees. The following excerpts are taken from that page.

"You can be well protected from hunter's guns if only you are willing to submit yourself to the following precautionary measures."

"Posters and signs warning hunters of the presence of enrollees will be posted at least one half mile from the camp or work project."

"All enrollees will be instructed in the dangers of working, hiking or being in the territory subject to hunting and will be restricted from leaving protected areas without advising proper authorities such as foremen or commanding officer."

"All enrollees exposed in unprotected areas for work or any other purpose will be supplied with a suitable such as a colored head band or a red cloth which is pinned on the back and somewhere about the head."

"Enrollees will be prohibited from hunting of their own accord except by special permission of the commanding officer."

"All enrollees on the work project shall report to the foreman in charge before leaving the location of the job as there is extreme danger of going into the woods without ample care being taken."

It would seem to me the measures indicated above were certainly good advice and apparently were also well adhered to by the enrollees, as nowhere do I find any notes, documents, or report of any kind indicating any incidents involving hunting-related accidents involving Civilian Conservation Corps enrollees during the entire period of time the camp in Poe Valley was operational.

WOODWARD SHOOTING MATCH

More than bragging rights would be taken away from a shooting match held in the nearby town of Woodward, where personnel from the Poe Valley camp would try their hand in a shooting competition. The following story is taken from the January 1937 camp newsletter:

> In the town of Woodward some time ago there was staged a shooting match, and some of our personnel division attended, namely; Capt. Edward R. Ayres, and Supt. Weaver and Sr. Foreman, Frankenberger of the Forestry Staff.
>
> Supt Weaver proved ability as a marksman, by winning a fine beagle hound, and Capt. Ayres displaying his art in handling a rifle won a nice fat turkey. Of course, Frankenberger, had to match those wares, with the turkey and guinea hen he received as a reward for his timely shooting.
>
> There seems to be a story connected with Frankenbergers prize Viz.—he expects to use the turkey as an alarm clock for those fouls seem to instinctively make a series of noises around 5 O'clock in the morning. Good luck in the new adventure.

CRITTERS AND PETS

The camp was situated in the remote mountains of Central Pennsylvania where wildlife was in abundance. Here was where on any given day while on work detail the enrollees would encounter much of the native wildlife of the region.

I was told many stories by veterans about their encounter with wildlife. They told of their first-ever look at a deer or their first visual of a wild turkey and its brood of chicks and their many encounters with raccoons, opossums, porcupine, and every other critter living in its native environment.

They also told of their young eagerness to take in an injured and displaced critter and attempt to nurse it back to health and sometimes wanting to make it a camp pet. They also told of the times when they simply trapped a critter for their own amusement. It is easy to understand how Civilian Conservation Corps officials were quite opposed to the holding of any wildlife for any purpose.

Foresters were directed to educate the enrollees on the natural order of life in the wild and to be the point person on assuring critters were not harassed in any way and to teach these young, eager enrollees to leave the critters alone.

It is also easy to understand how the enrollees took in a stray or nursed a weakened critter, using their many resources to hide

Camp personalities posing with captured deer. In addition to enrollees the photo includes the camp Superintendent, two Foremen, one Barracks Leader, and one Assistant Barracks Leader.

146

Camp pet and her pups

their mischievous ways, in effort to amuse themselves, all the while believing they were performing a kind act for the animal kingdom.

There were numerous directives issued repeatedly by Civilian Conservation Corps officials instructing camp administration personnel to not allow any wildlife to be captured and held in the camps. I have no way of knowing how effective these directives were, however, I know they had several violators from time to time as the veterans told of their various miscreant activities. I do know they were willing to allow a photo opportunity to occur when the captured prize was maybe too cute to let go, as is suggested in the photo on the facing page.

I suspect the camp administration personnel would turn a blind eye from time to time as is suggested in the photo.

What is known, is men young and old alike have from the beginning of time found comfort in the company of a pet. I suspect the many young enrollees far from home living in the mountains found a bit of comfort lost, which a pet provides to its temporary owner.

VISITING CAMP

The establishment of the camp was like so many others around the state. It was swift and created a small-town-like environment the boys would call home. Unlike home, however, there would be no visit for Sunday dinner by the rest of the family, nor would longtime hometown friends visit and go to the movies or double date with their favorite girl.

Visitors were a most-welcomed sight, and visitation to the camps was encouraged by administrators and many camp commanders. Visitation in the early days of the camp was very light to mostly nonexistent. Simply, people did not have extra money to fill the tank for a Sunday drive, and the camps were still in the initial stage of demystifying what was "going on" back in the woods. It would take more than a year before the local communities understood the camp was not home to undesirable, troubled youths and criminals sent there from the "city." Once a few locals who had enrolled and were sent into Poe Valley and a few dances had occurred where the local girls had been invited, the word got around that the camp was "quite a sight," telling friends go get a look for yourself.

The boys were proud of their home away from home and accomplishments made and wanted to make sure visitors felt welcome. They made and erected signs welcoming visitors to camp and built a very elaborate gate topper for all to enter through.

Gate topper at camp entrance

The construction of the dam was a significant event for the region. There was no manmade lake of any size within a hundred miles of Poe Valley at the time. The arrival of the steam-powered shovel at the railroad station in nearby Coburn to be used on the site was met with more than fifty onlookers; however, no one followed the shovel under its own power when it left the station to see where it was going.

While the dam construction was underway, the public expressed limited interest, as there was little to no advertising of the dam works nor was a "recreation park site" fully determined to become part of the work by state officials.

Visitors who did come in to take a look quickly learned the roads leading down to the dam construction area were little more than rutted paths used heavily by the camp's heavy construction trucks coming and going, making the trip a "rough one."

The later years of the camp operations saw a significant increase in camp visitation, particularly after completion of the dam, which created the twenty-seven-acre lake made available to the public for recreational bathing and picnicking. Camp commanders also invited technical personnel members' families and guests to share the Sunday midday meal in the Mess Hall with the boys. This provided opportunity to show off the work projects completed by the camp, and in particular the picturesque dam and lake.

CAMP EXCHANGE

On a military post, the building where items are for sale, such as sundries, clothing, candy, soda pop, cigarettes, and general-store items, is called the "post exchange," or more commonly the PX. In a Civilian Conservation Corps camp, those desired items were made available in the "camp exchange." The camp exchange was more commonly called the "canteen." These differing names were interchangeable, serving the same purpose. In the CCC canteen, books were available to the men and sold for the sum of $1.00 each. These canteen books had tear-out stamps in increments of $0.05, to be used for purchases made in the camp exchange. The canteen books were issued by the company commander. The canteen books had a security advantage, in that they could be held by the camp commander's clerk on the holder's behalf, minimizing loss.

Camp exchange booklet

Commanders in the camps were known to make the offer of a free canteen book as a way to initiate incentive for accomplishment and also a way to provide award when merited. There are several articles in the *Poe Valley Ravin* about commanders in Poe Valley using this method.

In the April 1939 issue, the camp commander initiated a "camp improvement contest" with the winner to receive a "free canteen book." He gave the following rules:

Starts May 1 end May 5

All enrollees of this camp have chance to win above prize by submitting ten suggestions on how this camp could be

Camp exchange area inside of Recreation Building

improved. 2. Just simply write down on a sheet of paper ten (10) suggestions on how to improve our camp. 3. Submit your suggestions to the Ed. Office not any later than May 5, 1939. 4. Neatness and legibility will not count in determining the winners. 5. The verdict of the following judges will be final. The judges will be Lt. Fox—Mr. Hutt—Mr. Dean

In the July 1939 issue the camp commander initiates:

"Neatest Equipment Awards Aids Barracks"

PRIZES SPUR ENROLLEES TO IMPROVE LIVING QUARTERS

July 28—Lt. Fox has introduced a novel means of having the enrollees of this camp improve the barracks in which they live. Two weeks ago he started the practice of awarding a canteen book each week to the representative in each barrack who presented the neatest array of equipment in beds, shoes, raincoats, lockers and other things that are attracted to the eyes of some one on a tour of inspection. This new plan has aided the barrack appearance one hundred percent.

CHAPTER 7

WHO WERE THESE BOYS, COMMANDERS, AND CAMP ADMINISTRATORS?

In 1983 I had an idea to have a reunion of my grandfather's boys and anyone else who may have an interest in attending a reunion to share old memories and catch up with old friends. I knew of several veterans who resided in the Central Pennsylvania area where I lived, and I thought if I could get an article written in a regional newspaper about the camp and use some of the information I had, maybe a gathering could develop. I met with a reporter for a regional paper known at the time as the *Grit*, which was published weekly in Williamsport, PA.

The reporter chose to take in all of the information I presented and researched the Civilian Conservation Corps program's history, and subsequently an article was indeed written. The article published included my name and my contact information. I knew the article was to appear on a given Sunday morning.

My hope was to reach out and maybe touch base with a few other local and regional veterans and maybe get together, allowing me to learn more about the program my grandfather had been part of.

My hopes were fulfilled by 7:30 A.M. that particular Sunday morning as my phone started ringing at 5:45 A.M. and continued to ring intermittently for a few days. Calls came in from far and wide: New York, Ohio, Texas, Nevada, Virginia, Maryland, and Pennsylvania. With the help of my wife, my mother, and a few local veterans, a successful reunion was planned and held in June of 1983 in Poe Valley with more than fifty veterans attending.

Veterans showed up from more than fourteen states, having been notified through the effort of one article placed in one paper published and issued one day a week. Annual reunions were to follow for the next thirteen years.

During these reunion times, much was shared and learned about the operation of the camp, and for me, the camaraderie was strikingly similar to that of any military company reunion, as these men quickly went back in time to a date about fifty years prior, their memories quick and clear.

The most significant challenge faced when organizing the reunions and gatherings currently being held on behalf of Camp S-63 was how to reach out to make those former members and extended family aware of the scheduled event. A repository of rosters of CCC member names associated to a specific campsite is generally not available. State and federal government records providing rosters of individual camp names, hometowns, and other contact information generally no longer exists for the enrollees.

There is a national archive of individual enrollee records, however, access to these records was generally unknown thirty years ago. Today, these records are readily accessible, but there is a fee to look up an enrollee, and the records are maintained in alphabetical order without the benefit of any breakdown by company number or camp number, or even just a by-state identification or other alternate listing.

Among the numerous items found in my grandfather's box were two Christmas holiday menu cards. A holiday theme was illustrated on the front of the menu card. An itemized menu for the Christmas day celebration meal was provided on the inside of the card indicating more than fifteen items were to be provided, a most bountiful feast for these young men helping to ease the loneliness of being away from home and family at Christmas time.

Additionally, on the inside of the card was a complete alphabetized roster of all of the members, including their hometown and state. We were able to use these names and hometown references to send notices to local newspapers announcing the scheduled event.

This means of notification did indeed make some former members aware of the reunions, as many former members went back to their hometowns after their enlistment periods, where they settled, worked, married, had families of their own, and served their communities. We also learned conversely in this process that the vast majority of members had moved on in life's journey and settled elsewhere throughout the country.

One of the things learned during the reunions and attempts to locate former members was the impact World War Two had on the hometown locations where former members took up residence.

Many members had joined or had been drafted into the various armed services during World War Two, continuing to serve their country most honorably. After returning back to the states after their war service, they found opportunity for employment and had opportunity to experience visitation to other regions throughout the country where attraction to these differing regions would lead them to remain away from their original hometowns.

I am herein including the names of the technical personnel, military commanders, and the enrollees available to me. These names are made available from the various textural documents left to me by my grandfather and the numerous materials I have collected over the years.

The lists of the technical personnel and military commanders is believed to be complete. The lists of enrollee names is incomplete; unfortunately, no records are available providing a roster of each enrollee who was assigned to the Poe Valley camp.

My hope will be for anyone reading this book to possibly disseminate these names into the old-time method of social networking, when people contacted people direct with news they thought someone else may be interested in, and also to use the means of social networking now available to us like the Internet, Facebook, Twitter, etc. so that family, friends, and others will come to know these men had part in such a grand endeavor and share the legacy of their part in the Civilian Conservation Corps.

Military - Company Commanders

US Army Captain Charles H. McNair . . . (*June 1933 - December 1933)
US Army Captain Gilbert E. Bixby . . . . . (*December 1933 - February 1935)
US Army Captain Lingle . . . . (*March 1935 - August 1935)
US Army Captain Malcom V. Coates . . . (*September 1935 - February 1936)
US Army Captain Edward R. Ayres . . . . (*March 1936 - April 1937)
US Army Lieutenant E.P. Curtain . . . . . (*May 1937 - February 1939)
USMC First Lieutenant Lee Fox . . . . (*March 1939 - ** July 1941)

* Dates served as camp commander.
** Date shown is believed to be the date the camp closed, although this date is uncertain.

Forestry Service - Technical Personnel

Auman, Frank . . . . Foreman
Auman, Robert . . . . Blacksmith

Bennett, Amos .... Engineer
Bradford, Paul E. .... Foreman
Bressler, Miles .... Foreman
Dean, Homer .... Education Advisor
Frankenberger, Sumner .... Senior Foreman
Guisewite, Harold .... Machine Operator—Bulldozer
Grenoble, Irvin .... Foreman
Holcomb, Newton .... Education Advisor
Hoyt, Edwin F. .... Engineer
Hutt, Charles H. .... Camp Superintendent
Johnson, F. K. .... Foreman
Kerstetter, Wilmer .... Foreman
Knepp, D. .... Foreman
Korman, Warren T. .... Foreman
Kramer, Harry .... Vocational Teacher
Lewis, Oscar .... Engineer
McPherson, B. D. .... Forester
MIller, George W. .... Foreman
Neese, Harry S. .... Mechanic
Sherwood, Leroy E. .... Mechanic
Smith, John E. .... First Camp Forester
Smull, Herbert E. .... Mason
Steel, Samuel .... Foreman
Throstle, William .... Foreman
Vonada, Paul .... Machine Operator—Steam Shovel
Weaver, Luther .... Camp Superintendent (first)
Wert, Ralph .... Foreman
Wilson, L. E. .... Engineer (first camp engineer)
Ziegler, Paul .... Recreational Teacher

* The dates of service for each of the Technical Personnel listed is unknown.
* For some of these men, limited service dates and alternate locations of service is noted in other chapters of the book.

The 1933 camp Christmas card noted the menu to be served for the Christmas meal and the camp roster.

Captain Gilbert E. Bixby, Calvary, Company Commander
1st Lt Alfred G. Gillis, M. C.1
2nd Lt. David T. Carter, Inf.

Mr. Luther L. Weaver, Camp Superintendent
First Sergeant, Glen W. Comer
Mess Sergeant, Charlie W. Palmore
Fred H. Grafting, Engineer
John E. Smith, Forester

Foremen:

Sumner Frankenberger	Miles Bressler
W. J. Throssell	W. J. Korman
C. J. Grenoble	C. D. Knepp
W. C. Kerstetter	E. R. Auman
F. B. Auman	

The roster listed the following enrollees.

Leaders:
Brown, Lewis I.
Carlson, Iner
Croftcheck, John

Fee, Edwin O.
Hartzell, Merle R.
Immel, Roy S. B.

Jackson, Walter W.
Snyder, Miles E.
Tate, Lester W.

Assistant Leaders:
Beck, Gerald P.
Benson, Rudolph
Blose, Loyne C.
Brown, Paul E.
Brown, Raymond E.

Calligaro, Arthur
Campbell, Norman B.
Foernsler, Robert William
McMillen, John
Miller Carl G.

Miller, Fred
Myers, William
Ruggiers, John
Swabb, Paul D.

Members:
Adamik, Joseph J.
Adamson, George
Adamson, Hugh S.
Aley, Leon H.
Anderson, Wayne
Andrusko, Leslie C.
Archer, Austin W.
Balaban, John
Bailant, Frank
Banks, Henry R.
Belson, Thomas
Benninger, Gerald
Birk, Edward
Bojtos, Mike D. Jr.
Bonfilio, Peter S.
Bressler, Edward C.
Brooks, Raymond W.
Butters, Alvin L.
Caldwell, Foster
Callahan, Jesse W.
Cannan, Jacob E.
Casey, Harry W.
Cepegi, Stephen J.
Childs, Thomas R.
Chion, Joseph M. Jr.
Coble, John
Col, Daniel (maybe
  Coll, Daniel)
Coll, Donald L.
Collier, John V.
Coss, Harry E.
Coughenour, Lorian
Cousins, Clyde T.
Dannenhauer, G. K.
Deargi, Michael
Davis, Norman
Dean, Frank
DeGarmo, Eugene S.
Deranzo, Frank A.
Drozda, James

Duboy, Andrew
Easton, Carl
Eisenhuth, Ened J.
Emery, Homer Jr.
Evans, Delbert
Fantozzi, Armanda
Fazzari, Anthony
Federico, Phillip E.
Fields, William H.
Filchock, Martin
Franks, Chad N.
Gable, Paul
Gales, William E.
Garden, John O.
Garee, Delmer H.
Garrett, Henry
Gathers, Benjamin
Getsy, Mike
Gochenauer, John E.
Gochenauer, Paul L.
Grim, Reuben G.
Grimm, Everett
Guesman, Leonard
Guy, Clarence W.
Haefner, Henry
Hagan, Claude M. Jr.
Hall, Joe C.
Harrington, Garfield
Hartosh, Mike R.
Haught, Ulysses G.
Harrington, Jesse C.
Hetrick, Clarance H.
Hoffman, John
Hoffmaster, Charles
Hoover, Edward
Hugghes, Michael B.
Hulings, Frederick
Joseph, Daniel
Keiser, Chester W.
Keiser, William G.

Kiec, Stanley C.
Knapick, John
Kissinger, Frank S.
Kovall, Paul
Kughn, Walter F.
Layton, Russell E.
Lenox, Edwin
Liezak, Paul
Lochrie, Richard N.
Lopotosky, Andy
Lowther, David G.
Lucus, Terrill M.
McCullough, Lawrence J.
McEllhenny, Clear
McKnight, Robert
McLaughlin, Leroy H.
McWilliams, Phay C.
Malone, Basil M.
Messenger, Louis W.
Miller, Edward H.
Mikan, Mike
Morris, Jesse J.
Morris, John R.
Mountjoy, Albert E.
Newkirk, James M.
Nigro, Alphonso
Obitko, John
Oppelt, Floyd
Usmer, Arthur L.
Parke, Samuel
Parker, Alfred C.
Petrusik, John
Pollock, Thomas S.
Pontoriero, Frank
Porter, Harry M.
Preamble, Michael
Rakushin, Mike
Reed, George K.
Reed, Herbert L.
Reel, Andrew

Reider, Earl L.	Shultz, Harry Lowell	VanAulen, Robert
Reikard, George	Slater, John T.	Wagner, Carl L.
Rinehart, Roy S.	Smith, Arthur	Wagner, Martin L.
Roberts, John	Smith, Eugene B.	Watson, David
Roberts, Raymond Jr.	Smith, Robert J.	Wentzel, Leroy F.
Robson, Orval P.	Stanley, James	Wingard, Henry F.
Rohanna, kali P.	Stewart, Raymond J.	Wolff, Eugene (maybe
Rohrer, Russell	Tassone, Victor	Wolfe, Eugene)
Ruble, William J.	Teasdale, Harold L.	Worry, James L.
Rucker, Woodrew E.	Temple, David L.	Young, Lowell J.
Rumbaugh, Merle H.	Thomas, George E.	Zettle, Robert
Scherick, Orange E.	Thomas, Robert	Zook, John C.
Seibert, Charles C.	Tshudy, Raymond G.	Lewis, Eugene
Shaffer, Donald	Valencheck, Henry	

The 1934 camp Christmas card noted the menu to be served for the Christmas meal and the camp roster.

Captain Gilbert E. Bixby, Calvary, Company Commander
1st Lt William S. Miller M. C. R.
1st. Lt. John T. Brown Strode, M. D.
1st. Lt. James F. Carroll
2nd Lt. Willard N. Wallace

Mr. Luther L. Weaver, Camp Superintendent
First Sergeant, Lewis I. Brown
Mess Sergeant, John Balaban
A. T. Bennett, Engineer
John E. Smith, Forester

Foremen:

W. J. Throssell	Miles Bressler
C. J. Grenoble	W. J. Korman
W. C. Kerstetter	C. D. Knupp
F. B. Auman	E. R. Auman
Sumner Frankenberger	H. S. Guisewite

The roster listed the following enrollees:

Leaders:

Copenhaver, Merrill T.	Immel, Roy S. B.	Wert, Ralph
Degarmo, Eugene S.	Malone, Basil M.	Wheelan, Stephen

Assistant Leaders:

Brooks, Raymond W.	Dannenhauer, Gottfried	Stanton, Joseph
Corcoran, James	Kelly, Merrill W.	Zettle, Robert
Croyle, Joseph A.	Saloma, Stephen	Zimmerman, Edwin H.

Members:

Adminski, Mike	Baroni, Arthur	Bucknarish, Paul
Ahlgren, Golden	Beatty, Arthur	Budziszewski, Michael
Albright, Wesley	Brandt, Billy	Callahan, Thomas Wm.
Barnhart, William	Bryant, Richard	Cannon, Billy

Conway, Patrick
Coolican, Francis
Crader, Clarence F.
Decker, George S.
DeStephano, Umbert
Dexter, Wesley
Dunn, Kenneth
Engel, Walter
Eufusia, Aldo
Euken, Joe
Evans, Leo
Fecowicz, John
Filer, Raymond
Fisher, Robert
Fryer, Charles
Glasgow, Woodrow M.
Glass, Raymond L.
Gramley, Henry
Halahan, John D.
Haley, Phillip
Hallowell, Ralph
Hannum, John D.
Hansen, Ralph
Hart, Robert
Hassinger, Irvin
Hazel, Ray E.
Heckman, William
Heffner, Andrew
Hoffman, James
Hopkins, William
Horsmon, Thomas
Immel, Sandy
Jacobs, Esley
Jakuboski, Alex
Johnson, Clifton
Jones, Edward
Josefezyk, John
Juba, Charles
Kalajuta, Michael
Kerrick, John
Kerstetter, C. F.
Kirin, Marko
Kondak, Frank
Koretsky, Steve
Korn, Edward
Kozlowski, Charles
Krichovetz, Myer
Kuznar, Stanley
Laih, Earl
Landers, Wm. Jr.

Lathrop, Lawrence
Lindsey, Harry
Lublinski, Alex
McCalmont, Paul
McCormick, Arthur
McCreary, Albert
McDonnough, Ray
McKinsey, Roderick
Mahon, Ray
Mansfield, Gerald
Marquardt, Bern.
Marquardt, John
Merion, Benjamin
Metarko, John
Mills, John
Mohney, Harry
Montauge, Russell
Moran, Orsell
Muirey, Frank
Muscalus, Wm.
Musser, Ellwd.
Myslinski, Louis
Mysliwiec, Henry
Nappe, Alphonso
Nemchak, Joseph
Noyes, Harry
Offi, Robert
Omachel, Edward
O'Neill, Joseph
Ott, Dana W.
Oyler, Bernard
Patricca, Tony
Pavlock, Leo
Payne, Gordon
Payne, Robert
Perock, Stanley
Perrone, Mike
Pletcher, Arthur
Pociunas, John
Ponick, Anthony
Pura, Andrew
Quil, William
Ream, Paul
Rebic, Joseph
Reese, Elliott
Reightler, Melvin
Rhine, Edwin O.
Robbins, Francis
Roller, Hugh
Russell, John

Russell, John A.
Selnick, Joseph
Sandor, Joseph
Sattizahn, Clark
Schell, Floyd
Schohn, Edward
Scott, Pete
Seleni, Edward
Serine, James
Shandor, Peter
Shatto, Harry
Shawver, Walter
Singer, John A.
Slack, George
Slack, Kenneth
Slatwitch, Chester
Smith, Walter
Springer, Robert
Steiger, Rufus
Stolt, Theron
Stoyka, Charles
Stoyko, John
Swain, Richard
Thompson, David
Todd, Paul
Toscano, Anthony
Towey, Thomas
Turray, Mike
Veasey, Phillip
Veneziale, John
Vensick, Wm.
Verbus, Joseph
Vogel, John Jr.
Wasko, John
Weir, William
Weiss, Theodore
Wellner, Jack
Whomsley, Arthur
Wilson, Ralph C.
Winkelblech, Wm. J.
Wise, Samuel A.
Wisnesky, Alex
Yeosky, Frank
Yost, Joseph
Zettle, Norman E.
Zukovich, Hicholas
Zupon, Joseph
Zurusky, Anthony

The 1935 camp Christmas card noted the menu to be served for the Christmas meal and the camp roster. The camp roster listed the following enrollees.

Leaders:

Brown, Lewis I.
Brooks, Raymond W.
Coperhaver, Merrill T. (believed a typo and should read: Copenhaver)

Immel, Roy S. B.
Malone Basil M.
Marquardt, John
Sattizahn, Clark E.

Wert, Ralph
Wheelman, Stephen
Zimmerman, Edwin H.

Assistant Leaders:

Beahm, Guy A.
Croyle, Joseph A.
Danneehauer, Gottfried K.
Graham, Thomas G.
Grassi, Oliver J.

Halahan, John David
Kaiser, Joseph F.
Landers, Wm. Jr.
Malesic, Anthony
Perrone, Mike
Quil, William

Saloma, Stephen
Steiger, Rufus
Wise, Samuel A.
Zettle, Robert

Members:

Andrus, John F.
Aruscavage, John Joseph
Baird, Benjamin
Baroni, Arthur
Beatty, Arthur
Bedich, John
Bochan, Andrew
Bonci, Delpho R.
Briggs, Clarence I.
Burkholder, Frank A.
Cable, John E.
Callahan, Thomas Wm.
Cherrozzi, Dominick
Chorba, Frank R.
Civils, Clair E.
Conway, Patrick
Crabtree, John L.
Crader, Clarence F.
Crawford, Paul G.
Crawford, William A.
Cypher, George J.
Czyzyk, Leo S.
Daniels, Joseph L.
Davis, William J.
DeTullio, Dan P.
Diggins, George E.
Eckard, Gerald
Fiochetti, Lewis E.
Fleck, Donavan R.
Florcik, Stanley
Gillis, Leo
Grabill, Paul E.

Groce, William J.
Haley, Phillip
Hamm, Robert G.
Heffner, Andrew
Hildebrand, Lyman D.
Hilton, Robert A.
Hollabaugh, Herbert B.
Hopkins, William M.
Horchar, Joseph J.
Rorish, Walter A.
Immel, Sandy
Jagerski, Anthony J.
Josefczyk, John
Kidd, Alfred Jr.
Kirin, Marko
Kopchak, Peter
Koretsky, Steve
Krell, John C.
Kuback, John
Kushmider, John H.
Lamoreaux, Rolland A.
LaRossa, Joseph
Lee, Theodore W.
Lockard, Paul E.
Longstreth, George L.
Loomis, Joseph
Nostalgia, Patsy N.
Love, John S.
MacDonald, Winford A.
McMillen, Harold A.
Maciak, Felix
Mahalchick, Joseph M.
Mandry, William

Manos, Stanley
Mariano, Tony
Marquardt, Bernard
Mars, Gilbert
Martin, Robert L.
Mateer, Earl T.
Mavrich, Matt
Meinhart, Clair E.
Mike, Jacob P.
Minarik, John
Modolo, Olimpio
Montague, Russell
Moore, James E.
Moran, Orsell
Mowery, Alfred C.
Murphy, Harold A.
Myers, Robert S.
Mysliwiec, Henry
Nazarevich, Steve
Nearhoof, Frederick L.
Nelson, Donald J.
Nido, Mike J.
Obuchowski, Adam
Oluschak, Pete,
Olzonitski, Mike
Omachel, Edward
Ormanowski, Henry J.
Ostrich, John
Panisuicz, Stanley J.
Parks, Harry C.
Pavlakovich, Nick
Polignone, Raymond
Porter, Raymond C.

159

Reed, James V.	Singer, John A.	Watson, Archibald M.
Reimer, Byron E.	Skoff, Christian L.	Wazelle, Marcel R.
Rhine, Edwin O.	Slatwitch, Chester	Welch, Chester F.
Richardson, John A.	Sluscavage, Michael	Wells, David P.
Roller, Hugh	Smith, Harry C.	Wheaton, Joseph S.
Romanowski, Leonard F.	Snare, Frank Jr.	Widmeyer, John C.
Rupeka, Nick	Springer, Robert Jr.	Wilczinski, John A.
Rupert, George L.	Stachefsky, Joseph J.	Williams, Harold
Ruscio, Joe,	Stevens, Charles F.	Wilson, Ralph C.
Rynkiewicz, Peter S.	Tennis, Fred J.	Wisnesky, Alex
Sabino, John T.	Thayer John W.	Wojnasski, Stanley
Sandor, Joseph	Thayer, Joseph E.	Yanchick, Alec
Schaul, John L.	Thomas, Paul P.	Yenchis, Joseph
Schohn, Edward	Towey, Thomas	Yeosky, Frank
Scott, Cecil H.	Turay, Mike	Yost, Joseph Jr.
Scyrek, Felix S.	Vantroba, Joseph	Zaborchak, Michael
Serine, James	Varcho, Steve R.	Zabroski, Francis
Shatto, Harry	Vogel, John Jr.	Zalot, John Henry
Sherwood, leroy	Vrabel, Joseph	Zapalsky, Charles S.
Shugarts, Everett E.	Warner, Andrew J.	Zapotechne, Andy
Shumbris, Edmund G.	Warner, Conrad L.	Zaryczry, Frank

The June 1936 issue of the *Poe Valley Ravin* newsletter listed the following enrollees arriving in camp from disbanded Company 1385 (first name not provided).

Leaders:
Javorsky
Varan

Assistant Leaders:
Bekelja
Kubej

Members:

Wilchinski	Fesko	Heckman
Sromovski	Kreydatus	Colby
Prenovitz	Morley	Buranyk
Perschau	Schnaufer	Brutz
Yagloski	Donnelly	Bauthman
Maylock	Cryder	Miller
Luce	Cetera	Orth
Laseaski	Boback	Serini
Jabronowski	Williams	

The June 1936 issue of the *Poe Valley Ravin* newsletter listed the following enrollees arriving in camp from Ft. George G. Meade (first name not provided).

Onderika	Neveras	Russin
Nicklas	Okonieski	Rovnak
Roche	Smith	Rohrbach

Ringes	Radzinowicz	Petrini
Ricci	Radnovich	Petchul
Reid	Pozza	
Rakowski	Peterson	

The September 1936 issue of the *Poe Valley Ravin* newsletter listed the following enrollees departing camp on September 30, 1936, at the end of their enlistment.

Leaders:
Marquardt, J.
Zimmerman, E.

Assistant Leaders:

Kuback, J.	Heckman, H.	Colby, R.
Landers, W.	Montgomery, B.	Luce, S.
Wise, S. A.	Petrini, R.	McDonald, W.
Members	Perchau, R.	Wolcott, H.
Golecki, E.	Orth, C.	Florcik, S.
Gudus, E.	Morley, J.	Brutz, J.
Slater, E.	Baughman, K.	Boback, S.
Kelleher, C.	Chorba, F.	Mariano, T.
Miklowcic, A.	Zapetechne, A.	Maylock, E.
Vantroba, J.	Mowery, A.	Ringes, S.
Cetera, S.	Fleck, D.	Benarick, P.
Loomis, J.	Zidik, M.	Civils, C.
Grabill, P.	Rimbey, L.	Lasecki, C.
Prenovitz, A.	Kudgus, E.	Wales, R.
Yessen, M.	Evans, A.	Williams, M.
Lewandowski, J.	Suponcic, J.	Miller, W.

The 1936 camp Christmas card noted the menu to be served for the Christmas meal and the camp roster.

Captain Edward R. Ayres . . . . Cav-Res., Commanding
Lt. James F. Carroll . . . . CAC-Res., Adjutant
Lt. Edward Kelly, Med-Res. . . . . Camp Surgeon
Newton Holcomb . . . . Educational Advisor
C. Paul Ziegler . . . . W.P.A. Recreational Teacher
Harry Kreamer . . . . W.P.A. Vocational Teacher
Luther Weaver . . . . Camp Superintendent
J. E. Smith . . . . Forester
S. Frankenberger . . . . Foreman
F. B. Auman . . . . Foreman
Miles Bressler . . . . Foreman
W. Throstle . . . . Foreman
Ralph I. Wert . . . . Foreman
H. Neese . . . . Mechanic
E. R. Auman . . . . Blacksmith
H. Guisewite . . . . Operator

The roster listed the following enrollees:

Leaders:

Brown, Lewis I.
Copenhaver, Merrill T.
Croyle, Joseph A.

Immel, Roy S. B.
Malesic, Anthony
Quill, William

Welch, Chester F.

Assistant Leaders:

Bekelja, John A.
Donnelly, Francis P.
Halahan, John D.
Kirin, Marko

Mars, Gilbert E.
Myers, Robert S.
Reimer, Byron
Martin, Robert L.

Shugarts, Everett E.
Steiger, Rufus

Members:

Aley, Leon H.
Berkstresser, R. D.
Cryder, Charles C.
David, William J.
Diggins, George E.
Ferguson, Roy
Herrig, Harold K.
Hilton, Robert A.
Horchar, Joseph J.
Horn, Ralph A.
Huetger, Charles J.
Huff, George E.
Immel, Sandy
Jabronowski, Walter
Janson, George L.
Judkis, Frank J.
Kachmarsky, Nick
Kehoe, Joseph P.
Kellett, John J.
Knowles, Edward
Kopchak, Peter
Kotlarsky, Walter
Kreydatus, Joseph
Kushmider, John H.
Lafferty, Archie
Lameroux, Rolland A.
Lawless, Joseph J.
Lemmo, Andrew N.
Lindmar, William T.
Link, Edward R.
Lipsack, John J.
Mace, Elmer W.
Mandry, William
Marzucco, Michael
May, George
McCreery, Joseph
McDonald, Howard
McGehean, Joseph E.

McGuigan, Francis J.
McMillen, Harold A.
McMullen, James E.
Mike, Jacob P.
Moore, Wilson W.
Minarik, John
Morczyski, Chester
Murphy, Joseph
Napoli, Fred
Nearhoof, Fredrick L.
Neveras, George J.
Nicklas, Bruno R.
Okonieski, Joseph
Olzonitski, Mike
Opprouseck, Walter
Ostrich, John
Perry, Jack P.
Petchul, John J.
Peterson, Harry W.
Petrus, Charles
Planinchek, Ignatz
Powell, Leonard W.
Proto, Vincent R.
Pye, Arthur P.
Polinski, John
Pozza, Lewis
Rafalko, Henry
Radnovich, Anthony
Radzinowicz, F. L.
Rapp, Louis
Rasimovich, Alphonso
Reed, James
Reid, Daniel W.
Ricci, Peter P.
Rocho, Andrew J.
Radichock, Frank P.
Rogozus, Stanley W.
Rohrback, David

Rokus, Joseph
Rupeka, Nick
Rupert, George L.
Russin, Frank
Scepura, John J.
Schaul, John L.
Sczyrek, Felix S.
Serine, Frank
Serine, James
Sherlock, Kenneth
Sherwood, Leroy E.
Slatwich, Chester
Smith, Clyde
Smith, Joseph
Sromovski, John A.
Stark, Roland
Sorochinsky, Mike
Sviatko, Michael
Tennis, Fred J.
Varcho, Steve R.
Vischansky, Westly
Vonada, Reuben
Warholic, Harry
Warner, Andrew J.
Warner, Conrad L.
Watson, Archibald M.
Wilchinski, Paul
Wilson, Ralph C.
Wilson, Theodore R.
Wisnesky, Alex
Wojnasski, Stanley
Wosny, Anthony
Yakorsky, George
Zaborchak, Mike
Zalot, John
Zapalsky, Charles
Zelesniker, Henry

Note the above roster of names is generally known to be enrollees from Pennsylvania. The early years of most camp rosters is widely known to be young men from the same state as where the camp is situated. The limited roster of names including hometown addresses indicates most of the enrollees in the Poe Valley camp were from Pennsylvania.

The 1936 district yearbook listed the following roster for Company 1333. There are company photographs included in the yearbook (see pages 166-167). The clothing being worn suggests the weather is cool, indicating the photo was taken in the late fall. The roster also included the hometown of the enrollee member.

Technical Personnel:

Weaver, L. L.	Superintendent
Lewis, O.	Engineer
Smith, J. E.	Forester
Frankenberger, S.	Foreman
Auman, F. B.	Foreman
Bressler, M.	Foreman
Throssle, W.	Foreman
Wert, R. L.	Foreman
Neese, H. S.	Mechanic
Auman, E. R.	Blacksmith
Guisewite H. G.	Machine Operator

Leaders:

Brown, L.	Millheim, PA
Copenhaver, M. T.	S. M., PA
Croyle, J. A.	S. Fork, PA
Immel, R. S.	R'burg, PA
Malesic, A.	Enhaut, PA
Quill, W.	Pittsburgh, PA
Welch, C. F.	Tyrone, PA

Assistant Leaders:

Bekelja, J. A.	Bressler, PA
Donnelly, F. P.	Exeter, PA
Halahan, J. D.	N. B'dock, PA
Kirin, M.	Columbus, PA
Mars, G. E.	Harrisburg, PA
Martin, R. L.	Altoona, PA
Myers, R. S.	Tyrone, PA
Reimer, B. E.	D'ville, PA
Shugarts, E. E.	Dubois, PA
Steiger, R.	Coburn, PA

Members:

Aley, L.	Jacksonville, PA
Berkstresser, R. D.	R'rg, PA
Baroni, A.	Pittsburgh, PA

Cryder, C. C. . . . . Weatherly, PA
Davis, W. J. Parsons, PA
Diggins, G. E. . . . . Altoona, PA
Ferguson, R. Canton, PA
Hering, H. K. Powell, PA
Hilton, R. A. Altoona, PA
Horchar, J. J. . . . . S'yersville, PA
Horn, R. A. . . . . Philadelphia, PA
Huetger, C. J. . . . . Philadelphia, PA
Huff, G. E. . . . . Philadelphia, PA
Immel, S. . . . . Rebersburg, PA
Jabronowski, W. . . . . Wilkes Barre, PA
Janson, G. L. Philadelphia, PA
Judkis, F. J. Philadelphia, PA
Kachmarsky, N. . . . . Lopez, PA
Kehoe, J. P. Philadelphia, PA
Kellett, J. J. Philadelphia, PA
Knowles, E. . . . . Philadelphia, PA
Kopchak, P. F'mansburg, PA
Kotlarsky, W. . . . . S'ville, PA
Kreydatus, J. Saxton, PA
Kushmider, J. H. . . . . H'ton, PA
Lafferty, A. . . . . Philadelphia, PA
Lamoreaux, R. A. . . . . K'ton, PA
Lawless, J. J. Philadelphia, PA
Lee, T. W. . . . . Altoona, PA
Lemmo, A. N. Philadelphia, PA
Lindmar, W. T. . . . . Philadelphia, PA
Link, E. R. . . . . Forest City, PA
Lipsack, J. J. Philadelphia, PA
Mace, E. W. Philadelphia, PA
Mandry, W. . . . . Pittston, PA
Marzucco, M. Philadelphia, PA
May, G. . . . . Philadelphia, PA
McCreery, J. Philadelphia, PA
McDonald, H. Philadelphia, PA
McGehean, J. E. . . . . Philadelphia, PA
McGuigan, F. J. . . . . Philadelphia, PA
McMillen, H. A. . . . . Dubois, PA
McMullin, J. E. . . . . Philadelphia, PA
Mike, J. P. . . . . New Castle, PA
Moore, W. W. Philadelphia, PA
Minarik, J. . . . . Easton, PA
Morczyski, C. Philadelphia, PA
Murphy, J. J. Philadelphia, PA
Napoli, F. . . . . Philadelphia, PA
Nearhoof, F. L. . . . . Tyrone, PA
Nelson, C. . . . . Philadelphia, PA
Neveras, G. J. . . . . W. H'ton, PA
Nicklas, B. R. Kane, PA
Okonieski, J. Pond Hill, PA
Olzinitski, M. Butler, PA
Oprouseck, W. . . . . Philadelphia, PA

Ostrich, J. . . . . Vanport, PA
Parks, H. C. B'mingham, PA
Perry, J. P. . . . . Philadelphia, PA
Petchul, J. J. B'ard, PA
Peterson, H. W. . . . . B'ard, PA
Petrus, C. . . . . Forest City, PA
Planinshek, I. Forest City, PA
Pomrink, J. H. . . . . Philadelphia, PA
Powell, L. W. Philadelphia, PA
Proto, V. R. . . . . Philadelphia, PA
Pye, A. T. . . . . Philadelphia, PA
Pozza, L. . . . . Hazelton, PA
Rafalko, H. . . . . Forest City, PA
Radnovich, A. . . . . Pringle, PA
Radzinowicz, F. L. . . . . S'kin, PA
Reed, J. . . . . Fredonia, PA
Reid, D. W. . . . . Taylor, PA
Russin, E. E. B'chard, PA
Ricci, P. P. . . . . Shickshinny, PA
Roche, A. J. . . . . Scranton, PA
Radichock, F. P. . . . . Philadelphia, PA
Rogozus, S. W. . . . . U'dale, PA
Rohrback, D. Freeland, PA
Rokus, J. . . . . Mildred, PA
Rupeka, N. . . . . Mines, PA
Rupert, G. L. Altoona, PA
Scepura, J. J. Forest City, PA
Schaul, J. L. Tyrone, PA
Sczyrek, F. S. . . . . Nanticoke, PA
Serine, F. . . . . Dunmore, PA
Serine, J. . . . . Dunmore, PA
Sherwood, L. E. . . . . McClure, PA
Slatwich, C. . . . . Frackville, PA
Snare, F. . . . . Williamsburg, PA
Sromovski, J. G'town, PA
Stark, R. . . . . Uniondale, PA
Tennis, F. J. . . . . Tyrone, PA
Varcho, S. R. Larksville, PA
Vischansky, W. . . . . Powell, PA
Vonada, R. . . . . Coburn, PA
Warner, A. J. Wilkes Barre, PA
Warner, C. L. Wilkes Barre, PA
Wilchihski, P. Inkerman, PA
Wilson, R. C. Fairchance, PA
Wilson, T. R. Millheim, PA
Wisnesky, A. Eynon, PA
Wojnasski, S. Larksville, PA
Wozny, A. . . . . Heidleburg, PA
Zaborchak, M. . . . . M. Mills, PA
Zalot, J. . . . . Nanticoke, PA
Zapalsky, C. . . . . Kingston, PA
Zelesniker, H. F. City, PA
Watson, A. . . . . DuBois, PA

These company 1333 photographs were included in the 1936 district yearbook as noted on page 163 . A roster of technical personnel and enrollee member names including their respective hometown are also included in the district yearbook for Company 1333. The names, however, are listed alphabetically and thus do not provide any reference of order for the individuals depicted in the photographs.

The March 1937 issue of the *Poe Valley Ravin* listed the following enrollees departing camp at the end of their enrollment period:

Perry, Jack P.	Lafferty, Archie	Malesic, Anthony
Morczyski, Chester	Powell, Leonard	Mars, Gilbert
Martin, James	McGuigan, Francis	Polinsky, John
Judkis, Stanley	Knowles, Edward	Kreydatus, Joseph
Huff, George E.	Proto, Vincent	Sorochinsky, Mike
Kellett, John	Jabronowski, Walter	Zelesnikar, Henry
Wagner, Louis	Kushmider, John	Reid, Daniel
Horn, Ralph	Okonieski, Joseph	Reed, James
McGehean, Joseph	Donnelly, Francis	Mike, Jacob
Lemmo, Andrew	Wilchinski, Paul	Vischansky, Wesley
Napoli, Fred	Zapalsky, Charles	Pye, Arthur
McCrossin, Thomas	Bekelja, John	Rokus, Joseph

The April 1937 issue of the *Poe Valley Ravin* listed the following new men arriving from Wilkes Barre, PA, the morning of April 14th:

Cox, J.	Bodek, A.	Halushka, S.
McCarroll, E.	Burowsky, V.	Penko, L.
Pilecki, L.	Evans, W.	Price, D.
Sheridan, J.	Evans, G.	Rupp, L.
Slatky, J.	Gilroy, J.	Shraeder, J.
Szulewski, F.	Gabriel, B.	Segeta, G.
Torpak, G.	Stanton, G.	Aguris, W.
Tolensky, J.	Velgus, J.	Berginski, S.
Tomko, G.	Waypa, M.	Anzalone, J.
Zaberney, P.	Mondulik, F.	Herridge, E.
Zukowski, E.	Pelepko, L.	Kasilis, A.
Keska, P.	Tomasavage, W.	Mazeika, A.
Klimko, S.	Washington, P.	Mustulis, A.
Matishak, W.	Zgliniki, A.	Stanikinis, J.
Boyle, J.	Zupeck, G.	Mickolas, C.
Kochinski, J.	Pauska, E.	Urban, J.
Ropietski, J.	Vernac, C.	Snarski, A.
Harris, T.	Weiskerger, S.	Zabiegalski, B.
Rocofski, A.	Baldoni, L.	Kelly, R.
Thompson, R.	Zankowski, J.	Delmont, M.
Wanto, M.	Brown, F.	Mudrie, J. (transferred
Wosilius, E.	Massenous, C.	from Company 308)
Balavago, A.	Zatorski, J.	
Barge, M.	Brobeck, G.	

The following L.E.M.s were enrolled:

Stover, B.	Ertel, R.
Vonada, G.	Wilson, A.
Kling, I.	

Members W. Ledford and E. Stafford transferred from Cooks and Bakers School.

The September 1937 issue of the *Poe Valley Ravin* listed the following enrollees:

Enrollees leaving on September 30th are as follows:

Leaders:
Halahan, John D. (supply Sergeant) 1710 Murdough St., No. Braddock, Pa.
Immel, Sandy C. Rebersburg, Pa.
Nicklas, Bruno R., RFD #2 Kane, Pa.

Assistant Leaders:
Moran, Michael J. (forestry clerk) 2047 Prico St., Scranton, Pa.
Mudrie, John (company clerk) Dunbar, Pa.
Noveras, George J., (army truck driver) 508 W. Green St., West Hazleton, Pa.
Evans, George (CAEA) 317 Fremont St., West Pittston, Pa.

Members:
Aley, Leon H., Jacksonville, Pa.
Baldoni, Louis P., 28 Amber Lane, Wilkes Barre, Pa.
Berginski, Stanley J., 321 River St., Duryea, Pa.
Burowsky, Vitor, 128 Susquehanna Ave., Wyoming, Pa.
Davis, William J., 228 Hollenback Ave., Parsons, Pa.
Ertel, Randall G., Coburn, Pa.
Gabriel, Barney, 119 Davenport St., Plymouth, Pa.
Horridge, Enoch Jr., 8 Wharncliff St., Laurel Run, Wilkes Barre, Pa.
Janson, George L., 523 E. Dupont St., Philadelphia, Pa.
Keska, Peter P., 415 Pittston Ave., Avoca, Pa.
Kling, Ira A., 15 Mill St., Lewistown, Pa.
Lamereaux, Rolland A., 15 Mill St., Lewistown, Pa.
Peterson, Harry W., 8 N. Mill St., West Nanticoke, Pa.
Quil, William, 4523 Filmore St., Pittsburgh, Pa.
Ramer, Howard J., Reedsville, Pa.
Schaul, John L., (canteen steward) RD#2 Tyrone, Pa.
Sheridan, John C., 59 Reynolds St., Plymouth, Pa.
Wilson, Ralph C., Box 234 Fairchance, Pa.
Yaworsky, George, Freeland, Pa.
Cryder, Charles C., 542 Main St., Weatherly, Pa.
Sweeney, Edward, 1524 S. Hollywood St. Philadelphia, Pa.
Tomascavage, Walter, 106 Newport St., Glen Lyon, Pa.

The following is a list of enrollees who will reenroll for the next enrollment period:

Leaders:
Cohan, Benjamin F., (1st cook) Philadelphia, Pa.
Ledford, William J., (mess steward) 146 Carlisle St., Hanover, Pa.
McCreery, Joseph, (senior leader) 3106 Amber St., Philadelphia, Pa.
Planninshek, Ignatz, 433 Maple St., Forest City, Pa.
Serine, Frank, (1st cook) 110 Franklin St., Dunmore, Pa.

Assistant Leaders:
Diggins, George E., (2nd cook) 901 Eighth Ave., Altoona, Pa.
Hering, Harold K., Powell, Pa.
Lawless, Joseph J., (2nd cook) 2432 Alder St., Philadelphia, Pa.
Mace, Elmer W., Pottsville St. Wiconisco, Pa.

Pozza, Lewis 272, S. Laurel St. Hazleton, Pa.
Radzinowicz, Leroy E., McClure, Pa. RD#1 (Belltown)
Smith, Clyde J., (shower house attendant) Broad Top, Pa.

Members:
Anzalone, Joseph C., 117 Pine St., Pittston, Pa.
Balavage, Andrew, 327 Colley St., Lynwood, Hanover Twp., Pa.
Beals, Orlando E., Phillipsburg, Pa.
Beckwith, Raymond L., RD#3 Tyrone, Pa.
Bodek, Albert J., 112 Newport St., Sheatown, Nanticoke, Pa.
Boob, Stanley G., Spring Mills, Pa
Brandt, Ralph Donald, Coburn, Pa.
Brodbeck, Gilbert W., 27 Center St. Hughestown, Pittston, Pa.
Brown, Greenville, Williamsburg, Pa.
Byrne, Joseph A., 817 Second Ave., Juniata, Pa.
Doren, Joseph, RD#2 box 132 Osceola Mills, Pa.
Evans William, 161 Moyallen St. Wilkes Barre, Pa.
Ferguson, Roy, RD#1 Canton, Pa.
Fogleman, Charles, Mill and Hazel Sts., Milesburg, Pa.
Gilroy, John E., 29 Rutz St. Preston, Ashley, Pa.
Gotwalt, George D., Manchester, Pa.
Haluska, Stephen, 423 Carver St. Larksville, Pa.
Hazzard, John W., Moshannon, Pa.
Hirt, Ralph W., 204 Fifth Ave., Altoona, Pa.
Hughes, James W., 300 Fourth Ave., Altoona, Pa.
Kachmarsky, Nick, Lopez, Pa.
Kasilas, Alex, 47 Main St., Inkerman, Pittston, Pa.
Kerilla, George C., Clarence, Pa.
Kliensorge, Fredrick, 418 Northampton St. Edwardsville, Pa.
Klimko, Stanley A., 56 Berlin Ave. Pittston, Pa.
Klekus, Joseph, 219 Mill St. Miners Mills, Pa.
Kochinski, Joseph A., 282 Orchard St. Plymouth, Pa.
Kulikowski, Stanley, 116 Cleveland St. Hudson, Pa.
Kutzler, William F., 145 Lemon St. Reading, Pa.
Link, Edward R., 822 Delaware St. Forest City, Pa.
Marzucco, Michael, 4024 N. Reese St. Philadelphia, Pa.
Mandry, William, RD#1 Pittston, Pa.
McGuigan, Francis G., 2805 Rosehill St. Philadelphia, Pa
McCool, Clarence J., Spring Mills, Pa.
McMullin, James E., 1933N. Palethrope Dt. Philadelphia, Pa.
Massenous, Charles, 5 Market St., Inkerman, Pittston, Pa.
Mazeika, Anthony M., 5 Union St., Inkerman, Pittston, Pa.
Miller, Newell O., Spring Mills, Pa.
Motovidlak, Thomas J., 147 S. Walnut St., Georgetown, Wilkes Barre, Pa.
Moore, Michael F., 2742 Titan St. Philadelphia, Pa.
Moore, Owen J., RD#1, Camp Hill, Pa.
Morre, Wilson W., 4951 Odgen St. Philadelphia, Pa.
Murphy, James H., RD#2 Box 84, Osceola Mills, Pa.
Mustalis, Anthony, 38 Union St., Inkerman, Pittston, Pa.
Pelepko, Michael, 149 Diamond St. Wilkes Barre, Pa.
Penko, Leonard M., 86 George St. West Nanticoke, Pa.
Peterson, Harry W., 8 North Mill St. West Nanticoke, Pa.
Pilecki, Lawrence J., 51 Chamberlain St. Hilldale, Pa.
Price, Daniel, 11 Kidder St. Wilkes Barre, Pa.
Quill, William, 4523 Filmore St. Pittsburgh, Pa.

Radnovich, Anthony, 32 Nugent St. Pringle, Pa.
Rafalko, Henry, RD#2 Springville, Pa.
Rasimovich, Alphonse, 359 Dooley St., Lynwood, Hanover Township, Pa.
Regeci, Joseph G., 74 Ashley Rd. Wilkes Barre, Pa.
Ricci, Peter Paul, 19 North Canal St. Shickshinny, Pa.
Rodichok, Frank P., Pottsville St. Wiconisco, Pa.
Rogozus, Stanley, RD#2 Uniondale, Pa.
Rohrbach, David A., 458 Washington St., Freeland, Pa.
Rosebaum, Michael J., 6141 Glenmore Ave. Philadelphia, Pa.
Royer, William H., RD#1 Box 279 Bellefonte, Pa.
Russin, Frank E., 1713 River Road Pt. Blanchard, Pa.
Scepura, John J., 400 Susquehanna Ave. Forest City, Pa.
Schrader, Joseph, R. 4 Spring St. Glen Lyon, Pa.
Sczyreka, Felix S., 408 East Ridge St. Nanticoke, Pa
Segeda, George, 20 Miller St. Pt. Blanchard, Pa.
Serine, James, 110 Franklin St. Dunmore, Pa.
Sheffer, Dennis A., RD#1 Dillsburgh, Pa.
Sherlock, Kenneth, Saxton, Pa.
Shuey, Joseph A., Bellefonte, Pa.
Smith, James S., 428 Wharton Ave., Lakemont, Altoona, Pa.
Snarski, Alfred, 521 S. Main St. Parsons, Pa.
Spangler, George H., Blanchard, Pa.
Spangler, William M., Blanchard, Pa.
Sromovsky, John A., 825 Summit St., Geo., Wilkes Barre, Pa.
Strausbaugh, Leonard E., RD#2 East Berlin, Pa.
Szlewski, Frank J., 129 Main St. Dupont, Pa.
Tomko, George F., 21 Charles St. Geo., Wilkes Barre, Pa.
Veneziono, Paul, Clarence, Pa.
Velgus, John A., 637 W. State St. Larksville, Pa.
Vermac, Casimir, 921 Grove St. Avoca, Pa.
Vincer, Chester P., RD#2 Osceola Mills, Pa.
Walker, Ardell, Moshannon, Pa.
Walker, Harold, Julian, Pa.
Walsh, Richard W., Milesburg, Pa.
Wanyo, Martin A., 21 Brown St. Larksville, Pa.
Warner, Andrew J., 213 N. River St. Wilkes Barre, Pa.
Weiskerger, Sheldon, F., 215 Rock St., Hughestown, Pittston, Pa.
Wingard, Clair F., Spring Mills, Pa
Wingard, Norman A., Coburn, Pa.
Williams, Carlton, S., RD#1 Mt. Wolf, Pa.
Williams Charles J., Julian, Pa.
Wolfe, Kermit A., Spring Mills, Pa.
Wosilius, Edward, RD#1 Wapwallopen, Pa.
Zabielgaski, John S., 36 Coal St. Nanticoke, Pa
Zaborney, Pascal, 340 W. Union St. Nanticoke, Pa.
Zankowski, John S., 23 Hillman St., Miners Mills, Wilkes Barre, Pa.
Zatorski, John S., 254 River St. Nanticoke, Pa.
Zglinicki, Andrew S., 9 Orchard St. Glen Lyon, Pa.

The January 1938 issue of the *Poe Valley Ravin* listed the arrival of the following enrollees relocated from Camp SP-12, Farrington, PA:

Julius Kronick, Uniontown, Penna.
Glenn Forsythe, Uniontown, Penna.
Martin Maisey, Phila., Penna.
Joseph Zabawa, Phila., Penna.
William Regan, Scranton, Penna.
Steve Lasch, Republic, Penna.
Ralph Rundelli, Republic, Penna.
George, Kolessar, Republic, Penna.
A. Petlansky, Conemaugh, Penna.
Michael Obsharsky, Youngstown, Penna.
Steve Balas, Lansford, Penna.
G. Galushka, Conemaugh, Penna.
Michael Miller, Dunbar, Penna.

J. Wolshinsky, Seabrights, Penna.
A. Leniek, Park Hill, Penna.
R. Markwell, Natrona, Penna.
G. Moschak, Smoke Run, Penna.
William Lewis, Winstead, Penna.
E. Hernansky, New Salem, Penna.
Frances Fair, Home, Penna.
C. Dubrecka, Masontown, Penna.
R. Lynn, Charleroi, Penna.
A. Angeli, Mt. Carmel, Penna.
L. Pasqualini, Burgettstown, Penna.
Pete Zopchak, Meadowland, Penna.
A. Pengrac, Uniontown, Penna.

The March 1938 issue of the *Poe Valley Ravin* listed the following men to be discharged on March 31st due to expiration of term of enrollment:

Markwell, Raymond P., Pittsburgh, Pa.
Streyle, Robert, Erie, Pa.
Anzalone, Joseph C., Wilkes Barre, Pa.
Brodbeck, Gilbert W., Wilkes Barre, Pa.
Ferguson, Roy, Towanda, Pa.
Fioravanti, Louis J., Beaver Falls, Pa.
Gergely, John P., Greensburg, Pa.
Gilroy, John E., Wilkes Barre, Pa.
Gromalskie, William, Gilberton, Pa.
Kleinsorge, Frederick, Wilkes Barre, Pa.
Knipp, Charles, Ashland, Pa.
Kachmarsky, Nick, Dushore, Pa.
Lynn, Richard H., Washington, Pa.

Mineard, Robert G., Beaver Falls, Pa.
Obsharsky, Mike P., Washington, Pa.
Pilecki, Lawrence J., Wilkes Barre, Pa.
Pintur, Nicholas, Beaver Falls, Pa.
Penko, Leonard M., Wilkes Barre, Pa.
Russin, Frank E., Wilkes Barre, Pa.
Serine, James, Scranton, Pa.
Baney, Vincent R., Bellefonte, Pa.
Bucha, Mike, Bellefonte, Pa.
Conaway, Charles M., Bellefonte, Pa.
Decker, Elmer O., Bellefonte, Pa.
Rishell, Russell P., Bellefonte, Pa.

The September 1939 issue of the *Poe Valley Ravin* listed the following men to be discharged on September 29th due to expiration of term of enrollment:

James Harford
Michael Andrusky
Samuel Broudy
Clay Cogar
Robert Day
James DelSignore
John Francis
John Horum
Jesse Kefover
Kenneth Keith

Malcom Kunes
Max Lose
Michael Luketic
Thomas Montel
Joseph Novak
Stephen Radonich
Malcom Packer
Lawrence Rogers
Michael Roll
Stephen Ruskiewich

Charles Saltys
Erward Sodusky
Stanley Sokalsky
John Syrek
Joseph Tiberio
Elmer Torre
Anton Valencia
Orville Yauger
Stanley Dudek

The November 1939 issue of the *Poe Valley Ravin* listed the following roster of enrollees:

Senior Leader:
Carl Klein

Leaders:

Carl Fomich
Hyman Goldstein
Polycarp Karpinski

Leroy Pelka
Ignatz Planishek
Howard Ramer

Albert Slother
Thomas Wodusky

Assistant Leaders:

Joseph Casher
Carl Chessie
Harold Corman
Mike Gallo
Stephen Hornack
Joseph Karbinas

Joseph Kupchick
George Mandell
Edward McCloskey
Nicholas Pitiak
Robert Robson
John Sabo

Clyde Smith
Robert Smull
Harold Unger
Paul Yetter

Members:

Charles Armstrong
Michael Augustine
William Auman
Clyde Bennett
John Bennett
Millard Benton
Robert Barnhart
Arthur Bickel
Wendell Booher
John Boyle
Jack Burkey
Anthony Butkus
Glenn Butler
William Casper
Anthony Campana
Ralph Coviello
John Ciesienski
Edward Ciewod
Joseph Cingol
Ernest Collins
Nevin Crater
Paul Cunningham
Andrew Danish
John Demchak
Arthur Derk
John Drochak
George Dubesky
Joseph Duke
Clarence Durandetto
Robert Evans
Frank Evanitsky
James Fisher
John Flock
Bruce Freeman
Russell Gates

Andrew Gavlock
Paul Gaughan
Paul Gardner
Stephen Gible
Michael Gidick
Stephen Gomola
John Hazzard
Frank Hanusosky
Stephen Havick
Edwin Halicki
Kenneth Harter
Paul Hendricks
Theodore Helonski
James Holt
Walter Hook
Michael Hramotnik
Raymond Hoynoski
Morris Houser
Edward Houdeshell
George Jodynski
Charles Jodrziewski
Dominic Jendrisak
Stephen kadash
Leonard Kelley
Frederick Kelser
Lloyd King
Albert Kaskie
Larue Kramer
Michael Koleno
Stephen Kormanico
Stephen Krisko
Francis Krupa
John Legnosky
Paul Lowery
Michael Luketic

William Lupton
Andrew Magont
Stephen Matejeik
John Massengill
Joseph McCarthy
Francis McCloskey
Walter McCloskey
Walter McCracken
Cecil Milton
John Milton
David McDowell
Floyd Meeker
John Mondell
Joseph Motichak
Robert Mull
Edward Muirhoad
Harry Murphy
Harold Musser
Norman Noll
Cornelius O'Brien
John Panco
Andy Panick
John Ponish
Kenneth Phillips
Albert Puhalla
Thomas Racan
John Raffacz
Andrew Ramertick
Russell Rishell
Lee Riva
Byard Rupert
Wright Snyder
John Russell
James Saltards
Stephen Schaffer

Walter Schaoffer	Pete Timko	Chester Welsh
Joseph Sofchick	Milton Timms	Robert Woiland
Clifford Schofield	Robert Thompson	Adolph Williams
Isador Soprish	George Ulich	Paul Williams
James Sharkey	Joseph Volla	Ralph Wilkinson
Alfred Shively	Henry Vornava	Joseph Woloslaglo
George Show	Ardell Vonada	Leroy Wolfe
Paul Smith	William Vroman	Howard Wykoff
Walter Speck	Guy Walker	George Yewcic
Gilbert Stank	Nevin Walters	Michael Yosefik
Joseph Suchy	Marshall Wance	Ivan Zalac
Richard Summors	Elwood Ward	Joseph Zelinko
George Summerson	Marlin Watson	Stanley Zelinski
Michael Svancer	Harry Weakland	George Zema
Robert Tatsch	Donald Weaver	

The same issue of the *Ravin* newsletter gave credit to the Mess Hall staff as follows:

Mess Steward:
Polycarp Karpinski

Dining Room:
George Show
Leroy Wolfe

First Cooks:
Albert Slother
Thomas Wodusky

Officers' Orderly:
Bruce Freeman

Second Cooks:
Joseph Karbinas
Edward McCloskey

Technical Service Orderly:
Francis McCloskey

Student Cooks:
Richard Salyards
Gilbert Stank

Scullery Department:
Robert Barnhart
Ernest Collins
John Hazzard
Walter McCracken
Joseph Zelinko

The December 1939 issue of the *Poe Valley Ravin* announces "twenty four enrollees end stay in CCC" and a "two year limit forces three into cold cruel world. Those who must leave due to the two year limit are" as follows:

John Hazzard
James Sharkey
Leroy Wolfe

The others leaving are as follows:

Ralph Coviello	Frank Hanusosky	David McDowell
Paul Dennis	Stephen Havick	Cecil Milton
Arthur Derk	Albert Kaskie	John Milton
Edwin Halicki	Fred Kelser	John Mondell

Norman Noll	Richard Summers	Paul Williams
John Panco	Gilbert Stank	Ivan Zalac
Byard Rupert	Robert Thompson	Stanley Zelinski

The January 1940 issue of the *Poe Valley Ravin* listed the following roster of new enrollees arriving on January 22, 1940, from Centre, Juniata, Huntington, and Mifflin counties:

Paul Alexander	Paul Kliem	William Robison
Martin Baranyek	John Kossik	Donald Ross
Harold Bitner	Albert Laird	Elmer Rutter
William Bloom	Robert Martin	Irvin Schnarrs
Lewis Branty	Grant Mayes	Blair Sheets
Nick Catherine	Raymond Milton	Charles Shingler
John Clark	John Morrison	Paul Smith
Joseph Comitz	Raymond Musser	Joseph Spella
Norman Confer	Harman Myers	Homer Swartz
Samuel Croyle	Steve Padisak	Irvin Watson
Charles Decker	Donald Peck	John Wilks
John Casper	Samuel Powell	Sydney Williamson
George Gearhart	Martin Reckova	George Yeatter
Robert Grafius	Clyde Rhodes	Theodore Yingling
Elmer Grenoble	Lloyd Rhoades	

In the January 1940 camp newsletter, the editor offered the following regarding the forty-four new enrollees.

"Thus begins an adventurous portion in the lives of these young men unable to cope with the unemployment situation of the outside world. May their stay be long and pleasant, and they are certain to be better equipped to face the world upon termination of the CCC enlistments."

The September 1940 issue of the *Poe Valley Ravin* listed the following men to be discharged on September 30th due to expiration of term of enrollment and/or of their own accord:

Leaders: **Assistant Leader:**

Leaders:		Assistant Leader:
Seprish		Luketic
Slother		

Members:

Balent	Mabus	Styers
Dunlap	Motichak	Suchy, A.
Halliday	Racan	Suntich
Hicks	Russell, J.	Tanney
Houdeshell	Scaheffer	Vanaskie
Johnson	Shinskie	Walker, G.
Kiersnowski	Smith, P.	Welch
Longo	Stecker	

In the same camp newsletter, the editor offered the following regarding the twenty-six men leaving camp:

> On this date once again men will leave the C.C.C. for civilian life but better fitted to meet this hard world than they would have been had they not entered the camp. They will have learned how to work and to obey orders and some of them will have learned a trade while they were in camp which will help them immensely for they will need all this and perhaps more to compete with the outside world. The boys of Company 1333 wish these men the best of luck and we are sure they will all make good.

The December 1940 issue of the *Poe Valley Ravin* listed the following men to be discharged on December 23rd due to expiration of term of enrollment and/or of their own accord:

Charles Armstrong	Elmer Rutter	DElmar Schnars
Edward Ciewed	Mike Ben	Emery Stash
John Ciesienski	Frank Berenty	Harry Vaughn
Robert Evans	Marvin Fanning	Harold Waite
Theodore Helenski	Joseph Kosky	

The January 1941 issue of the *Poe Valley Ravin* listed the following roster of fifty-seven new enrollees arriving from Pittsburgh, Bellefonte, and New Castle:

Alvin Gay	Dale Haffey	Benny Caravagio
William Hughes	Robert Herr	Charles Clayton
Joseph Tomezek	Robert Huntington	Edward Cournan
Paul Welch	David Koshko	Lawrence Flower
Lawrence White	John McGarry	Harry Gentile
Russell Winkler	Edward Nolan	James Hiler
Joseph Winterhalter	Kohn Noonan	John Juricich
James Almond	Pete Padisak	John Lewchenko
Lawrence Ammerman	John Rager	Frank Maxwell
Robert Buckwalter	William Spangler	Bob Nail
Chester Burns	John Spicer	Charles Palmer
Steve Chessie	Grover Spotts	Jack Passente
Norman Confer	Miles Steele	Russell Paswell
Earl Cretzer	Richard Summers	John Prekopi
James Crownover	Samuel Vaughn	Paul Snare
Joseph Demchak	James Wagner	William Stewart
Charles Fike	Howard Walk	Jerry Terilla
John Finnegan	Tony Canami	
Harry Fye	Albert Cervone	

In the same camp newsletter, the editor offered the following regarding the fifty-seven new enrollees, "May their stay be long and pleasant and they are certain to be better equipped to face the world when their enrollment period is up."

The March 1941 issue of the *Poe Valley Ravin* noted the following:

March 31—Today forty-four men in all will leave this company. These men have served their term of enrollment and have decided to go out voluntarily or because their two years are up. We hope that these men when they reach the outside life find them-selves better trained than they were before they entered the CCC. The men who have two years in this company are as follows:

Joe Vella	John Massengill
John Raffacz	Joe Suchy
Robert Tatsch	George Ulich
Henry Vernava	Ralph Wilkinson

The men who are leaving voluntarily are as follows:

Max McBryan	William Smith	Andy Ramertick
Walter Hook	Donald Weaver	Donald Walker
George Zima	Nevin walters	Henry Deemer
Paul Cunningham	John Hoculock	Peter Witt
Leo Riva	Vincent Bores	Marshall Wance
Clarance Bunnell	Robert Elliott	Kenith Harter (known to
Mike Swancer	Steve Moses	be Kenneth Harter)
Joe Knapick	Steve Gomola	John Latovich
John Nazarek	Steve Bucha	Steve Toth
John Kosarek	Edward Gummo	John Fiderra
William Merrell	John Yereb	Walter Sshaffer
Raymond Cassick	Robert Weiland	Jack Gulitck

The April 1941 issue of the *Poe Valley Ravin* listed the following roster of new enrollees arriving on April 10, 1940, from the vicinity of Shamokin and Bellefonte:

Shamokin:

Joseph Deklinski	Frank Maliszewski
Edward Peter Dunchok	James Vincent Nestico
Frank Gratti	Enoch Plust
Edward Anthony Gusick	Joseph George Verschak
Michael Kodack	

Bellefonte:

William Anderson	John Lego
Arthur Brown	Richard Peters
Paul Billett	Andy Salvanish
Jacob Fryer	Mike Staco
Mike Gasper	Nevin Ulrich
Edward Howard	Lewis Williamson
Walter Kosko	

The following are listings of personnel in the Poe Valley camp taken from a booklet titled *Pictorial Review, Civilian Conservation Corps, Northern District, Company 1333, Camp Poe Valley, S-63 Pa., Coburn, Pennsylvania.*

To date, these are the only group camp photographs to include an organized roster of enrollees' names known to the author. The booklet, though not dated, is believed to have been published in 1940.

Company Commander: Subaltern: Educational Advisor:
Lee Fox, 1st Lt., U.S.M.C. - Res.   D. P. Camp   Mr. Homer A. Dean

Technical Personnel: (All of these men are believed to be foremen, except for Mr. Hutt.) First row: E. F. Hoyt, P. E. Bradford, C. H. Hutt, Superintendent, L. E. Sherwood, F. B. Auman, E. R. Auman. Second row: B. D. McPherson, R. L. Wert, G. W. Miller, L. L. Weaver, F. K. Johnson.

Army and Technical Overhead (*): First row: George Mandell, Leroy Pelka, George Dubesky, Joe Comitz, John Demchak. Second row: Joseph Suchy, Robert Mull, Angelo Russell, Kenneth Harter, Steve Matias. Third row: Francis Bennett, Steve Baranyak, Max McBryan, Marlyn Watson, Albert Bodek.

Special Duty Group (*): First row: Dominic Venziano, Russell Passwell, John Lewchenko, Paul Snare, Lewis Gentile. Second row: John Prepori, Ben Carvaggio, Pete Padisak.

(*) Unknown to the author are these descriptive headings. It is believed these headings describe the more commonly known terminology being "Enrollee Leaders" and "Enrollee Assistant Leaders."

Barrack No. 1: First row: Frank Maxwell, Jerry Ferilla, Clarence Durandetta, John Belfanti, Mike Svancer, John Shinskie, Ugo Degano, Eddie Radzinowicz, Francis Bennett, Paul Welch. Second row: Robert Nail, Charles Conner, Bill Steward, Steve Toth, Eddie Voytovich, Oscar Hoover, Albert Cervone, William Merrill, Alvin Gay. Third row: John Linton, John Massingill, Martin Rackovan, John Nazaruk, Max McBryan, Joe Tomczak, Andrew Magent, Leroy Hull, Theodore Yingling. Fourth row: Joe Mills, Alex Koshubra, Millard Benton, John Shinonovich, Clarence Girton, James Hiler, Edward Courman.

Barrack No. 2: First row: Steve Kormanice, Lawrence White, John Bohn, Isador Seprish, Robert Tatsch, Lawrence Flower, John McGarry, Joe Winterhalter. Second row: Henry Deemer, Vincent Bores, Nick Catherine, John Clark, Donald Ferry, Andrew Ramertick, William Hughes, Andrew Alexander. Third row: Robert Elliott, Emery Chaplin, Burton Lyscas, John Hosculock, Robert Weiland, Walter Schaeffer, John Kossik, Raymond Hess, Ebon Stricker.

Barrack No. 3: First row: Taylor Watson, John Latovich, Russell Winkle, Marshall Wance, Raymond Musser, Elwood Ward, Steve Matias, William Poorman, Guy Winters, Nevin Walters. Second row: Edward Gummo, Howard Wykoff, John Rager, Steve Shufran, Eugene Burns, Harry Fry, Richard Summers, Russell Stellfox, Samuel Vaughn, Donald Weaver. Third row: Gervis Corman, Miles Steele, John Juricich, Richard Cassik, Earl Crotzer, John Nooman, Edward Keiack, Dale Haffley, Kenneth Harter, Lawrence Ammerman. Fourth row: John Spicer, Randall Boob, John Fedorra, John Yereb, Joe Demchak, Floyd Crotzer.

Barrack No. 4: First row: Tony Canabi, Robert Herr, John Ponish, Steve Gibel, Steve Moses, James Beck, Grover Spotts, James Crownover, John Tomaseski, Albert Bodek. Second row: Andrew Pachipko, Robert Huntington, William Spangler, Chester Burns, William Robison, Lewis Berenty, Charles Fike, David Koshko. Third row: Loyd Packer, Gerald Lomison, John Gasper, Charles Palmer, Steven Gomolo, William Lesavage, Steve Bucha, William Smith, James Wagner. Fourth row: Samuel Powell, Ralph Wilkinson.

Barrack No. 5: First row: Robert Buckwalter, Frank Krout, Russell Fryer, George Ulich, Edward Tekely, Glen Bowersox, George Zimmerman. Second row: Edward Nolan, Steve Chessie, Norman Confer, Donald Walker, Norman Myers, Peter Witt, Clarence Phillips.

Company 1333 group photograph, circa 1935

Company 1333 group photograph, circa 1934

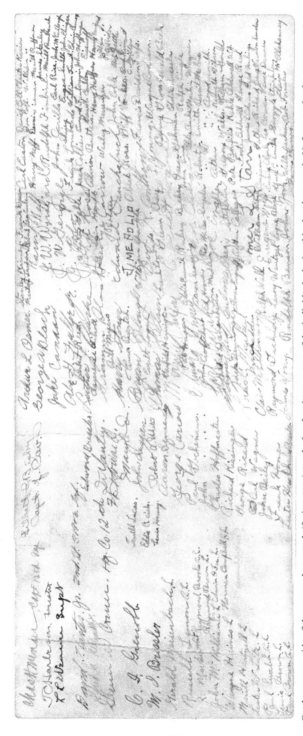

On the reverse side of the group photograph (facing page) are the hand-written names of the individuals depicted in the photograph. Unfortunately, the names are not listed in descriptive order

CHAPTER 8

SAFETY

The Civilian Conservation Corps was organized quickly, however, it was part of a government program, and any government program is developed with organizational structure and mandated requirements and responsibilities. In the case of the Civilian Conservation Corps, it was able to use organizational support from the department of labor to put a safety program into effect. As such, many policies established by the department of labor for the protection of workers and safety plans for the time were readily available to be put into play in the CCC.

A few of the written policies regarding camp safety requirements were found in my grandfather's possessions. One of these policies provides instruction to establish a "safety assistant to the superintendent." The camp superintendent was responsible for developing a "camp safety committee." The committee included the designated "safety assistant." The safety assistant was to be assigned by the chief foreman of the camp or, as was typical, the chief foreman or senior foreman would be the designated "safety assistant."

Therein, my grandfather, the camp senior foreman, was the designated safety assistant. In the documents he kept were numerous copies of minutes maintained by the committee. These minutes reflect the safety meetings that were conducted weekly and were attended by a representative from the camp's military officers, the camps education advisor, a representative from the forestry department, a representative from the foremen, and a representative from the enrollees. These records indicate the enrollees' representative was typically a selected barracks leader or barracks assistant leader. These minutes describe numerous

THE AMERICAN NATIONAL RED CROSS

✚

THIS CERTIFIES THAT

Sumner Frankenburger

HAS COMPLETED THE ___Standard___ COURSE
OF INSTRUCTION IN FIRST AID TO THE INJURED UNDER THE
AUSPICES OF _C.C.C. Camp, S-63, Co. 1333_
Coburn, _Pennsylvania_
August 26, 1935 _Harold F Calow_

DIRECTOR, FIRST AID AND LIFE SAVING

Foreman's First Aid card

sprains and strains and what medical attention was needed and subsequently provided.

The foremen were directed to provide basic instruction on work practices to mitigate the sprains and strains and keep these young men safe, as was the general practice of the times.

There was no such thing as an Occupation Safety and Health Administration program in play in the 1930s providing specific mandates for safety practices on construction project sites, as is in place today. Basic first-aid training was required to be administered to all camp foremen as part of the camp's military administrators and camp superintendents safety program.

The April 1937 safety committee meeting minutes describe an injury sustained to an enrollee, wherein the enrollee was run over by a dual-wheeled dump truck (see incident report on page 188). The first thought coming to mind when hearing of this type of accident is a severe injury or death will be the most likely outcome; should the victim be alive, a ride in an ambulance to a hospital would certainly occur. The victim in this incident was enrollee Leon Aley. An incident report written by my grandfather tells the story. In the camp Lost Time Accidents Report for 1937 for the period Jan. 1 to June 30, 1937 the following is recorded under Item d. *"- Member Leon E. Aley-Run over by truck (Forestry) while putting chains on rear wheel of same. Suffered the following injuries - Dislocation of Coccyx, Wounds, contused and abraision hip, right thigh, left and right knee, shock. Tis accident occurred in camp at 12:45 P.M. Injured enrollee returned to duty on April 30, 1937. Loss time ten (10) days- Complications NONE."*

April 20, 1937
Camp S-63, Coburn, Penna.

I _Sumner Frankenberger_, Assistant Safety
Inspector at this camp, swear the following statement to be true
and correct to the best of my knowledge.

I was talking to Lewis Rapp, a Leader at this camp, about
12:50 P.M. I heard someone shout, "Stop? I turned around and saw
the truck run over the body of Leon Aley. I ran to the truck and
helped carry the injured man into the Camp Hospital.

I began an investigation and found that the injured member,
Leon Aley, was trying to tighten the chains of his truck. He had
asked Louis Baldoni who was standing along side the truck, to get
in the truck and move it backward. Louis Baldoni evidently became
confused by the Reo gear shift and moved the truck the wrong way,
thus causing the accident.

I find that the following Safety rules were ignored, Louis
Baldoni was asked to drive by the injured member Leon Aley, although
he had not a license to drive a truck and was unfamiliar with the
gear shift of the Reo trucks.

Accident report

The meeting minutes would typically describe the current conditions subject to an enrollee who had been injured and was recorded in previous minutes and the recommendations discussed by the committee so as to mitigate the described cause for the injury sustained to the enrollee. These recommendations were then given to the foremen to be initiated in the camp. Additionally, the minutes would reflect whether the injury was to be recorded as a lost-time or non-lost-time injury, and the minutes would describe whether the injury was to be deemed avoidable or unavoidable.

Various notes, recordings in the minutes of scheduled safety meetings, and the camp newsletters indicate safety was a most serious issue among the management staff in Poe Valley, and significant effort was put into the avoidance of accidents through several measures.

There was a monthly safety bulletin published and distributed by the CCC to all camps. The bulletin described typical injuries sustained by enrollees, statistics on recorded injuries, lost-time data, and recommendations to reduce injuries. Monthly mass safety meetings were conducted in the camp, wherein all enrollees were required to attend. Motion pictures depicting safety topics were secured and shown to the enrollees. Enrollees prepared and presented safety programs in the form of plays, which were presented on the stage in the Recreation Hall.

As the program evolved, manuals for camp operations were published and distributed, such as "Emergency Conservation Work Safety Regulations." The camp received a copy of the safety manual in October of 1935. The contents of the manual included mandatory rules, specifications, and suggested safety measures to be taken.

Within the contents is a description for the safe handling and storage of explosives. During the era of the CCC, there were no controls imposed on the procurement or use of dynamite. Dynamite was used for many purposes in the camp, such as the movement of stone while road building, loosening of large tree stumps, and the blasting of stone when building the dam. In all of the safety records there is no mention of any injury resultant of dynamite usage.

The manual included a "Monthly Accident Summary" form to be submitted monthly by the camp commander.

Additionally, the editors of the camp newsletters apparently felt safety was an item to be kept ever present in the minds of the enrollees, and thus, almost every issue of the *Ravin* included articles about safety measures and eventually "safety" was a feature item in each publication.

The safety topics mentioned in the camp newsletters was extensive, and several would be repeated due to the constant change in personnel, as would be mandated by enrollment terms. Some of the topics included were proper lifting of heavy items, handling stone, snake bites, snow slides on company streets, trash disposal, handling dynamite, felling trees, jumping from trucks before stopping, fire extinguishers, handling axes, loose handles on tools, survey duty safety in the woods, handling of tools, sun stroke, heat exhaustion, hunting safety, sitting down while riding in trucks, and truck driving.

Numerous notes in safety meeting minutes describe various measures to be taken to reduce the numerous accidents. Many of the minor accidents were noted to be the result of "horseplay" and failure of enrollees to follow established safety tips and recommendations given to the enrollees in the various means described.

Of the repeated injuries, it seems axes were involved. The January 5, 1937, safety meeting minutes record the following:

> Member Daniel Reid (CC-3-51162) sustained a cut on the knee when his axe slipped from his hand while enrollee was walking while at work.
>
> Camp Commander Captain Ayres questioned Mr. Frankenberger whether there was a specific way of carrying an axe, at which Mr. Frankenberger replied that his instruction to the foreman and men was to carry the axe in the hand and not on the shoulder as he had seen a few do. Captain Ayres suggested that it would be advisable to set a standard in carrying axes, with the hand up close to the bit. Carried in this manner, the axe can be much more easily handled in case of a fall. The committee highly approved this suggestion, and Mr. Frankenberger would see that it was carried out.

In the December 1939 *Poe Valley Ravin* in a featured article titled "Use and Care of Various Tools" appears the following section titled "How To Carry An Axe." "When going through the forest or brush or rough country, the best way to carry an axe whether single or double bitted, is to carry it in the hand, grasping the handle close to the head, with the bit at right angles to the ground. Never carry a double bitted axe on your shoulder in rough country."

These same safety meeting minutes also recorded the following:

> John Lipsack (CC-3-195225) was injured while getting off a truck at the work project. The exact cause of the injury was not reported at the meeting, but Mr. Frankenberger mentioned that he believes that member Lipsack slipped from the truck in endeavoring to get out in a hurry, and sprained his wrist. It was not unduly slippery at the time he alighted from the truck, and due to the fact that enrollees are repeatedly warned as to the dangers of carelessness in getting on and off trucks, Mr. Frankenberger classes this accident as carelessness on part of enrollee concerned.

Also in these meeting minutes, the following is recorded:

> Captain Ayres stated that a Mass Safety Meeting would be held
> on January 14, 1937, and the entire company would attend.
> At this meeting, he mentioned, Mr. Frankenberger, Ass't
> Safety Engineer, Dr. Kelly, camp Surgeon, Mr. Holcomb, Camp
> Education Adviser and Captain Ayres, Commanding Officer will
> preside.
> Each of the above-named men will give a talk on Safety
> Topics of discussion as follows:
>
> Captain Ayres . . . . . . "General talk on Safety"
> Mr. Frankenberger . . "Care and handling of Tools"
> Lt. Kelly. . . . . "Prevention of Colds"
> Mr. Holcomb . . . . "Care and conduct of enrollees" and
>   "While using trucks in transportation"
>
> Mr. Holcomb will also read excerpts from the November
> Safety Bulletin published by the Safety Division, CCC, E.C.W.

Fire was an ever present safety matter. The barracks and all
of the other structures were heated by wood and coal-fired stoves.
Left unattended, sparks and hot embers falling out of these heat-
ing stoves could quickly ignite the wooden structures. The news of
fire occurrences, particularly in barracks buildings in other CCC
camps, had spread quickly throughout the camps in the early
days of the program. To mitigate the chance of fire, a watchman
was maintained at all times when these stoves were in operation.
The watchmen were enrollees, this duty would be assigned on a
rotational basis by the barracks leader.

A fire suppression system was developed consisting of fifty-
five-gallon drums filled with water positioned outside of each of
the barracks and other camp buildings. Maintaining these drums
full of water was performed by the enrollees, which was also assigned on a rotational basis by the barracks leader.

A fire alarm was maintained in the camp in the form of a
cast-iron bell. It was positioned atop of a stone foundation in the
center area of the camp and was known to resonate well and
could be heard several miles from camp.

Later, the fire alarm bell was relocated and hung from a wood
frame positioned adjacent to Headquarters.

Veteran William Koren told this story:

A couple of the fellows had missed the truck providing transportation back to camp from a Saturday night in Millheim, where they apparently had a touch of liquor. After walking all the way back to camp they thought it was a good idea to announce their arrival by "ringing the bell" and needless to say the rest of camp was not pleased with the false late night bell ringing. After "sleeping it off" the pranksters were "selected" to perform fire watch duty every other night for 30 days.

My grandfather departed Poe Valley in the early part of 1938 to be a senior foreman at Camp S-118 in Clearfield County where he assisted in the construction of another earthen masonry dam similar in design to the dam successfully completed in Poe Valley. This second dam he worked on was the rebuild of a failed wood crib dam at Parker Dam State Park. The dam failure was the result of extensive flood waters occurring throughout the state in 1936. The individual who took over my grandfather's safety assistant duties would be foreman Mr. Ralph L. Wert.

Mr. Wert was a Civilian Conservation Corps success story for the Poe Valley camp. Mr. Wert became a squad foreman in Poe Valley in June of 1936 after having been an enrollee in the Poe Valley camp for more than two years and would later be appointed to the position of junior foreman. The records indicate Mr. Wert was granted enrollment extensions in 1934 and 1935, an exception to the typical six-month enrollment periods early in the life of the CCC. A roster of all camp members in the 1935 camp Christmas card list Ralph L. Wert as an enrollee "leader." Mr. Wert went on to remain in the Poe Valley camp in the position of foreman for the remainder of time the camp was in operation through June 1941.

The records indicate Mr. Wert was the only enrollee in Poe Valley to "fully climb the ladder" entering camp as an "enrollee," becoming an "enrollee leader," and going on to become a "squad foreman" and then "junior foreman."

An article in the May 1941 camp newsletter indicates the efforts to constantly maintain safety in the minds of the camp paid off as "the camp was awarded the Civilian Conservation Corps division safety championship and were awarded a banner in testament."

Recorded safety infractions, recorded injuries, issues, and what was described as a less than effective program within the Civilian

Conservation Corps in more than one publication suggested the program was fraught with injuries and deaths due to ineffective safety training and execution by improperly trained personnel who were responsible to train a group of young, energetic individuals who were swinging axes and blasting rocks in some cases only a day or two after arriving in camp was mostly correct.

The recorded injury types between one camp location to another generally were similar as one might expect, due to the similarity of the work assignments, yet the number of recorded injuries between one camp and another varied significantly. The record ultimately reflected the recorded injuries resulting in "lost time" in Poe Valley were typically lower than most other camps in the district. This information was taken from excerpts posted in the camp newsletters.

SAFETY CONTEST

The recognition of the necessity for safety awareness in the camp is well-documented. Elimination of pain and suffering was always primary; secondary, a positive safety program kept men on the job and reduced loss in productive time and the time required to handle paperwork associated with any injury.

During the winter period of 1940-41, the foremen rolled up their sleeves and came up with a way to increase safety awareness in camp by putting pen to paper and created a "safety contest." The safety contest provided an opportunity for the enrollees under the direction and guidance of the foreman to further better their safety awareness and knowledge of how to properly prepare for and perform the tasks associated with their respective jobs to eliminate injury.

Typically, individual camp projects were assigned to a particular foreman who would take an assigned number of enrollees out on a given day to perform the work assignment. These individual foremen and enrollee assignments were more commonly referred to as a "crew." For the contest, these crews formed individual teams using the foreman's name as the team name.

Four teams, Auman's crew, Bradford's crew, Weaver's crew, and Wert's crew, took part in the contest. Safety questions were prepared by the enrollees of the company under the guidance of the military and technical personnel and the education advisor. These questions were in turn asked of the individual team members with award being given to the team member with the correct answer.

Round one had Bradford's crew competing against Wert's crew with Bradford's crew coming out on top thirty-two points to twenty-one points.

Round two had Weaver's crew competing against Auman's crew with Weaver's crew coming out on top twenty-nine points to fourteen points.

The final round of the contest had Mr. Weaver's crew competing against Mr. Bradford's crew.

The February 1941 issue of the camp newsletter announced the safety contest winner after the final round:

> After a hard fought battle the total number of points were added up and the total showed that Mr. Weaver's crew were the victors. Mr. weaver's crew had a total of 88 points to Mr. Bradford's crew who had 86.
>
> The prizes for the winning crew were announced to be a half-day off for each member of the winning crew in round one and round two and a pack of cigarettes for each member of the losing crew in round one and two.
>
> The prize for the winner of the final round would also be a half-day off work for each winning crew member and a pack [of] cigarettes to each member of the losing crew in the final round.

INFIRMARY

As was the way of the Army, a Civilian Conservation Corps camp organization structure included a camp surgeon. This position was filled by one of the military's Medical Corps assigned to the camp.

Additionally, an infirmary structure was made a part of the camp. These structures had the same look of a barrack building.

Each morning after breakfast the barrack leaders would allow any enrollee to report to the infirmary if it was felt the man needed to seek medical attention

Here basic medical services were administered and proper medical attention was given for any injury that may occur. When enrollees had sustained any type of severe injury or illness, such as appendicitis requiring hospitalization, typically enrollees were shuttled off to military hospitals. The nearby emergency service hospital for the Poe Valley camp was located twenty-four miles away in nearby Lewistown, PA.

When there was a shortage of available Army Medical Corps officers, the program would contract local doctors to temporarily fill the vacancy while awaiting arrival of a Medical Corps doctor. This would be the case in Poe Valley for a temporary period of time during the month of February 1939 when Doctor Thissell, whose practice was located in nearby Millheim, would become the camps resident doctor.

A new camp surgeon, Lieutenant Pennes, Army Medical Corps, was assigned to the camp in March 1939. After the arrival of Lieutenant Pennes, Doctor Thissell returned to his practice in Millheim.

Again, early in the year 1940 a contract surgeon was required. Dr. William Simpson filled the vacancy. Dr. Simpson served two separate Civilian Conservation Corps camps at this time, splitting full time between the two different camps.

The military supplied Army ambulances to the camps. One of these Army ambulances was assigned to the Poe Valley camp.

Army transport ambulance

The camp newsletter kept the members apprised of those who would require medical attention, as is noted in the March 1937 issue of the *Poe Valley Ravin*:

> "Removed To Hospital"
> It is with regret that we learn of the departure of Leader Roy S.B. Immel, ex First Cook and present Mess Steward, for the United States Naval Hospital in Philadelphia, Pa. for further treatment of a fractured ankle. We wish you a speedy recovery Roy and hurry back. We'll miss you.
> This swells the number of patients from this camp in the Naval Hospital to six. This camp has been extremely unfortunate in having so many of its, members in being hospitalized.

Safety committee records and notices in the camp newsletters indicate enrollees were hospitalized in nearby Lewistown. They were also sent to the US Naval Hospital in Philadelphia, Walter Reed Medical Center in Washington, DC, and the hospital at District Headquarters in New Cumberland.

Basic first-aid training was required to be administered to all camp foremen as part of the camp's military administrative requirements.

The infirmary was also where a visiting dentist would provide basic dental care for the enrollees. For many enrollees, this was where they had their first encounter with a dentist. It is unknown what the specific rotation schedule for these dentists were, however, documents and notices in the camp newsletters suggest a dentist was in camp approximately every two months and in some instances more frequent.

The June 1940 issue of the *Poe Valley Ravin* includes an article about the dentist.

"Camp dentist here again. June 21 Albert Rigsberg the camp dentist visited camp for a two day stay. While here Dr. Rigsberg will do extracting only.

"Dentist Rigsberg again pulled approximately 50 teeth, this makes close to a hundred that he has pulled this month for S-63."

Another dentist who served in Poe Valley was sub-district dental surgeon Lt. H. B. Fitch. Dr. Fitch also had a dental office in the nearby town of Millheim.

Like so many CCC camps, Poe Valley was located in rugged, mountainous terrain with limited access to major roadways. It is believed administrators would choose to assign a single camp-dedicated military medical officer to these locations. This is believed to be the case in Poe Valley where a single camp-dedicated military medical officer managed the camp infirmary. These medical officers rotated in and out of the camp on a six-month basis. Medical officers brought with them special skills based upon their respective education, experience, and technical skills. While one medical officer may be a skilled surgeon, not all medical officers were skilled surgeons. These medical officers performed differing medical services in the camp infirmary based upon their respective capabilities.

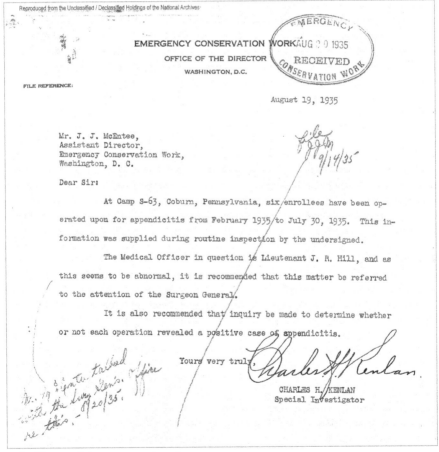

Federal Inspector's letter on camp surgeries

When an enrollee came into the infirmary needing medical attention, the medical officer would determine the needs and treatment for the patient. When the medical attention required was beyond the camp surgeon's capability, the patient was typically sent by ambulance to a military hospital.

Apparently, medical officer Lt. J. R. Hill was a skilled surgeon and believed himself quite capable of performing appendectomy surgery in the Poe Valley camp infirmary. A letter written on Emergency Conservation Work stationary by a special investigator dated August 19, 1935, indicates Lieutenant Hill had performed six such surgeries in camp and believed this to be quite abnormal and recommended a review be performed by the surgeon general (see letter on page 197). Furthermore, the letter recommended inquiry be made to verify the need for the operations.

This letter is believed to be the only document in regards to this matter maintained in the National Archive files. No follow-up letters were found to know if any investigation was conducted.

At no time during any of the reunions was I made aware of any discussion or stories shared by veterans regarding the "appendicitis-breakout" of 1935 in Poe Valley.

HAIR CUTS

Maintaining cleanliness and developing good personal hygienic habits has always been part of the US Army. The enrollees in the Civilian Conservation Corps camps were encouraged to maintain these same standards. Showering, shaving, dental care, wearing clean clothing, maintaining clean bedding, and keeping hair groomed were part of everyday life in the camp. In particular, during inspections military commanders were known to be on the lookout for well-groomed hair. Well-groomed hair, a neat bunk, and a recommendation from a barrack leader or foreman gave an enrollee a leg up whenever selections were being made to fill various perceived "cushy jobs" in camp versus assignment to a crew heading out to pick and shovel road-building duty.

Camp commanders were known to seek out enrollees who may have experience at cutting hair and take advantage of this in-camp opportunity and conduct the proverbial lineup of enrollees on a scheduled basis for haircuts. These haircuts, at no charge, were not the "high and tight" or "buzz" cuts the Army is well-known for. The enrollees were not in the Army, they were in the Civilian Conservation Corps where conventional Army ways were more relaxed.

Enrollee Joseph Kreydatus was known for cutting hair, so the camp commander allowed him the opportunity to cut hair in camp. The camp barber shop was located in the infirmary during Enrollee Kreydatus's stay. Enrollee Kreydatus was quite good at his trade as is exhibited in a letter of recommendation generated by the camp commander. (Please see letter below.)

Enrollee Kreydatus was also one of the members who was somehow able to get extensions on his enlistment term, as the letter states he had been providing barbering services in the camp for a period of thirty-two months.

1335rd Company CCC
Poe Valley Camp S-63
Coburn, Pa.

March 31, 1937.

TO WHOM IT MAY CONCERN:

This is to certify that Joseph Kreydatus has served as CCC Camp barber for a period of 32 months.

He has occupied the camp barber shop which is maintained under the rigid rules of the U.S. Army as to cleanliness, equipment, etc. He has averaged one hundred twenty-five haircuts a month. These were accomplished during evenings and other spare time of this member without any loss of time on his regular work.

His haircuts have been very neat and satisfactory in every detail. In fact they are better than the average of CCC Camp barbers.

EDWARD R. AYRES,
Capt. Cav-Res.,
Commanding.

Commander's letter on Krydatus haircutting

Haircut time rain or shine or snow

When there was no one with haircutting experience available in camp, commanders would seek out a local barber to come into camp, as was the case in Poe Valley. Harold Benfer, sole proprietor of Benfer's Barbershop in nearby Millheim would periodically come into camp and attend to the barbering needs of the enrollees.

Benfer's Barbershop was frequented by some of the enrollees, particularly on payday weekend. At the town barbershop, one could receive an "after shave" cologne treatment not available in the camp barbershop. The enrollees desired to have this treatment prior to spending the evening on the town, hoping to receive the attention of the local girls for a date.

GIMME THE BUTT

One of the more common topics of discussion by veterans at reunions was smoking. Smoking was described as a way of exhibiting being older than you actually were and being a tough guy, meaning you do not want to mess with me, as I smoke and as such will kick your butt. While I'm not sure I exhibited the tough-guy part, I know I did feel I was exhibiting a more mature self when I was a teenager and tried my hand at smoking. For me, the smoking thing did not stick, as I simply did not enjoy it. During my brief teenage smoking period, I easily remember having friend and non-friend alike asking to "bum" a smoke.

During my hitch in the Army, smoking was most popular and a significant deal. Smoke breaks were either granted or requested all the time. Either granted for good behavior or withheld for poor performance. As a young platoon leader who did not smoke, I would easily forget about granting smoke breaks and would quickly be reminded by the guys who smoked about the desire to have "that" smoke.

I could easily understand the general gist of many a story about smoking being told by Poe Valley veterans during reunions. They told stories about the high value of a single cigarette when trading for other items.

Veteran William Koren remembered how the trade of four or five Lucky Strikes would get a "whole week of barrack orderly services." Other veterans told of how foremen, who like me did not smoke, failed to allow time for smoke breaks. They told of how many enrollees who came into camp with a smoking habit would "kick" the habit due to economic reasons; they could not afford the $0.22 for a pack of cigarettes.

Smoking has been a part of America since the very beginning. In current times, smoking has been a base for placing one's health at risk for multiple reasons shared by some and in some cases by almost everyone. Leading into The Great Depression era, smoking was conventionally shared by almost everyone and generally accepted by all. The medical community in the early part of the twentieth century had expressed the risks associated with smoking. This for the most part had a small community of acceptance willing to acknowledge the smoking's harmful effects.

We came to know the harmful effects of smoking when one of the top news stories of 1964 was the surgeon general's findings released in the first report of the Advisory Committee on Smoking and Health and the subsequent Federal Cigarette Labeling and Advertising Act. The health risks associated with cigarette smoking were now known to every household in America. I remember well how divided my own family members were regarding their individual belief in the validity of the information expressed in the reports released by the surgeon general.

Thirty years prior to the surgeon general's report, the knowledge of risks associated with smoking were getting press time in Poe Valley. The February 1939 issue of the *Poe Valley Ravin* had a full-page editorial release on the health risks associated with cigarette smoking titled "Gimme the Butt." The article is as follows:

> "Gimme the butt" is the most ignominious saying used in camp. It is a by phrase in the barrack, rec hall, going to work — everywhere. The danger from the habit that leads to this saying should be obvious to every one, and yet the habit increases each month.
>
> There are two great dangers to this habit: possibility of contracting germs which may lead to illness, and the danger from the cigarette itself.
>
> When one person accepts a butt from another, the one who had the cigarette first has had his lips on the cigarette first. If the person has a cold, sore throat, or even tuberculosis or syphilis, the germs are present in his mouth. The germs may die in the open air in a very few minutes, but the receiver of the butt instantly puts it in his mouth and begins to heave on it vigorously.
>
> The next danger is the one concealed in the cigarette itself. As we know a cigarette contains a large amount of nicotine, that is, large enough to be dangerous. It is also true the nicotine in three cigarettes is sufficient to KILL a man. But when some one is smoking, the butt end of the cigarette acts as a filter to the deadly poison. For that reason a cigarette should be thrown away before it is two-thirds consumed.
>
> Now it is easy to see that some one who is continually accepting butts is subjecting himself to the dangers that scientists spend their lives attempting to overcome. All the dangerous poisons of the cigarette are in the butt end, and as the butt becomes shorter, there must be an outlet for these poisons. The butt smokers mouth is the only exit.
>
> Why run the unnecessary risk that accompanies the acceptance of a butt? Do without until canteen books are issued, until pay day comes, or even borrow the money to buy cigarettes; but in any case we should all make an earnest effort to do away with the ominous "Gimme the Butt."
>
> Robert Robson
> Editor

It is easy to understand how this practice became so popular at a time when so many were not able to afford cigarettes. Wanting to make friends, keep friends, and let their buddies have that last drag had to have been a significant contributing factor when saying yes to the "Gimme the Butt" request. It is even more easy to understand how cigarettes would get into the hands of enrollees when we read the following article published in the September 1939 issue of the *Poe Valley Ravin.*

> "Enrollees Sample Popular Cigarettes"
> September 18 a representative of the American Tobacco Company made a jaunt into Poe Valley today and made a determined effort to convince the enrollees of the merits of his product.
> He arrived in time for the evening meal, and the company listened to the recordings of Kay Kayser (Kyser) and Mark Warnow while they were eating.
> Each enrollee was given a sample of the cigarettes made by the American Tobacco Company.

KEEPING THE PEACE

Whenever there are young, healthy men grouped together for any extended period of time, discourse and disagreement will ensue. Misinterpretation of words spoken and outright derogatory statements often lead to confrontation. For most enrollees, their new-found home came with unknown and unanticipated assigned tasks to maintain neatness and cleanliness. Most would settle into the new assignments without much angst. For some, following direction was met with ambivalence and in some cases outright refusal to comply. For many others, this was their first experience at being grouped together with others from unfamiliar, diverse backgrounds.

The US Army is well-known for punishing the whole for the sins of one. An example of this would be to have everyone in the barracks clean the entire barracks two and three times over because one individual had not cleaned up his own mess, all the while having the individual responsible stand and watch everyone else perform the unquestioning added tasks. This means of discipline management, however, was not used in the CCC camps. The Army way to have unquestioning response to orders given was not necessary in a CCC work camp.

The Army adopted a modified chain of command policy in the camps. Each of the barracks was assigned a barracks leader and a barracks assistant leader. The company commander selected these individuals from the enrollees assigned to the camp. Barracks leaders received an additional $12.00 a month, and the assistant leader received $6.00 a month for their work. It would be the responsibility of these leaders to maintain order, assign duties, and keep the men in the barracks informed on the ways of life and expectations of camp administrators while in the confines of the camp. These leaders would typically be selected based upon age, temperament, and stature, as having the big man in charge usually had a positive impact on maintaining order. Whenever discourse and unacceptable behaviors occurred, it would be these leaders who were first in line to keep the peace.

During reunions, I heard stories about a particular "skirmish" whenever a barracks leader was setting an enrollee straight on camp or barracks law and order. I learned that most times whenever a case of homesickness was affecting the performance of an enrollee or an argument was about to lead to a physical altercation, the barracks leaders were expected to step in and keep the peace. Whenever an enrollee was faced with a personal matter or a severe infraction of camp rules had occurred, it was the barracks leader who would take the matter at hand to the camp commander for review and disposition. I did not hear of any specific problematic matters requiring excessive or extensive peacekeeping.

I heard on more than one occasion the enrollees in Poe Valley were pretty well "worn out" at the end of a day's work, and everyone was in the "same boat" dealing with the economic hardships of the times and subsequently developed a camaraderie in getting along.

Camp commanders had the responsibility of organizing and running the camp in accordance with rules and regulations established by the program director's offices in Washington, DC. These rules and regulations were in play within the confines of the camp. When the enrollees were turned over to the camp superintendent for work projects out in the forests beyond the confines of the camp, it would be the responsibility of the camp superintendent and his staff of foremen to keep the peace.

The camp superintendent and his staff of foremen had no authority to discipline enrollees. When enrollees were disruptive during the work day and the foremen or superintendent were not able to resolve the issue at hand, the name of the enrollee who was "causing trouble" was typically given to the barracks leader in an effort to get resolution. When warranted, the foremen turned the matter over to the camp superintendent, who could in turn take the matter to the camp commander for review and disposition. The camp commander, in turn, doled out appropriate discipline; in most cases, the infraction did not merit a harsh discipline, and for these minor offenses some measure of extra duty, like added fire watch time or some other unwanted task for an assigned time period was handed down. For more severe infractions, disciplinary measures could be a loss of weekend privileges or supplemental duty assigned to be performed during the enrollee's free time. The most severe disciplinary action would be to recommend the enrollee be discharged from the CCC, receiving a dishonorable discharge.

The following is taken from the enrollee John P. Shinskie's autobiography:

> It was December, 1940, and Christmas was just a few days away. I had been granted leave to spend the Christmas at home with my family. Mom, Dad, and my sister and brother were excited about my coming home and more so because Pat would be spending several days of the holiday season with us too. My Christmas furlough was to begin on the Saturday before Christmas and that almost didn't happen. On Friday during our evening meal in the camp mess hall, someone put a handful of brown bombers in the coffee pitcher on our table. Brown bombers were the most potent laxative ever invented and ingesting just one of them could keep a person running for several days. By Saturday morning several members of our table reported to sick call in search of relief. Of the eight persons sitting at our table on Friday evening, everyone had a bad case of the skitters on Saturday morning. The dispensary attendant called this to the attention of the senior leader and he reported it to the company commander. All eight members who sat at our table on Friday evening and drank that brown bomber laden coffee were called to the company office to face the wrath of Marine First Lieutenant Lee Fox. It would be my first and only one-on-one confrontation with him. He did the talking and his ultimatum was "there will be no Christmas

leave for any one of you until I find out who is guilty of this. Right then I decided Lt. Fox was crazy or at least temporarily insane. I asked him for permission to speak and he granted it. I asked one question - "Why would every person at our table drink the coffee if one of us was guilty of putting the brown bombers in the pot?" He responded by saying that "if one of us didn't do it then one of us knew who did." After that I really began to question his mentality. He dismissed us and we either headed for the barracks or the latrine.

It was close to noon and I was feeling bad about the prospect of spending Christmas in camp and then I became angry about the unfairness of it all. I went back to the orderly room and asked for permission to speak with Lt. Fox again. When I walked into his office, I was fighting to control my anger but had already decided to have my say. I said I was innocent of any wrongdoing and was entitled to my furlough and spending Christmas with my family. He of course, disagreed. I then asked him what my punishment would be if I went home without leave. He said it would be severe. I asked if it would result in a dishonorable discharge. He said no, but only because it would be my first infraction of the rules. Right then I made up my mind to go home for Christmas with or without Lt. Fox's blessing and I did. I had a wonderful time for seven days and then I reported back to camp. I again asked for permission to speak to Lt. Fox. When I entered his office I didn't know what to expect. He asked me if I had a nice Christmas with my family and I said I did and that I was now ready to accept any punishment he deemed necessary. Punish me he did.

Remember it was wintertime. I was to be responsible for filling every coal bin at each building for the next 30 days – after I had finished my regular day's work in the mountains. I would also be confined to camp for those thirty days. After that I would have to clean the kitchen grease trap on the Saturday following the coal punishment. Well, I had plenty of coal shoveling experience before entering the CCC's, so filling the coal bins was no problem except for the time t would take. After the first couple days I would load up my wheelbarrow with coal from the stock pile and push it up to a coal bin by one of the buildings only to find it was full. You see the fellows knew that the punishment was not warranted and it was their way of showing it. They filled up their own coal bins – after it got dark.

The grease trap was a different story. It was not the hardest job to do, but it was the stinkiest dirty job I ever did. I got no help there. When someone got the grease trap to clean as punishment, Lt. Fox always came by to inspect the job and to more or less watch the fellow squirm and sometimes throw up because of the smell. I made up my mind that he wouldn't do that to me. My good friend and first cook, Angelo Russell asked me if I was hungry and then he laughed because no one ever ate when they cleaned the trap. He really looked surprised when I asked him what he had to offer. Angelo said "I have anything you want, old buddy and if I don't have it, I'll send someone to town for it." I told him I'd like a couple oranges peeled and sectioned in a large bowl and a clean fork and more importantly, to let me know when Lt. Fox entered the mess hall. I turned a clean bucket upside down and put the bowl of orange slices on it and busied myself with cleaning the trap. The grease trap was located outside. Angelo left me know that Lt. Fox was on his way and when he walked out the kitchen door, I was standing there eating the orange slices. He asked me how it was going with what I thought was a smirk on his face. I said, "Fine just fine, but this kind of work makes a person hungry." It was his first turn to think I was crazy. As I was popping another orange slice into my mouth, Lt. Fox looked at me, shook his head as if bewildered and walked away. That ended my punishment and Lt. Fox wiped my record clean. The camp senior leader, Leroy Pelka, told me that when Lt. Fox returned to his office after inspecting my effort at cleaning the grease trap he remarked that "the Shinskie kid is one tough cookie". Lt. Fox is deceased so I can't ask him, but I wonder if my record was wiped clean because of my positive attitude of accepting my punishment without complaining. I must admit Lt. Fox was one "tough cookie" too.

CHAPTER 9

In addition to the multiple forestry work projects undertaken by the enrollees, the two-year project constructing the dam creating Poe Valley Lake, and the construction of more than thirty miles of roads that included construction of more than ten bridges, there were numerous other projects undertaken by the boys of Company 1333. Unknown are all of the projects these boys worked on throughout the life of the camp. Most of the tasks and projects performed by the boys in the Poe Valley camp throughout the state-owned Bald Eagle Forest were duplicated in many of the other CCC camps situated on state-owned lands. During the era of the CCC restoration, management of lands having been subject to fire was performed. Additionally, many forest fires were hard fought by CCC enrollees. The CCC is credited with saving tens of thousands of acres of valuable forests from loss due to fire throughout the country.

Sadly, during the life of the CCC, enrollees lost their lives while valiantly fighting forest fires. In many cases where lives were lost, limited or no proper training on firefighting was listed as a contributory cause. Early on in the program, enrollees were engaged in fighting forest fires without being properly trained. Other writings describe some of these losses and tell of how the CCC quickly put together proper forest-fire fighting training for the enrollees.

Fighting of forest fires by enrollees is noted in numerous *Poe Valley Ravin* newsletters.

FIRE TOWER AND WATCHERS CABIN

Early detection of forest fires, particularly those caused by lightning strikes, is key to saving acreage from the devastation caused by fire. The Department of Forest and Waters chose multiple sites to have eighty- and one-hundred-foot tall lookout towers erected to

FORESTRY

Spring in Poe Valley

Spring and the approach of summer aids Poe Valley to become a scenic splendor of Natural Beauty. The newly constructed dam built by Camp S-63, offers a recreational center for the lovers of the out-doors. The recent stocking of the lake with 4,800 game fish of legal size allows the fisherman a real sport. Boating and swimming in the clear mountain water

New Projects

The razing of abandoned Camps S-62 and S-65 are practically complete. Several new projects have been started. The building of a road and bridge around Poe Valley Dam already has begun. It will be on the opposite side of the dam and will run back again to meet Poe Valley Road at the Junction. This will enable the fishermen and bathers to get to the other side where a park area, beach and shelter will be constructed. Many of the roads entering the Valley have been repaired and shaled and will offer more riding pleasure for the tourists.

Forest Fire

Several weeks ago Bailey Auman's crew was the first to test their ability for fighting fires. Their quick responsive action and cooperation soon put the fire under control. The fire occurred on the North side of Poe Tower Mountain. Approximately forty acres were burned over. The origination was not known.

Thousands of Trees Planted

Bill Throssel's crew has planted approximately 50,000 trees in the past few weeks. A variety of White Spruce, Red Pine, and Pitch Pine were planted in various areas of Poe Valley and Green's Valley. The places planted were where deer seldom frequent. As the deer always chew the tops off from the young greens, there-by stunting their growth.

Fire At Penn's View

On April 30th Bailey Aumans' crew was again called to defend the forest from destruction by fire. The fire was below Penn's View although it was not a very big fire it was a stubborn one, taking about six hours to extinguish it completely. It also took two crews of men working alternately to extinguish the blaze. Many new men, never before at a Forest Fire alone battling one were on the side of the defenders. And were throughly initated in the work.

Forestry Classes

The following classes are taught by members of the Forestry personel of this company; Practical Engineering, Saw Filing, Auto Mechanics, Blacksmithing, Everyday Problems, Leadership Training and Road Construction. For further information see the Class Schedule on the Bulletin Board

Enrollees firefighting services described in April 1938 camp newsletter monitor fire conditions. Poe Mountain was one of the sites selected to have a tower erected, as the elevation provides an excellent, sweeping view of the Seven Mountains region. The boys of Camp S-63 were tasked with the construction of the lookout tower.

Performing the task of looking out for fires was the job of a "watcher." The watcher was employed by the Department of Forest and Waters. In addition to the salary received by the watcher, a cabin was made available in which to reside while on duty.

The boys of Camp S-63 were also tasked with constructing the watcher's cabin. The cabin is a single-story structure constructed primarily of stone masonry. The cabin floorplan included a large living room with a stone fireplace, a kitchen area, and columned front porch.

The end of service for the lookout tower happened in 1966, and the tower was demolished in 1970.

The watcher's cabin remains standing today without any assigned use at this time. In testament to the construction skills of the enrollees and the foreman's instruction, the structure while

Enrollees "hanging out" on the fire tower they constructed

receiving limited maintenance and now more than seventy-five years old, is in good condition and looks much the same as it did when it was constructed.

View of watchers cabin taken from atop of the fire tower

View of watchers cabin as it stands today

When I was eleven or twelve years old, I remember my buddies and I would hike up to the top of Poe Mountain where the tower stood while pretending to play army. After careful battle planning, we would storm the enemy who had taken up position atop of the tower. You should know each and every time we stormed the enemy, the enemy was sure to lose the battle as soon as we reached the top of the stairs. Rarely would we sustain any casualties during these raids.

The stairs took you up to a small, enclosed lookout room. The room was locked and at no time did I ever have the opportunity to gain access into the room to look out upon the mountain scenery.

CAMP SIGN

During a gathering to celebrate the legacy of Poe Valley Civilian Conservation Corps, Company 1333 in 2012, I nervously awaited while attendees filtered in. Not knowing how many people may show for a gathering focusing on extended family members of former enrollees, I was pleased to see a turnout exceeding seventy-five people. While I was observing those who were filtering in prior to commencement of the program, I noticed a woman in the crowd who seemed familiar to me. After another brief eye contact, I was fairly certain this woman might be a former high school classmate of mine, but her name totally escaped me.

Knowing this woman knew my name, as it was provided on the flyer sent out regarding the event, it was now my turn to learn hers. I went over and introduced myself, and after introductions I learned she was indeed a high school classmate. We reacquainted ourselves after having not seen each other for quite a lengthy time. I learned her married name to be Mary Jane Smith, and she is the daughter of Enrollee Elwood Ward.

Mary Jane reminded me of the passing of her father when we were seniors in high school. She then went on to tell me she had only recently learned her father was an enrollee in the Poe Valley CCC camp. She could not remember her father ever telling of his time in the camp and told me her mother had recently moved into a nearby retirement facility, after which the family was looking through collections of items in their mother's house. They came upon documents indicating their father had been an enrollee of the Poe Valley camp. Further inquiry on the part of the family confirmed he had indeed been in the camp from October 1939 through September 1941.

While my grandfather and my classmate's father had served time in the Poe Valley camp at different times, each had separately been part of a large collective accomplishment known to all who have visited Poe Valley State Park in the seventy-five years following the closing of the camp.

Circumstance joining coincidence around a common issue seems to occur more often than we expect. Around the same time-frame Mary Jane was learning her father was a part of the Poe Valley camp, I was purchasing a photo album online advertised to contain photographs of the Poe Valley camp. We soon learned two photographs in this album depicted her father in camp. What are the chances?

The one photograph depicts Mary Jane's father, Enrollee Elwood Ward, posing in front of the camp welcome sign.

Enrollee Elwood Ward at camp sign

The second photograph depicts Enrollee Ward sitting on the porch railing of the newly constructed masonry watchers cabin suggesting he had helped construct this cabin (see top of facing page).

TEN BRIDGES

The June 1936 *Poe Valley Ravin* lists ten bridges having been constructed by the boys of Company 1333 between the period June 1933 and June 1936. I have no documentation providing the specifications for the materials used to construct the bridges,

Enrollee Elwood Ward on right at watchers cabin

nor do I have any details or plans showing how the bridges were constructed.

After conducting a tour of all the roadways into, out of, and throughout the Poe Valley region where the CCC boys were engaged in various road construction projects, I was able to locate several of the original bridge construction assemblies, which remain in service today.

One of the bridges constructed by enrollees still in service today

More bridges constructed by enrollees still in service today

The stone bridge abutments remaining in service today are a testament to the proper selection of materials indigenous to the area and competency of the foremen directing the labor performed by these greenhorn bridge building boys of Company 1333.

The bridge construction works of the Poe Valley boys was recognized in the CCC national newsletter, *Happy Days*, in the October 24, 1940 issue.

Bridge construction article posted in the national CCC newsletter *Happy Days*

THE MILK RUN

While sitting with veteran Randall Boob, he told me the milk run story.

Randall was a local enrollee, having grown up in the nearby town of Coburn. Randall, like so many, had joined the Civilian Conservation Corps so as to have a job or in his case to have continuous, full-time employment.

At this time, the local dairy farmers had their milk, in milk cans, collected and transported to the regional milk processing plant by a trucking service. The processing plant was located adjacent to the railroad station, allowing easy transport to the train station, thereby moving the milk products quickly onto general commerce.

Randall explained he had a few odd jobs prior to joining the Civilian Conservation Corps and one of these odd jobs was to help transport milk from nearby farms. His father had one of the few trucks in the area transporting milk from the farm direct to the processing plant, and he helped his father from time to time; in doing so, he had learned the routes and also learned how to drive the milk truck.

Transporting the milk on schedule was most critical, as this was at a time when commercial refrigeration was not yet in place and farmers used ice as an interim means of refrigeration and heavily relied on milk haulers to pick up their fresh milk and get it to the processing plant prior to spoilage.

Randall went on to explain one day when he was in camp he was told to report to the company commander's office on a Friday afternoon without any idea of why he was to report to the "Top Man's" office. He went to see the commander and was told the camp had received a phone call from home, requesting Randall be allowed to come home as early as possible on Saturday to handle the milk run, as his father had fallen ill. After Randall explained the importance of the milk run, the company commander allowed Randall to go home for the milk run and subsequently allowed Randall to help out a few other times when the request was made.

He remembered one of the camp foremen gave him a ride out of camp that first time but was not able to remember the foreman's name.

THE POULTRY PROJECT

An article in the March 1940 issue of the *Poe Valley Ravin* tells of a newly proposed camp project. The spring of 1940 was to bring a new and different education-sponsored program to the camp. This project was a dual-purpose education and food service program. It was to be known as the "poultry project." Here the enrollees learned the fundamentals of "poultry husbandry" and provided a supply of eggs and meat for the Mess Hall. The project included construction of a chicken house, subsequent operation of the facility, and supply of eggs and meat. The project started with one hundred chicks and subsequently added one hundred chicks in following months.

I am not certain if this project ever came to fruition, as none of the enrollees ever mentioned this program during reunions and gatherings.

I have no knowledge of egg production, however, I believe a significant effort would be required to provide the quantity of eggs needed in a CCC camp on a weekly basis. Average egg consumption in a CCC camp was known to be about 120 dozen per week.

POE PADDY PARK

In the latter part of the eighteenth century the mountains of Pennsylvania provided opportunity for lumberman to move in and start cutting. The demand for lumber was at an all-time high. The mountains surrounding Poe Valley were ripe for the cutting. Standing timber, plentiful in this region, supported the development of a small lumbering community to become known as Poe Mills in 1880. At its peak, Poe Mills had a population of more than 300 and was located approximately six miles east of the site where Camp S-63 was located. A railroad spur was constructed into Poe Mills to move lumber out of the area. Penns Creek flowed adjacent to Poe Mills, supporting the town and lumbering operation needs. Here would be where the Poe Valley Lake feeder stream, Big Poe Creek, would flow into Penns Creek. Lumbering operations dried up around 1901, and Poe Mills became a place to be remembered. A signboard stands today telling the story of the short life of Poe Mills.

Penns Creek today is most well-known as a fishing stream where fly-fishing anglers from far and wide come to challenge the native trout during the nationally known annual "green drake fly hatch" time.

Sign board posted in Poe Paddy Park at the site of the Poe Mills lumbering center

Ten acres of grounds adjacent to the area where the once-pros-perous Poe Mills stood was selected to be developed into a small picnic area by Camp S-63. I do not remember my grandfather specifically mentioning the development of this area. Documents, however, tells us the area was developed by mid-year 1936 and prior to dam construction activity where all hands were working.

Development of the site provided an area for camping and picnicking. Two pavilions were constructed in the log-frame style that included picnic tables and a masonry fireplace for cooking. Parking areas and sites for tent erection were made part of the work, and masonry fire rings where "stories of the night" could be passed from generation to generation were constructed. Other works included roadway improvement, bridge construction, and stream improvement to support fish growth and the popular sport of fishing. All of this development work and construction was suc-cessfully completed by a "bunch of kids" from the city, as these enrollees were on more than one occasion referred to by locals and the public at large.

Initially, the site was named Poe Paddy, a site for camping and picnicking. Poe Paddy is named for Poe Mountain to the west and Paddy Mountain to the east. After initial development by the CCC boys, Poe Paddy was listed as a State Forest Picnic Area. Today, Poe Paddy is officially listed as a state park.

Today the two original pavilions erected by the CCC boys in the 1930s remain in service. The masonry fireplaces still provide a place to cook the family picnic meal. Current modernization

Picnic pavilion constructed by enrollees

The picnic pavilion as it stands today

includes updated toilet facilities and a new bridge to cross over Big Poe Creek.

Poe Paddy Park today looks much the same in its majestic, rustic form as it did upon its completion more than seventy-five years ago. It has had the pleasure to serve a vast and mostly unknowing public regarding how it came to be.

OPEN HOUSE CELEBRATION

An article appears in the March 1939 *Poe Valley Ravin* inviting all to celebrate the sixth anniversary of the Civilian Conservation Corps:

> March 20 - On Palm Sunday, April 2, the public is invited to visit Poe Valley Camp S-63 at the open house in celebration of the sixth anniversary of the Civilian Conservation Corps. Visiting hours will be from 10:00 A.M. to 4:00 P.M., and a lunch will be served for the guests at 12:30 P.M.
>
> Many recreational spots, roads fire trails, towers, as well as improvement of forests have been done by the boys, of which they are proud and anxious for the public to see. Enrollees are urged to invite parents and friends to the festivities.

I have no knowledge about how well-attended the celebration may have been. What is known is that by the springtime of 1939, America had started to find its way out of The Depression, allowing family motoring to occur and visitation to those recreational parks being created by those "boys back in the woods."

William Kelly, one of two military officers I met while attending reunions who served in Poe Valley, enjoyed sharing his remembrances of his time spent. He told me the Army in particular encouraged camp commanders to host an "open house" or "camp dance," giving visitors every opportunity to visit the camp, so as to allow themselves a firsthand look into the camp setup. Many rumors were spread among "locals" about how these "boys" were back there in the woods "being mind controlled" under influence of military commanders. He went on to say it would be during these visits that folks learned how military commanders were mostly behind the scenes, unknown administrators and that the foremen in camp knew their sons by name, having more day-to-day interaction with the enrollees than military commanders.

VISTAS

Whenever friends and family from out of town came to Coburn to visit my parents, conversation almost always included what sites the area had to offer visitors. Usually, first on the list was a suggested visit to famed Penns Cave, believed to be America's only all-water cavern where visitors tour the cave by boat. Next would be Woodward Cave, one of Pennsylvania's largest caves, known as the "Big One."

A road trip into Poe Valley was always suggested and on most occasions would occur. We would pile into the family station wagon for the ride into Poe Valley. Along the way, the first stop would be near the top of Second Mountain at the first lookout sight to be seen along the way. This first stop was at Bells Majestic View. From this spot could be seen the small town of Spring Mills and a grand view of the farmlands of Penns Valley.

The next stop would be Penns View. Penns View is situated atop of Slide Mountain. Slide mountain derived its name from the early logging days, where trees felled off of the area known as "Little Flat" were dragged by mules to the mountain edge and sent on down the mountain on a log slide. From here could be seen the town of Millheim and my own hometown, Coburn. Unfortunately, one could not see my house from here.

From this same lookout, the famed catch-and-release fly fishing stream, Penns Creek, can be seen at the foot of the mountain. Anglers have been coming to the region for decades to wade the waters and challenge the native trout in this stretch of water from Coburn to Weikert. The same view provides a look at a short section of the then Lewisburg & Tyrone Railway line, a subsidiary of the Pennsylvania Railroad. The same view provides a look of the railroad line crossing over Penns Creek on an elevated trestle bridge and then passing through a tunnel in Tunnel Mountain, south of Coburn. This same rail line had the short branch that ran into Poe Mills back at the end of the nineteenth century.

Trains ran this line section for the last time mid-summer of 1972 when Hurricane Agnes dumped torrential rains resulting in extensive damage to rail beds and bridge structures; subsequently, the steel rails and wooden ties were removed ending any train run through the region. Today, thanks to conservancy efforts, the old rail bed is part of the "Penns Creek Rail Trail."

The roads and trails leading to and from these sites and the clearing of the area providing the vistas for all to enjoy was performed by the foremen's boys out of the Poe Valley camp. Now, more than seventy-five years later, these vistas and roads built mostly by hand with limited support of motorized machinery remain in service, allowing visitors today to enjoy the same wonderful views my parents shared with friends and family more than fifty years ago.

CHAPTER 10

SIDE CAMP

In our current time when government and corporate action programs are presented to the public, these programs typically have been subject to extensive and exhaustive development. The extensive development usually included input from multiple agencies and sources requiring rewrite, revision, and additional review, and in most instances the time from program concept to program implementation can be years in the making. There are other instances when some programs are rolled out without the benefit of the exhaustive development; these programs are typically referred to as being a "work in progress."

I believe the success of the Civilian Conservation Corps program can vastly be attributed to it being a work in progress. The ability of so many to cooperatively move forward and make things happen, all while doing the work of program development for the better good of an entire nation was unprecedented. Certainly, program development did not go blissfully smooth and bump free every step of the way, as agreement will forever be met with disagreement and no singular thing can be accomplished using one singular approach.

Many changes in program operations occurred, such as in the program's requirements for enrollment. Many more changes were made at the camp level, so many in fact a recording of these changes was in most cases never made. These changes were made to support opportunity for employment of young men at a time when employment opportunity was dismal.

Much change occurred at a rapid pace in camp operations and development of the various individual projects to be undertaken within a district and at the camp level throughout the state. In Poe Valley one of the changes was to have men assigned to the

Poe Valley camp perform work at another camp location while still assigned to the Poe Valley camp. This action also occurred at other camp locations and was commonly known as setting up a "side camp."

The May and July 1939 issues of the *Poe Valley Ravin* included articles on the side camp activities. This side camp was established nearby at the former site of abandoned Civilian Conservation Corps Camp SCS-62. Here the men of Company SCS-62 completed construction on a small dam and manmade lake and a small recreation park open to the public.

The May 1939 issue tells us approximately thirty men occupied the grounds for three months commencing on or about June 20. The men were quartered and fed in the former camp's recreation hall.

The July 1939 issue reads:

> The rumor that a side camp would be established at the site of former Camp S-62 became a reality today as Mr. Wert and his crew moved to the spot adjacent to the Penn-Roosevelt dam.
>
> The crew consists of twenty five enrollees, including Edward McCloskey, who is taking care of the feeding problems.
>
> Abe Planishek, leader on Bailey Auman's crew, has been transferred to Mr. Wert's crew due to the lack of rated men on the latter's crew.
>
> The men who have two bridges to build and work on roads to do, are expected to be stationed in this side camp until the latter part of September. They return to this camp every weekend, however, and will enjoy recreation trips to Lewistown during the week.

I learned through a "confidential source" many bunkmates remaining back in the Poe Valley camp were envious of the side camp crew, as the Penn Roosevelt Park site had already become a popular park area where many local gals were known to don their bathing suits, enjoy sunny days and the cool waters, all the while gaining the admiration of those lucky side camp campers. My *confidential source* would not divulge any further information about any after-hours activities happening in the Penn Roosevelt Park other than to say boys have always enjoyed the company of girls.

WHAT DID THEY DO?

On numerous occasions when doing presentations on Camp S-63 I have been asked the same question: "What did these boys do in the camp?" In previous chapters, much of what they did in regards to work activities has been written. Chapter 4 tells much about the large-scale dam construction project, particularly in thanks to a daily log of activities maintained by the camp engineer.

Other general information about the work projects undertaken and described is provided based upon stories told by veterans, my grandfather, and passed-on information from locals who have been lifelong residents.

Unavailable are daily logs or any other written daily accounts that may have been maintained by military commanders, technical personnel, advisors, or others in the camp. The *Poe Valley Ravin* has been an invaluable source.

After the initial development of the camp structures, generally, the work projects undertaken prior to the dam construction project were road construction, trail development, forestry resource management, and bridge building. After completion of the dam construction, the work projects undertaken focused once again on the same projects prior to dam construction.

An article provided in the August 1940 camp newsletter titled "Project News" provides a description of ongoing work projects.

BRADFORD'S CREW

For the past several months the men of Bradford's crew have been working on the beautiful Poe Paddy Drive which winds from Poe Paddy Park to the top of Poe Mountain and then onto Penn's View. They have widened the road, built new head walls and culverts and posted signs of warning at every sharp turn. While working on the drive the crew has had the chance to see how dynamite is used and the work it can do. The men also had a chance to watch a "bull-dozer" cutting a road and then seeing the grader make the road smooth and easy to drive over.

BAILEY'S CREW

Bailey's men have recently finished the Ryder Hollow Road and have been working on the Sand Mountain Road. All the turns in the old road will be taken out and it will be very much straighter than before and also much easier driving. They have cut the right-a-way and have started to rip rap the ground up where the new road will go. This will give the men a chance to see how a road is made from the beginning and also practical experience. The road is expected to be finished sometime this winter.

McPHERSON'S CREW
McPherson's crew or the gooseberry crew as it is usually called has as you know been picking gooseberries for most of the summer. The berries when they are ripe dissolve into a powder and the powder is blown into pine trees and causes the trees to die. The men pick the gooseberries before they are ripe and destroy them. The men are now just finished with them and they will start a new project soon.

WEAVER'S CREW
Weaver's crew are now making an incinerator about half-way between te camp and the dam and will be used to burn the rubbish that is left lying by the picnickers and campers down at the dam. It is made of stone and the men will get a lot of experience in stone-masonry.

WERT'S CREW
Wert's crew is noted in this camp for its stone-masonry and bridge building. At the present time they are building a bridge in Panther Hollow which is about eight miles from camp. Luketic is the chief stone-mason but there are several more on the crew and more learning for this crew does most of the work.

Being in camp was similar to a regular job with limited supplemental requirements. Requirements included A.M. exercise, A.M./P.M. personal hygiene, fire watch, and maintaining personal space in barracks in a neat, clean, and orderly fashion, similar to the Army way. Basically, Monday through Friday after the day's work was accomplished and minimal duties were attended, the enrollees were on their own leisure time. Just as if they were back home, leisure time was fulfilled in many different ways. The following indicates many of the ways their leisure time was fulfilled.

The camp's recreation building was the main gathering place for after-hours activities. Here, the men would retire for the day and take time to write a letter back home to family and friends or just sit and read a book or magazine taken out of the camp's library stock to relax after the day's work. Games were a favorite way to pass the time, including card games, board games, table tennis, billiards and darts. A radio was eventually acquired and maintained in the recreation building. The radio kept the men entertained with music and current with the news and the shows common to radio broadcast at the time. During reunions, enrollees remembered listening in on weekly shows like *The Lone Ranger* and *The Shadow and Jack Armstrong*. They remembered easily enjoying music presented by Bing Crosby, The Mills Brothers, Guy Lombardo's Orchestra, and the Grand Old Opry. Listening in on baseball games was remembered as a favorite also.

The great outdoors provided sporting options for the men. Hiking, birdwatching, fishing, and swimming were a few of the activities to be conducted in the natural mountain environment surrounding the camp.

Sports provided a most popular means for recreation and exercise in camp. The games played included baseball, flag football, basketball, mushball, volleyball, and badminton.

Other recreational activities included movie night in camp and, most popular, camp dances. Camp dances were held on a non-scheduled basis, typically as a reward for a job well done by the camp commander or the celebration of a camp anniversary with an invitation being extended to the fairer sex from the surrounding communities. An orchestra and refreshments were even included.

The enrollees looked forward to the weekend just the same as the workforce of today. Saturday and Sunday were days off. The camp commander provided a truck and driver to take the boys to town on the weekends. The truck excursions were limited to the nearby towns of Millheim and Lewistown. This same truck returned at a scheduled time to pick them up and return them back to camp. During the summer months, going to town to take in the sites and entertainment at numerous carnivals and festivals was a favorite recreation.

A common theme in the camps was to further the education of the enrollees. Typically, this included the development and continued publishing of a camp newsletter. This theme was certainly maintained in Poe Valley. The education programs organized by the camp education director included multiple subjects like health & first aid, safety, citizenship, social courtesy, cooking, and many others.

Eventually, the education program in Poe Valley included a very full schedule.

The education program course offerings made available in camp were popular among the enrollees. These courses were offered during the enrollee's free time. The curriculum included publishing the camp newsletter. In-camp education programs were coordinated by the full-time education advisor. The following depicts the curriculum for the period July 1 through November 31, 1940.

CLASS SCHEDULE FOR THE PERIOD
July 1 to November 31, 1940

MONDAY	**7:00–8:00 AM**	
Blacksmithing	L. L. Weaver	Blacksmith Shop
Dynamiting	E. R. Auman	Educational Building
Blue Print Reading	C. H. Hutt	Library
Saw Filing	F. B. Auman	Blacksmith Shop
Auto Mechanics	L. E. Sherwood	Forestry Garage
Forestry	B. D. McPherson	Ed. Class Room
	5:30–6:30 PM	
Group Guidance	William Kelly	Ed. Class Room
Woodwork	Harry Kramer	Woodshop
TUESDAY	**7:45–8:30 AM**	
Safety	Ralph Wert	Recreation Hall
	4:15–4:50 PM	
Foremanship Training	C. H. Hutt	Forestry Office
	5:30–6:30 PM	
Health & Hygeine	Fox, Kelly, Dean, & Hutt	Ed. Class Room
Art	Harry Kramer	Art Room
WEDNESDAY	**7:00–8:00 AM**	
Truck Driving	Miller & Wert	Reading Room
Surveying	E. F. Hoyt	Educational Office
Road Construction	P. E. Bradford	Ed. Class Room
	5:30–6:00 PM	
First Aid	B. D. McPherson	Ed. Class Room
Woodwork	Harry Kramer	Woodshop
	7:30–8:30 PM	
Social Courtesy	Lee Fox	Recreation Hall
Motion Picture	Jones	Recreation Hall
THURSDAY	**5:30–6:30 PM**	
First Aid	Dr. Thissel	Library
Government	Homer A. Dean	Ed. Class Room
Woodwork	Harry Kramer	Woodshop
	6:30–7:30 PM	
Leadership Training	Foxx & Hutt	Ed. Class Room

CLASS SCHEDULE FOR THE PERIOD
July 1 to November 31, 1940

FRIDAY	4:15–4:45 PM	
Teachers Training	Homer A. Dean	Ed. Class Room
	5:30–6:30 PM	
Poultry Keeping	Homer A. Dean	Ed. Class Room

As the education program matured, courses of instruction were made available to the enrollees outside the confines of camp at nearby Lewistown High School and at the Pennsylvania College in State College. Various training films were developed by program officials in Washington and made available to the camps. Early on, prior to the camp acquiring its own projector, these films were shown to the enrollees in the theatre building in nearby Millheim. The education program was subject to constant change. Staff changes in education administrators, camp commanders, and foremen, all of whom were educators, resulted in curriculum changes to match the capabilities of the educators. Other contributing factors to change in curriculum were work projects and the desires of the enrollees.

GET THEM HOME

Mr. Larry Wert, son of camp foreman Ralph Wert, related the following story about how the foremen additionally "fathered" their charges as best they could as it was related to him by his father.

Foreman Wert and the other foremen used their family connections network throughout the state to help an enrollee get home whenever a family emergency would arise. The issue at hand would be the cost of transportation for an enrollee to get back home. At that time the normal means of transportation would be for an enrollee to take the train back home, as this was the conventional mode of transportation. Simply put, enrollees did not have the money for a train ticket to get back home. Here is where the foremen stepped in to do what they could when they could.

The foremen with the support of family and friend connections throughout the state would in a "hand them off" sort of way help those fortunate enrollees get home. The foremen took the enrollee after release by the company commander out of camp to a friend or family member in the region and "hand them off" to be ferried on to the next friend or family member along the way with repeated hand off, as may be necessary to reach the enrollee's hometown whenever feasible. Mr. Wert remembered his father telling him they had a network developed to Pittsburgh, Wilkes Barre, and Philadelphia and other towns along the way in route to these metro areas.

Another helping-them-get-home story is told in an article published in the August 1936 issue of the *Poe Valley Ravin*:

> Lt. Brock, camp physician, spent the week-end of August 22 visiting his wife and Mother-in-Law at Philadelphia. Mrs. Brocks' Mother is a patient at a Philadelphia hospital.
>
> Ralph Wilson and Pete Kopchak accompanied Lt. Brock as far as Philadelphia and then continued on to Camden N.J. to visit family. Anthony Malefic also accompanied the Dr. as far as Harrisburg.

The military officers who were in camp had motor cars. For the most part, anyone who had a car in camp was envied by every enrollee for more than one reason. These cars obviously were another means to get them home whenever an officer was willing to share the road.

Later drawings depicting the camp layout show a military garage where the officers' motor cars would be garaged. Here there was an enrollee assigned to maintain these vehicles, keep them clean, and on the ready at all times. I am sure being a military garage steward would have had a perk or two made available to the selected enrollee in this service.

ENROLLEE BECOMES FAVORED LEM

In April 1940 LEM Forestry Service mechanic Mr. Mike Neese resigned his position as the camp equipment mechanic, a position he had held since mid-1935. He announced he was starting his own garage in the nearby town of Millheim.

During his tenure as camp mechanic, he proved to be well-skilled and competent in performing his multiple tasks. He became highly regarded by so many enrollees who trained under his guidance while they were in camp, many of them leaving camp with the skill of junior motor mechanic acquired under his tutorship.

Under his guidance, he trained enrollee Leroy Sherwood. Leroy was nicknamed "Farmer," because he was a local enrollee coming into Poe Valley straight off the farm. Given his nickname, he was thought to be a typical farm boy who was thought to be able to milk a cow yet know little else. He would soon, however, become affectionately known as Farmer due to his quick wit, and he demonstrated a capable mechanical mind easily able to repair and fix most anything. He then became an assistant barrack leader and eventually a barrack leader. While in camp, he trained under the guidance of LEM Neese and became one of his best "graduates" most capable of maintaining and repairing anything with a motor in the camp. He had an excellent grasp of motor mechanics and did well on keeping the numerous trucks in camp in working order.

Mr. Sherwood departed Poe Valley and later acquired a position as an LEM mechanic in Civilian Conservation Corps Camp S-87 Cross Forks.

Then on May 1, 1940, guess who took over the position of LEM forestry service mechanic in Poe Valley. Yes, you are right, "Farmer" Leroy Sherwood returned to Poe Valley, becoming one of the success stories and favored mechanic.

SADNESS BEFALLS THE CAMP

Lieutenant Lee Fox was the only officer to serve as company commander in Poe Valley, coming from the ranks of the United States Marine Corps. His distinctly different uniform variation versus that of US Army commanders was admired throughout the camp. Soon after taking command of the camp in March of 1939, Lieutenant Fox quickly established himself as a friend and supporter of the enrollees by bettering camp life.

Early in December 1939, Lieutenant Fox learned his wife required an operation and was being admitted into Boehne Hospital back home in Evansville, Indiana. One week after the operation, Mrs. Fox's condition worsened, and Lieutenant Fox was summoned to her bedside. Mrs. Fox's condition improved, and Lieutenant Fox returned back to Poe Valley on December 8th.

On December 13, 1939, sorrow quickly spread throughout the camp after hearing news of the passing of the wife of its well-liked company commander. Lieutenant Fox, now on leave, immediately returned home to handle arrangements for his wife's memorial and burial services and tend to the couple's young son Donald Lee Fox.

During the absence of Lieutenant Fox, Lieutenant Henry G. Thomas US Army, Sub-Altern of Veterans Company 1394, Weikert, Pennsylvania, temporarily assumed command of the Poe Valley camp.

CHAPTER 11

CHANGE, ADDITIONS & CONDITIONS

Change was the way of the Civilian Conservation Corps. The very creation of the CCC came about due to the unprecedented change in the American economy. The name was a change from its origin name of Emergency Conservation Work.

Conservation measures to be executed in the Deep South were a change from those taken in the North, and certainly change was needed in other geographical regions to thwart the continued degradation of America's natural resources.

The overall development, management, and operations of Civilian Conservation Corps camps all across America necessitated change. In many instances, these changes took place on a daily basis.

So many changes occurred in the program throughout its existence, it would fill many volumes if these changes were to be documented. In most instances, these changes were required to fulfill the needs and challenges presented. On the part of the military, camp requirements were dictated by convention; everyone needed to be fed, clothed, housed, and their personal needs attended to on a daily basis. As one can imagine, in the winter months the clothing needs for enrollees in a South Florida camp would be much different than the needs in a Northern Pennsylvania camp.

In Poe Valley, many of the changes made are told to us in photographs, articles published in the *Poe Valley Ravin*, and other documents. One of the first significant changes in Poe Valley was the relocation of the enrollees from their temporary tent quarters into permanent wooden barracks.

Another chronology of photographs depicts stone-lined, dirt walkways between the barracks and other camp facilities to be upgraded to wooden walkways, then wooden walkways are replaced with large, flat stone laid down as the walkway surface.

The next chronology of photographs depict decorative, wooden fences having been installed along the edges of the walkways. In these same photographs can be seen the age-old tradition in which the Army will "spruce up the place." This age-old tradition is to white wash anything that does not move. White paint always plentiful in the Army store rooms is brushed on at the direction of those in charge. The painting work not only dresses up the place, it also, maybe more importantly, keeps idle hands busy.

I remember one of the veterans during a later reunion looking through photographs that were taken after he had departed camp seeing the newer, painted picket fencing remarked "my, my they sure did dress up the place."

Company street with wooden walkways

Walkway improvements now include stone-paved walkways

Walkway improvements now inlcude stone-lined walkways

Walkway improvements now include white-picket fencing

Common to all camps was the scheduled change of the military commanders and the enrollees' time in camp. For the first six months the faces in camp did not change. Rotation of all the enrollees and military personnel took place in January 1934. The forestry management personnel of the camp superintendent, foremen, and forester remained in service, as there was no required rotation of these personnel.

In Poe Valley, change occurred from the beginning through the entire time period the camp remained in operation.

Ever changing were the names of the military commanders in camp. The changes in military personnel brought change to camp operations and daily life. The military commanders had overall charge of the camp setup and camp operations during off-work hours.

When a new military commander came into camp, they brought with them differing experiences and philosophies. A particular commander brought with him a favor of baseball over basketball and subsequently directed baseball gear be procured for camp recreation in lieu of basketball gear. Conversely, another camp commander had a music background and pushed music learning programs versus other arts. These changes certainly brought diverse opportunity into the camp. The experience the enrollees shared between the various military commanders was similar yet constantly subject to change.

Every new commander brought with him a differing background, experience, and view of how camp operations should change or remain as previously administered. These commanders would typically rotate out approximately six months after arrival. Documents indicate the military commanders in Poe Valley mostly attempted to improve upon previously established camp conditions and operations.

It seems this was mostly a positive experience for Poe Valley. I do not remember my grandfather making many remarks about military commanders either to the negative or the positive.

A significant challenge for any military commander in a CCC camp was to maintain good morale among the enrollees. Documents and discussions with veterans and the locals reflect management of camp life maintained camp morale in a mostly positive manner. In Poe Valley, activities of all sorts were part of camp life, and camp-sponsored dances and receptions were frequent and well-attended by the public. Other activities were made available to the enrollees for their free time. The education programs were highly regarded and maintained a constant presence in the camp. Change was constant in the sporting activities; for instance, records indicate there was a bunch of guys wanting to have a basketball team in one winter period, but there was lack of interest the next winter, so no team followed the first.

One of the most positive ways to improve and maintain morale among the enrollees was to allow them to leave camp and go to town during weekend free time. Transportation for the enrollees was provided, utilizing camp-assigned Army trucks out of camp to town and back to camp for these leave periods.

There are no "handed-down" stories in the local communities indicating the boys were "serious trouble" when they came to town. It is easy to imagine and understand how doubting and concerned the parents of young, impressionable daughters would be when they learned these young boys were coming to town for recreation time. Many discussions at reunions among veterans were shared in polite conversation of how relationships with these daughters and the "boys" had developed. Also told were the stories about how these girls were repeatedly told they were in no way to associate with these *boys*.

One might think when a bunch of these boys went into the local towns, they also brought a certain measure of trouble with them. Locals who may not be so fond of having these unknown "boys" in their midst could make disparaging remarks regarding their presence and confrontation could ensue. Additionally, given the economic hardships of the times, it would not be a stretch to suspect minor petty crimes could be associated with these unknown visitors. For the most part, the boys visited the small town of Millheim to the north and the larger town of Lewistown to the south. There was not a police presence in Millheim and its immediate surroundings. A small police force kept the peace in Lewistown.

Growing up in Coburn and basically knowing most of the residents in Millheim afforded me the opportunity to hear any passed-on stories regarding the mischief perpetrated by the boys from Poe Valley, to which I never heard one story involving criminal behavior on the part of the boys. While I didn't have the same opportunity to hear of any passed-along stories from the townspeople in Lewistown and its surrounding communities, I suspect no criminal behavior was imposed on these folks by the boys from Poe Valley.

I am, however, not able to say no crimes were ever reported or criminal charges actually brought upon any enrollee from the Poe Valley camp in the towns local to the camp. What I am able to tell is this: During reunions, gatherings, or listening in on stories about the boys from Poe Valley, I heard they looked out for each other and did not want trouble of any kind. They felt any bad behavior on their part would reflect poorly, especially on the foremen and their families who were from these communities. Many had developed a bond with these foremen and camp commanders through a mutual respect for the purpose at hand.

During reunions and gatherings, I did not hear many stories about the military personnel assigned to the Poe Valley camp, other than positive comments about how the commanders seemed to be there to support the enrollees in any manner sought out by the enrollees. The general perception of these commanders was they had their job to do and would deal with the "bad apples" when necessary, recalled veteran Wendall Booher.

Poe Valley was widely regarded as a "highly satisfactory" camp and repeatedly received superior or satisfactory ratings from district- and regional-level military command inspectors indicative of positive command influence.

Conversely, change was not as significant in the camp technical personnel group. The names of the foremen and support technicians did not change for the first three years of camp operations in Poe Valley.

Within this group the change to occur took place when the specialized skill a technician brought to camp would no longer be required and the position would typically be vacated. Technical personnel would be added, particularly during the time period when the dam was being constructed. In the late-winter period of 1938, the largest change in camp technical administration personnel took place. A dam was to be constructed at the site of Camp S-116 Parker Dam, Clearfield County. This dam was similar in design to what was recently completed by Company 1333 in Poe Valley. To support this new project Senior Foreman Sumner Frankenberger, Machine Operator S. Immel, Steam Shovel Operator Paul Vonada, Camp Engineer Amos Bennett, and Camp Superintendent Luther Weaver all left Poe Valley and relocated to Camp S-116 to manage the construction of the new dam.

This group of five former Poe Valley CCC men remained at Camp S-116 until the successful completion of the dam construction project. My grandfather and three others resigned their positions in the CCC at this time and left the service of the Pennsylvania Department of Forest and Waters. Luther Weaver remained in the CCC and returned to Poe Valley after supervising the work and successful completion of the Parker Dam project. Mr. Weaver, the former Poe Valley camp superintendent, returned to Poe Valley in early 1941 taking up the position of senior foreman and remained in Poe Valley until the closing of the camp in 1941.

Another more significant change to be experienced in camp concerned the enrollees. Initially, they signed on for a six-month hitch. This six-month period was strictly enforced in the initial years of the Civilian Conservation Corps program. Change occurred when the enrollment periods were increased from six months to twelve months, and later on the enrollment period was increased to twenty-four months.

There were numerous reasons for the increase in enrollment periods. A common practice for enrollment extension would be recommended for members who demonstrated exemplary capability in technical service skills and/or strong leadership capabilities.

As time passed and the economy strengthened, enrollment numbers of new-enrollee signups back home were dropping. Many camps had work projects requiring a steady number of enrollees to maintain schedules and fulfill tasks. In order to maintain these established needs and goals in camp, enrollees desiring another six-month hitch would be given this opportunity.

The very first enrollees to arrive living in tents all woke each day with the same tentmates and fellows about camp. After barracks were erected and for approximately two and a half years, these enrollees continued to see the same faces as enrollment periods were maintained at six-month periods.

After this, initial enrollment periods were extended and faces changed. Enrollees saw change in their barrack mates during their enrollment periods, and they experienced the many changes that came about in camp work project assignments.

In the beginning of the program, officials directed enrollees be sent to camps away from their hometowns in an effort to minimize desertion rates, fearing that should enrollees be in a camp close to home they would simply walk home if "homesickness" could not be overcome. This requirement was lifted in later years, allowing enrollees to sign up and go into camps near their hometowns. Enrollment rates had started to slow, potential enrollees let officials know they would consider enrolling if they would be allowed to go into a camp nearby their hometowns. Word had spread about camp life that included things like freedom on weekends, sporting activities, movies being shown in the camp, camp dances, further enticing enrollment if allowed to be in a camp near home.

Another significant change was the appearance of the enrollee. After wearing Army surplus clothing for the first six years, the Civilian Conservation Corps shed itself from the surplus uniform attire of the US Army and was issued a uniform designed, detailed, and made just for them. The enrollees at Poe Valley received the first issue of these new uniforms on October 8, 1939.

A description of the new uniform is provided in the September 1939 issue of the camp newsletter.

> "Spruce green uniforms arrive, vast improvement over old O.D.s"
>
> The new outfits consist of spruce green trousers and coats, short coats, mackinaws and overseas style hats. The belts are also green. The shoes are black, and the present O.D. shirt will be worn with the new uniform. The coats are stylish cut with pleated backs and half way belts. The CCC insignia is on the shoulder of the coats and on the hats.

Change was a constant when it came to the education programs in the Civilian Conservation Corps in Poe Valley. Early enrollees in Poe Valley got the opportunity to learn carpentry skills, erecting their own barracks and the related camp service buildings. Enrollees in camp during the later years did not get this same opportunity, but instead got the opportunity to learn the trade of bridge building which was not available to the early enrollees in camp.

The education program of early years was comprised of more OJT (on job training), while the later years had a more organized classroom program with offerings not available in camp previously.

The forestry management training and works performed by enrollees, however, remained mostly constant during the operation life of the camp. Another major change to the education program came in June of 1938 when the camp celebrated the opening of a new education building.

Other facility changes were made through the life of camp. In addition to the construction of the new education building, a new temporary barrack building was erected in the fall of 1939 to accommodate additional enrollees being sent to Poe Valley to support the proposed work schedule. In the spring time of 1937 the Forestry Quarters facility received an addition that made it twice its original size. This addition was made to accommodate added technical personnel being brought into camp to facilitate

Forestry Quarters building with expansion

New tool room

scheduled work projects. At this same time, a new tool room was constructed.

The Recreation Hall was rededicated and named Oyler Hall in memory of Enrollee Bernard Oyler who was killed while on duty in service to the CCC.

Numerous facility changes were made during the life of the camp. In May of 1940 the Mess Hall was torn down to allow construction of a new, larger Mess Hall. This renovation included new kitchen equipment, new electric refrigeration units, and tile floors. A most significant change during the renovation included chinaware replacing the mess kit issue previously carried by each enrollee.

Records indicate the Mess Hall project was placed on a brief hold after construction commenced due to a funding issue.

The April 1941 issue of the camp newsletter tells the outdoor basketball court located behind the Officers' Quarters was being reconstructed into a tennis court, just once more, depicting the changes ongoing in the camp.

The enrollees in Poe Valley on day one were challenged with constructing the barracks and additional structures necessary for camp operations. Next, they constructed miles of roads

Renovated Mess Hall now including electric refrigerator and china service

Outside ball court

throughout the region, simultaneously performing forestry management works, cutting in trails, and eradicating unwanted vegetation. They then undertook the construction of the dam, creating a manmade lake for recreational activity; afterwards, the activities shifted again back to road improvement and construction activity that included bridge building. Also simultaneously, they constructed a 100-foot-tall fire tower, built a masonry watchers cabin, continued forestry management works, planted more than half a million seedlings, all the while creating what would become Poe Valley State Park for the recreational use of the public at large.

Change was constant in camp personnel at all levels during the life of the camp. The records reflect consistent change by way of positive improvement in camp development and camp operations during the full life of the Poe Valley camp.

The boys changed the landscape of a small, remote valley situated in the scenic mountains of Central Pennsylvania by the creation of a twenty-seven-acre, manmade lake. They developed roadways allowing the public to visit and enjoy the beauty of the natural, scenic, mountainous terrain and vistas previously inaccessible in the region and conducted forest improvement works on thousands of acres of forested lands surrounding the camp.

The changes made to the landscape of Poe Valley were from a small, minimally visited, remote, forested valley hosting a small stream fed by natural springs, flanked by mountains, providing scenic views and a small apple orchard farm into a magnificent State Park for the benefit of generations to follow.

Certainly, not all enrollees in camp were living a utopian life. These "unhappy campers" typically expressed their unhappiness through constant, negative commentary, poor personal hygiene, and poor work performance. Discussion among veterans described these mannerisms in a particular memory of an unhappy barrack bunkmate. The most common word used to describe these unhappy enrollees was "slacker" and "goldbricker."

Many veterans shared their discomforts and dissatisfactions. Food was an ever-common gripe, as the foods served were not to their liking or were served cold or without enough sugar or with too much salt or same menu items were served too often. While others described the food experience as being quite satisfactory, food being plentiful was noted by many. Many told me this was the first time in many years when they sat down for three meals a day seven days a week. I was also told by more than one veteran that they felt a bit of shame in knowing they were eating very well in camp, all the while knowing family back home were not sharing the same good fortune.

Another common gripe was the work detail they were assigned to. One of the shared dissatisfactions was the work demands required of the foremen. This is easy to understand, as these foremen came from a background of farm and forestry work where a hard eight or more hours was put in every day, and their expectations were that these strapping, young men should be able to give it a hard eight hours as well. For many enrollees, this was their first experience at employment; most of the jobs these young men were assigned were not paper-shuffling, office-environment tasks. Their tasks were muscle-building, body-strengthening acts like the swinging of axes, sledge hammers, and daily handling of pick and shovel.

Many enrollees who had come from a large-city environment found themselves in the middle of the forest in what was perceived as the "middle of nowhere." These city boys garnered confidence and gained limited comfort after becoming friends with the "local yokel," who knew their way around a mountain and were not unsettled by the scamper of animals and sounds of the forest. These city boys came to appreciate the yokels' keen sense of direction, in particular, being able to get back to camp without becoming lost.

Homesickness was a constant in camp, especially with newly arriving enrollees. For most, this was their first time away from home for more than a day or two.

Many veterans described their private feelings of being homesick during their early days in camp. For most, however, their first payday brought a new sense of accomplishment in themselves and in knowing they were now responsible for contributing to relieving the family plight back home. This new sense of pride and the developing camaraderie with bunk mates would for many help dissolve the discomforting edge of being homesick.

Others found their homesickness was too strong to overcome and went out "over the hill," never to return.

Enrollees had opportunity to express their thoughts about CCC life through conventional means, and they also had a newsletter where the opportunity to write their thoughts was provided.

Desertion rates in the camps varied dramatically from one region to another and from one camp to another in those regions. Numerous factors played a part in the desertion rates. There is limited information regarding desertion rates subject to the Poe Valley camp. The information available provides us with desertion rates listed on an itemized report for a five-day period conducted annually. The limited, incomplete information and discussions with veterans who were in camp at varying times indicates desertion of enrollees in Poe Valley was less than 2%.

Another significant factor contributing to the uncertainty of a desertion rate was that many times enrollees travel

ed home on a weekend and didn't return, having found gainful employment. While records management in the camps listed the enrollee absent, in many instances, a discharge certificate was issued, noting the enrollee had left camp for employment, particularly if a bunkmate or foreman or letter from the employer had information supporting the reason for absence.

While attending reunions, numerous enrollees described their experience as being one of the more exciting times in their lives. Many noted the combination of being away from home and having gainful employment contributed to their desire to sign up for another six-month hitch.

A noted change came decades after the closing of the Civilian Conservation Corps camps all across America: a recognition for

EDITORIAL

WHAT'S WRONG WITH THE C.C.C.

The main fault with the CCC at the present time is the influx of an overwhelming number of "kids" as substitutes for the many thousands of camp-wise men who were forced to leave due to the two year limit.

Naturally, in all enlistments, there were a great many kids who became enrollees of the CCC, but although great in numbers, in proportion to the number of older boys who entered before the two year law went into effect, the ratio was comparatively small. As the two year limit forces out in enormous numbers the enrollees who made the CCC, their places are being filled by these youngsters because there is no one else to fill them.

Compare the two types of enrollees: those who entered prior to the two year limit and those who fill the enlistments at the present time. Those who came in a couple of years ago entered at the height of the depression, and to them the CCC was a grand refuge from unemployment and the temptations of the streets. The average age of enrollees during 1934 was said to be over twenty five years. That is definite proof that the CCC was a means of aid for unemployed men. To these men the CCC was a home. These were the men who raised the hundreds of camps throughout the country to the standard they now maintain because the regarded their camps as their homes and showered upon it the treatment that should be given a home. And the present day enrollees proudly agree that it is 'his' camp although the aid obtained from him for its maintenance is only secured by the so-called "despotism" of his barrack leader. The majority of the boys who come into the CCC at the present time look forward to a hilarious six months with no work and all play and still hang on to this idea although it is impressed upon them from the start that a certain amount of work must be accomplished on the project and maintenance work must be done in the camp area. The same men are the ones who are untidy in their dress and the appearance of the area allotted them in the barrack and even neglect the clothing they wear to town.

It is not the fault of these men that they are here. In the first place the minimum age requirement is too low. In the second place the selecting agencies are too lenient in enforcing the minimum age ruling.

A remedy would be found for this situation by administering severe spankings to those laggards, packing them up, and shipping them home where they should be returned to high school and in many cases to junior high school where they should stay until their public school education is completed. By that time they should have learned the meaning of the word-"cooperation."

                                        Robert Robson, editor.

Enrollee thoughts about the CCC, published in the September 1939 issue of the camp newsletter the works performed by those who were the CCC in the long-ago closed campsites. In Pennsylvania, we have a state park system envied by many. The lion's share of these state parks were created by the Civilian Conservation Corps. I hosted my first reunion for veterans in the Poe Valley camp in 1983. At that time, there was very little information available in any library to learn about the CCC. Today, there are numerous publications in your local library to tell the story of the CCC, many written in just the last decade.

There are numerous reasons for the long-time coming in telling the story of the Civilian Conservation Corps and the huge contribution the program imparted on America during one of its darkest times—The Great Depression. Two of the most significant reasons are a strengthening economy and World War Two. Combined, these two conditions in large part took away much of the need for the Civilian Conservation Corps. I learned, however, while sharing during those reunions and gatherings how so many enrollees for decades spoke little of their experience or not at all. Many shared a common theme in their reluctance to talk of their time in the camps being a raw "shame" in being on county "relief roles." They told that when they went to their local county "relief" offices to sign up, they felt there was a certain stigma now attached to them in being on the "government dole" and not having made it on their own. This shared yet unspoken stigma between themselves led them to share little about their experience, and in many cases, they found themselves hesitant to tell of their time in camp as they moved on in life.

How sad it is for these veterans to have this feeling after facing the challenges of their time, all the while performing the required laboring works day after day. Many took the learned skills and training gained while in camp and developed lifelong, satisfying careers from this experience. It seems to me the shame is on those that would suggest anyone who had signed onto the program after giving us so much in return could possibly have been considered "being on the dole."

For myself, I found the most striking change to be the change that did not occur, this being the wage rate paid to the enrollees. Throughout the entire nine-year operational time of the CCC program, the enrollees' pay rate stayed constant at the rate of $1.00 a day.

CHAPTER 12

POE VALLEY—MAYBE NOT MEANT TO BE OR MAYBE BY ANOTHER NAME

Mr. A. T. Bennett, Poe Valley's longest serving camp engineer, was easily remembered by veterans for his engineering skills and expansive knowledge on many varied subjects. Numerous articles were included in the camp newsletters authored by Mr. Bennett on varied subjects that allowed the reader to easily understand or learn more about the subject at hand.

During discussions with veterans over the years, I at no time heard an unkind word spoken about Mr. Bennett. I did hear several veterans mention how Mr. Bennett maintained a brisk pace when walking uphill, over the rocks, and through the brush during work projects, making it somewhat difficult for some enrollees to keep pace. Highly respected, Mr. Bennett could maintain a spirited conversation with anyone on a vast array of topics.

My grandfather remained lifelong friends with Mr. Bennett after their time together in camp. He mentioned Mr. Bennett's name frequently, and always fondly, on the many occasions when my grandfather was telling a story of a time or event in camp.

One of the stories told by my grandfather when I was young only allows me to have just a hint of remembrance. This story was about the naming of the recreation area created by the construction of the dam. I could not tell any more other than remembering there were discussions in camp about the newly created park area not being named "Poe Valley." This memory had gone away completely until a few years ago when I was contacted by Penn State University professor John Shingler. Professor Shingler asked to meet with me to discuss the topic "Poe Valley." We met, and I learned Professor Shingler was doing research on Poe Valley at large, and he wanted to gain insight into the Civilian Conservation

Corps era, of which he learned I was a local Poe Valley Civilian Conservation Corps historian.

During our meeting, he advised he had during his research learned there was a time when state officials and Mr. Bennett in particular had discussions and shared correspondence on alternate names regarding the naming of the park at the time when construction of the dam project was nearing its end. Professor Shingler subsequently shared copies of specific correspondence between these state officials and Mr. Bennett he had acquired, outlining a proposed name change for Poe Valley.

Later, when doing research on my own at the state archives, I came across these same documents. While these documents do not provide a day-to-day accounting of the name change discussions, there seems to be sufficient information to provide a general story about how the park is so named "Poe Valley State Park."

In lieu of me trying to tell this particular story well beyond my capability to describe and even further beyond my knowledge of the history described in the referenced acquired correspondence, I herein include the correspondence to tell this story itself.

These letters are indicative of how well-read Mr. Bennett was and further describe his capability to ascribe and disseminate information about a particular topic.

POE VALLEY STATE PARK—(MAYBE) NOT TO BE

The small valley situated in the mountains of Central Pennsylvania had been inhabited by Indians long before exploration of the region in the latter part of the seventeenth century. These early explorers and eventual settlers to the region included the Poe family. The Poe name was ascribed to numerous elements in the region, such as Little Poe Creek, the small stream flowing through the valley that fed the lake created by the construction of the dam through the labors of the Civilian Conservation Corps. Also, Poe Mills was a small logging community of the 1880s and 1890s with a population greater than 300 people. The community, developed at a time when lumbering was booming business, located approximately six miles east of where Camp S-63 was located. Poe Mountain, heavily harvested for its timber, was positioned on the west side of the valley.

Poe Valley - Camp S-63, Civilian Conservation Corps was named in honor of the Poe family also. Eventually, Poe Valley

Camp CCC #S-63
Coburn, Pennsylvania
November 6, 1937

Mr. Paul H. Mulford
Assistant District Forester
Milroy, Pennsylvania

Dear Mr. Mulford:-

Complying with a suggestion of Mr. James Pates while you and he visited Poe Valley Park that another name be suggested for this Park, we suggest the Indian name Monsee or Lenape Park.

First, I should like to say that Poe Mountains, Poe Valley, Poe Valley Dam and Poe Creek all fill their purpose splendidly, but they suggest a dearth of names when applied to our park area.

Second: Colonel Henry W. Shoemaker, that intrepid thinker and venerable writer and author of "Allegheny Episodes" has been credited by scholars and statesmen, alike, as having done a noble piece of historic research work in our great state. There is a serious purpose to his labors even though colored with fanciful tales and romantic expressions of tradition.

I cite for you his chapter on the naming of the State Forest Areas of Pennsylvania in which Mr. Shoemaker says in part "It seemed fitting to give each a name of local and historic import, as well as a number. These names were to be of such distinctiveness that when mentioned the region in which the district was located would be instantly recognized."

It seems very apparent that sponsored by such eminent writers and authorities as Dr. J. T. Rothrock, Dr. Geo. P. Donahoo, Colonel Henry W. Shoemaker and others, that names rich in tradition give to some particular locality a deep living interest, "a picture of by gone days." Thus guided by precedent we ask that the name Monsee or Lenape be given to this park area.

Monsee is the name of the Wolf Clan of the Lenape Indians. Back of the name Monsee is a beautiful tradition which applies peculiarly and particularly to this Community. Indeed, Poe Valley is in the centre of the territory ruled over by Nita-Nee, their Indian Queen. Nita-Nee was the daughter of Chief Chun-Eh-Hoe, Nitany Mountains and Nitany Valley are named in her honor. Although Nita-Nee's father and his braves defended their beloved land to the last extremity, they were driven into the Seven Mountains, by the Tuscaroras and decisively defeated causing the death of their Chief Chun-Eh-Hoe. Thus Nita-Nee succeeded her father. The Monsees were later attacked by the Tuscaroras. Nita-Nee's forces showed no signs of advancing beyond the foot of Long Mountain, which the attacking tribe mistook for cowardice and they sent an attacking party to drive them out of this section. This party was completely "defeated in the gorge of Laurel Run above Milroy. Thus the right of the Monsees to the Karoondinha and the adjacent valleys was signed, sealed and delivered in blood."

In conclusion we wish to call attention to many other no less interesting tales coincident with and surrounding these "everlasting hills".

Very respectfully yours,

A. T. Bennett

Mr. Bennett's story on naming Poe Valley

Road, the main road accessing Poe Valley State Park, was also named in honor of the family.

In Poe Valley, the surrounding mountainous areas, and all across America, unchecked lumbering methods were performed without thought to reestablishment of this valued natural resource. Depletion of America's forests would in large part be one of the principal reasons for the establishment of the Civilian Conservation Corps to support the reestablishment of America's depleted forests.

By the latter part of 1937, Company 1333 - Camp S-63 had dedicated hundreds of thousands of man hours to the rehabilitation of the forests surrounding the camp. They constructed miles of trails and access roads to support the effort.

Fire management and eradication of unwanted and diseased vegetation was performed as part of the effort, including thousands of man days constructing the dam.

Water had not yet been allowed to build up and flow over the dam breast in the fall of 1937, as construction was not yet fully complete. Construction scheduling called for completion by years end 1937. Every enrollee now working on the dam project was hoping to see water for the first time roll over the spillway before their enlistment period came to an end. By this time, excitement in camp was high as all were anxious to see the fruition of their labor.

The boys in camp had developed a well-deserved sense of pride knowing their individual contribution to the effort would result in creation of a recreation site with a lake in the mountains of Central Pennsylvania, or so they believed this to be.

Dam construction was mostly completed by years end 1937. Water would roll over the spillway for the very first time at 4:15 A.M. on December 19, 1937. There was no celebration or ribbon cutting on this momentous day. Most boys working on the dam construction project were now being assigned to forestry improvement work details and roadway construction and improvement details. These forestry work details, most important to the reestablishment of vegetation and tree growth in mountains in the immediate region, were deemed by most to not be as important or as exciting, as was dam construction detail in the previous two years.

While forestry detail moved along at a brisk pace into early 1938 keeping all busy, talk in camp seemed to focus on what the new lake created by the dam construction was to be used for. Would it be a place to fish or go boating or a place to enjoy swimming in warm-weather periods, or would additional design soon follow converting the lake from a CCC camp worksite to a new state park site?

Acceptance by state officials, naming Poe Valley a state park, would be a crowning achievement for the boys of Company 1333, but it was yet unclear what the area where all of this effort had been expended was to be officially called.

Earlier in 1937, the Forestry Department announced the vicinity had been selected as a site for a newly proposed state park, however, more than a year after this announcement, official determination as to whether or not Poe Valley would be a state park had not been made.

Word was spreading throughout the Civilian Conservation Corps camp community the Pennsylvania Department of Parks was further developing lands now greatly improved by the boys in other camp locations. Subsequently, these sites were becoming new state parks having names like Halfway State Forest Park, Clear Creek State park, Greenwood Furnace State Park, and Promised Land State Park. Particularly, this was occurring in vicinities where Civilian Conservation Corps camp sites were situated on state-owned lands.

The boys in the Poe Valley camp were most proud of the camp's accomplishments to date, particularly the successful completion of the 660-foot-long, earthen dam and its 60-foot-wide masonry spillway. To date, the boys in the Poe Valley camp believed theirs was the largest dam project undertaken in Pennsylvania's CCC camp program. Word of the successful completion reported in many camp newsletters spread quickly throughout the camps, and congratulations were being offered to the boys of Camp S-63.

Inspections by program officials was commonplace in the camps. The program was layered with administrative personnel at state and federal levels in regional and district offices. In addition to visits by officials from these regional and district offices, there were military inspectors coming into the camps. Inspections by state officials and visits by officials, however, seemed to increase when dam construction was nearing completion, and some felt more than a fair share of inspectors had come to camp soon after completion of the dam. As it turned out, this was the case indeed; officials from Pennsylvania's Department of Parks were coming into the Poe Valley to get a look at the newly completed dam. Although construction of the dam had commenced now more than two years prior, several key state officials were not aware the dam had been under construction, let alone completed.

The growth of Pennsylvania's Department of Parks in the early years is partially attributed to recreational site development through efforts of the many Civilian Conservation Corps camps all around the state. Officials were focusing development of these new parks when the sites were situated nearer to metropolitan areas.

While overall general plans for a complete state park system had been developed by the Department of Parks, further development of Poe Valley as a state park beyond the initial works of the CCC boys, which included the construction of the dam, was not moving forward in the fall of 1937 as many in camp were anticipating. State officials were guarded in their decision making on moving forward with development of Poe Valley as a park in the fall of 1937.

In a Department of Parks internal memo dated October 20, 1937, officials expressed it to be the following:

"Extremely questionable to encourage any recreational developments at Poe Valley Dam at this time because,
1. The area is too remote from heavily populated areas to support itself.
2. There are areas in the vicinity, such as Greenwood Furnace, Whipple Dam, Snyder Middlesworth, Penn Roosevelt, Reeds Gap and Joyce Kilmer, that adequately take care of the demand now.
3. Nearby there is a picnic area known as Poe Paddy.
4. The adoption of a general plan to be worked upon ten years later is not good policy. Every year brings changing conditions and changing policies.

As to the design submitted: I feel that the simpler types of recreational facilities should be encouraged if such development is to be considered.

Picnicking and tenting rather than picnicking and cabins would involve less capital costs.

The entrance road should be confined to one outlet to permit practical control.

The trails are not wide enough for proper maintenance.

There are too many shelters for the size of the area.

Unless the parking area and the forest roads are oiled or surfaced with bituminous material I am afraid the picnickers would be eating dust all day.

Development of the immediate area surrounding the dam and lake was performed by the boys of Camp S-63 in the springtime of 1938. This work was limited to construction of a bath house and wooden dock. Locals and others were now starting to visit the park to enjoy the recreational opportunities created by the construction of the dam, and in particular to take a dip in the new Poe Valley Lake. They were also questioning when additional development of the park could be expected.

In another Department of Parks internal memo dated October 18, 1938, the same officials referenced in the October 20, 1937, memo noted the following:

> Note has been made of your memorandum to Mr. Emerick, dated October 4th, regarding the intensive development of the Poe Valley area.
>
> May I inform you that I have never been in favor of Park Development in Poe Valley, nor have I changed my mind to date. I feel that if it is desirable to put boats on this area, this may be done with a view to collecting revenue from those who wish to fish or swim. However, I do not believe we should establish picnic areas, or any other highly developed area which will require future maintenance costs.
>
> It must be realized at this time we are planning quite an extensive park program near the metropolitan sections of the State, and our efforts should be concentrated in that direction. Just because a dam has been built is no reason why we should increase maintenance costs by adding recreational facilities.

In another Department of Parks internal memo dated October 31, 1938, the same officials referenced in the October 18, 1938, memo noted the following:

> In discussing the future development of Poe Valley, I wish to state the following views upon the subject:
>
> I cannot seem to find out where the idea for the construction of Poe Valley Dam originated or why the Dam was built.

It now seems that some of the Federal men are being worried about the construction of the Dam since no use is made of it at the present time. This should have been looked into before the Dam was built. However, in view of the fact that the Dam is constructed, I believe that probably a certain amount of simple recreational facilities may be built. I understand that already a stockade bathhouse and two latrines are constructed. In order not to increase our maintenance costs, great restraint should be exercised as to the development of picnic areas. In fact, I do not believe such facilities a wise development at this time but I do feel that camping facilities would be very inexpensive and we would derive quite a good deal of revenue since the area is remote from any large center of population and those visiting it will naturally wish to stay for a week or so.

I, therefore, wish to advise that the field personnel may submit a plan a plan for a simple tenting area, indicating thereon water supply, circulation and control.

In conclusion, I would say that it would be a mistake to do anything before we are certain that there will be enough use to enable us to derive sufficient revenue to properly maintain the area.

Coincidentally, in the latter part of 1937 while officials were indecisive regarding development of the park, another form of indecision was ongoing regarding the area that eventually became Poe Valley State Park.

During visits by these same officials in Poe Valley after completion of the dam, many discussions were held between camp administration personnel and these officials regarding further development of the area.

A focus topic during these discussions regarded naming of the proposed park. A name that seemed to easily roll off the tongue for most was "Poe Valley State Park" in honor of the Poe family, the prominent, well-known early pioneers to the region and certainly to the name given the area where the park was positioned being Poe Valley.

The Poe Valley camp engineer, Amos Bennett, well-known for his intellect on a wide range of topics, was known to have an expansive knowledge of the history of the region and in particular its first inhabitants being the Indians. During a particular visit with then Director of Parks James Pates, Engineer Bennett held a conversation with Mr. Pates about naming the park something other than in respect to the Poe family. At the end of the conversation, Mr. Pates suggested Mr. Bennett forward his suggestions for naming of the park to the regional forester for consideration.

Subsequently, Mr. Bennett submitted a letter to the assistant forester, Paul Mulford, for consideration regarding naming of the park.

CCC #3-63
Coburn, Pa.
Nov. 20, 1937

CCC-3
Personnel
A. T. Bennett

Mr. Paul H. Mulford
Assistant District Forester
Milroy, Pennsylvania

Dear Sir:-

I regret very much that the tone of my letter relative to the renaming of Poe Valley was misleading.

Mr. Pates is correct in saying that I suggested the proposition of a new name.

I repeat here as in my other letter that Poe, Valley, Poe Mountain, Poe Creek, Poe Valley Dam, Poe Paddy Drive, Poe Paddy Park, Little Poe Valley, Little Poe Mountains suggest a dearth of names for a region that has such a rich tradition and historical background as this valley has.

Nor am I unmindful of the very kindly suggestion of Col. Henry W. Shoemaker that we cannot honor the name of Edgar Allan Poe too highly. I thoroughly agree with him but it seems unfortunate that such significant names as Allummapees-Lenape, Warrior King, Strong Heart, Jeanette Rau, the first white woman to visit the site, Walter Gherrity or Lena Walters after Poe's sweetheart.

I, hereby, ask him to accept my apology for inadvertently placing the emphasis on his part to the conversation. I was and am very anxious and hopeful that due consideration and honor be given to those who played such an important part in the pioneering days of this section. I thank him for submitting the proposition to the Historical Society of Pennsylvania.

I wish Mr. Pates to know that I elicited suggestions from Col. Henry W. Shoemaker to whom I am indebted for valuable information.

Very respectfully yours,

Amos T. Bennett Jr. Engr.
Engineer S-63

Mr. Bennett's letter on proposed name for Poe Valley

Prompt response to this letter submitted by Mr. Bennett came from several state officials. These letters in chronological order follow:

(Copy)

COMMONWEALTH OF PENNSYLVANIA
DEPARTMENT OF PUBLIC INSTRUCTION
State Library
Harrisburg

Room 222
Education Bldg.
Nov. 13, 1937

Mr. A. T. Bennett, Jr.
Coburn, Pa.

Dear Mr. Bennett, Jr.,

Your good letter of 6th., received, together with copy of communication sent to Mr. Mulford, Assistant district forester at Milroy.
As to the names you suggested there are Monsee and Lenape Parks all
over the State, but no other section honors the memory of the immor-
tal poet, Edgar Allan Poe, and the years he spent in Pennsylvania.
To my mind there can't be too much emphasis placed on the name of
Poe in Central Pennsylvania, a giant among writers and poets. If it
is felt the word "Poe" is over emphasized, the park might be called
after Poe's sweetheart in Poe Valley—Hellena Hallett; if that is
not favored then Virginia Clemin Park after the poet's child wife.
If an Indian name is used, Allummapees Park, after the Lenape King and warrior
warrior, or Strong-Heart Park would be acceptable, after the Indian
who had his hunting camp near where the Park Area is located, and
who perished trajically in the Veiled Lady's Cavern, near Grenoble-
Village, Centre County. Or Camp Jeannette, after Jeannette Rau, the
first white woman to visit the site, a missionary to the Indians. Or
Walter's Rest, after Walter Cherrity, the last of the Pennsylvania
hermits, who died recently.

Faithfully yours,

(signed)   H. W. Shoemaker

Copy to Mr. Jas. Pates.

COMMONWEALTH OF PENNSYLVANIA
DEPARTMENT OF FORESTS AND WATERS
EMERGENCY CONSERVATION WORK

CCC S-63
Coburn, Penna.
Nov. 15, 1937.

Mr. Paul H. Mulford
Assistant District Forester
Milroy, Pennsylvania.

Dear Mr. Mulford:-

Am inclosing copy of letter received
from Colonel Henry W. Shoemaker.

As you will note, this eminent gentleman
has deluged us with names. I bow in humble
submission to such eminent authority. May I ask
you to kindly send forward one copy of his letter
and to keep the other for your files.

Very cordially yours,

(Signed)

Amos T. Bennett
Eng. Camp S-63

ATB/hg

Copy to P. H. Mulford
      S. Kendrick Lichty

November 18, 1937

File No. 22
Subj: Change in Name

Major Frank W. Melvin, Chairman
Pennsylvania Historical Commission
Harrisburg, Pennsylvania.

Dear Major Melvin:

      The accompanying communications suggesting new names for the park in the Poe Valley of Centre County, are forwarded to you for consideration.

      Mr. Bennett's letter would indicate that I had suggested a change in the name, whereas it was his own idea and I asked him to put it in writing for submission to proper authorities.

      Any comments you may see fit to make will be appreciated.

      Very truly yours,

      James S. Pates
      Director of Parks

Enclosures
JSP SPG

Copy to Major Melvin
        S. Kendrick Lichty

November 18, 1937

File No. 42
Subj: Change in Name

Paul H. Mulford:

Your letter of November 13, 1937, with
enclosure of Mr. Bennett's letter, in regard to
naming of areas within your District, has been
received.

Mr. Bennett's letter would leave the
impression that I had originated the idea of
new names whereas the suggestion was his own
and I asked him to put it in a letter.

Your second memorandum, and a further
letter from Mr. Bennett and one from Colonel
Shoemaker, have been received.

There seems to be so much room for
controversy in the matter that I am referring
it to the Historical Commission for their consideration and comments.

James S. Pates
Director of Parks

JSP SEC

Attention of: Mr. Oas J. Pates.

COMMONWEALTH OF PENNSYLVANIA
DEPARTMENT OF FORESTS AND WATERS
HARRISBURG

Camp No. S-63
Address Coburn, Pa.
Date Now. 20, 1937.

Mr. Paul H. Mulford,
District Forester,
Milroy, Pa.

Dear Mr. Mulford:

Attached is letter relative to conversation regarding Poe Valley Park. I think it is self-explanatory and may I ask you to kindly forward a copy to Mr. Pates.

My enthusiasm relative to this proposition caused me inadvertently, to state the conversation as I did. I want to give due respect to such splendid gentlemen as Mr. Pates.

Very respectfully yours,

(Signed)
A. T. Bennett.

PREVENT FOREST FIRES---IT PAYS

COMMONWEALTH OF PENNSYLVANIA
PENNSYLVANIA HISTORICAL COMMISSION
EDUCATION BUILDING
HARRISBURG

November 22, 1937

Mr. James S. Pates
Director of Parks
Department of Forests and Waters
Harrisburg, Pennsylvania

My dear Mr. Pates:

Your communication of November 18 to Major Melvin has
been called to my attention. I have read the attached correspondence with interest. I am inclined to agree with Colonel
Shoemaker, who is the member of the Historical Commission most
responsible for such matters. I believe that his letter of
November 13 provides all the information necessary to settle
the question of naming the park.

Sincerely,

S. K. STEVENS
Historian
Pennsylvania Historical Commission

SKS-aw

These letters easily tell us how the naming of Poe Valley State Park came to be.

Had Mr. Bennett been able to persuade officials into honoring the Indians who were the first to see the area where the park was now positioned, Poe Valley State Park would maybe be by another name.

Had state officials stood their ground, not allowing development of the area immediate to and surrounding where the dam had been constructed, maybe there would not be a Poe Valley State Park.

AMOS T. BENNETT

(The following was shared by Matthew Townsend, great nephew of Mr. Bennett.)

Camp Engineer Amos T. Bennett was raised on a small farm outside of Gettysburg, PA, working the farm land and working in a sawmill aside his father when a young boy. Amos enjoyed attending school, however, his father was more in favor of his young son working the mill and the land. Often, Amos was punished with "the strap" for skipping out of work to attend school. He left home a young teenager and eventually attended Gettysburg College, receiving a civil engineering degree in 1899. Having little funds while attending college, Amos lived in a boxcar on the railroad siding near campus. While in college, he participated in various sports, including boxing, football, and the catcher for the baseball team. This baseball team featured the great Eddie Plank, future Hall-of-Fame pitcher who went on to win more than 300 games in the major leagues.

After college, Amos married and moved west. Employment opportunity kept the couple for extended stays in Indiana and Utah. In the mid-1920s, Amos retired from engineering, and the Bennett's returned back to York Springs, PA, purchasing a small farm owned by his wife's family. On this small farm Amos was able to indulge in his favorite pastimes—hunting, fishing, reading poetry, and doing calculus after dark.

Like most folks of the time, reverses brought on by the market crash of 1929, worsened by the lengthening Great Depression, required Mr. Bennett to emerge from retirement. Mr. Bennett became employed by the Department of Forest and Waters as a civil engineer and was assigned to the work in the Poe Valley CCC camp. Mr. Bennett was one of two engineers to serve in the Poe

Valley CCC camp. When construction of the Poe Valley dam he helped to design and supervise construction of was successfully completed in 1937, Mr. Bennett moved to Clearfield County, PA. There he served in the same capacity as company engineer in CCC Camp S-116, helping to design and supervise construction of Parker Dam.

After successful completion of Parker Dam, Mr. Bennett again retired, returning to York Springs, where he spent his remaining years on the farm.

The following was shared over the years:

Mr. Bennett 5'10" 180 lbs. was known to be a "wiry man who seemingly never tired." When excited or angered, he seemingly would have a burst of energy or "adrenaline rush." Many enrollees remembered their attempts to keep up with Mr. Bennett especially when assigned to a surveying crew under the direction of Mr. Bennett.

One story in particular went something like this: Enrollee Joe Rushio from Altoona, PA, known as "Tiger Joe" was a large man and purportedly was an amateur boxer. Foremen would tell of their dissatisfaction of Tiger Joe's disruptive manner to sit down and take a break whenever he chose to do so.

Mr. Bennett hearing this suggested Tiger Joe be assigned to his surveying crew. The next day's crew assignments found Tiger Joe on the surveying crew. Setting out at a brisk pace, the whole crew was traversing up and down one mountain and staring up another when Tiger Joe promptly stopped, sat down on a log to "take a break." Immediately, Mr. Bennett addressed Tiger Joe asking him, "Are you sick?" Tiger's response was, "No, I'm resting."

"We will rest at the top of this mountain," Mr. Bennett replied. "No, I'm resting now," said Tiger. With that, Mr. Bennett grabbed Tiger by the shirt, picked him up off of the log, shoved him around, then released him. Subsequently, Tiger fell backwards over the log onto the ground. "You will rest when I tell you, you will rest," stated Mr. Bennett. All expected a physical response from Tiger, but watched Tiger sit there, maybe in shock, get up slowly, pick up his tools, and proceed to walk on up the mountain. There was no further trouble from Tiger Joe.

CHAPTER 13

END OF CAMP

Very few original buildings remain standing at CCC campsites throughout the country today. The basic structures erected for the purposes of the Civilian Conservation Corps were designed and fabricated of materials for temporary occupancy.

Generally, they were single-story, wood-frame structures positioned atop of stone and wood piers with tarpaper wall and roof coverings.

Today in Poe Valley, two of the original camp structures remain standing. Both of these structures have been maintained as recreation camps in the woods by their owners. The remaining structures are the Officers' Quarters and the Forestry Quarters.

The Officers' Quarters structure has been added onto over the years, however, the front of the structure is easily recognized when comparing old photographs. The stone masonry supports for the front porch and front elevation wall are original construction elements. The original floor plan with the original diagonal-cut, hickory wood flooring remains in service, along with the original operating masonry fireplace.

Adjacent to the Officers' Quarters is the Forestry Quarters facility, also easily recognized when comparing old photographs, as the front elevation and particularly the front porch are original-construction elements.

The official end of the Civilian Conservation Corps came in June of 1942. Congress did not appropriate any funding for the continuance of the program that year. Then Director McEntee was allowed $8 million to close down the program. Closing down the program included disposition of the facilities erected on the campsites and disposition of all equipment positioned throughout the camp locations. The disposition of the facilities happened in many ways. Buildings were razed in most locations, and at other locations buildings were dismantled and relocated for differing purposes within government agencies. The Army took possession of many of the buildings and much of the equipment to assist in fulfilling the needs for involvement in World War Two.

At the time of this writing, the specific closing date of the Poe Valley camp when the last remaining enrollees were shipped out of camp is believed to be July 7, 1941.

Taken from Poe Valley Enrollee John P. Shinskie's autobiography: "On July 7, 1941, Company 1333, Camp S-63 was deactivated. I was transferred to Owls Gap Camp S-60 in Huntington County, Pennsylvania. I was probably the last enrollee to leave Poe Valley. I drove a truck to Camp S-60 and upon arrival I turned it over to the company commander."

All documents reviewed indicate the camp operations most likely came to an end in midsummer 1941. The last archived *Poe Valley Ravin* newsletter is dated June 1941.

This seemingly abrupt halt to operations of the Poe Valley camp I learned was not uncommon. Reorganization of camp operations by military command would in many instances abruptly shut down camps that had completed many of the projects developed by foresters and for not being able to "fill the barracks" due to low enrollment figures.

The disposition of the camps didn't follow a single prescribed method. Campsites situated on leased lands in the district, however, were mostly handled in similar fashion.

The Poe Valley camp was situated on leased lands. In Poe Valley, the disposition of the camp provided the land owner opportunity to purchase the buildings at a valuation prepared by program administrators.

Documents dated May 18, 1943, typed on Department of War letterhead indicate the camp structures remain standing and place a valuation on them at $5,730.00. This same document goes on to place an estimated value to return the property back to the land owner at $12,944.00. This being the estimated cost to dismantle the remaining buildings and for restoration of the grounds.

The camp at Poe Valley was positioned on leased private lands. The land agreement generally was a lease agreement, where upon at the end of the lease the property would be restored and returned to the land owner in the same condition as it was received.

This same document goes on to describe the final agreement between the land owner and the department to satisfy the lease agreement as follows:

END OF CAMP

The lessor of the camp site has submitted an offer of one hundred dollars ($100.00) for the property remaining on the camp site and will, upon acceptance of this offer, execute a supplemental agreement releasing the government from all obligations for the restoration of the camp site and any claims arising out of the use and occupation by the government of the premises.

ADDRESS REPLY TO
CHIEF OF ENGINEERS, U. S. ARMY
WASHINGTON, D. C.

REFER TO FILE NO. CE 324.5
(Third Service Command)–SPEUM

WAR DEPARTMENT
OFFICE OF THE CHIEF OF ENGINEERS
WASHINGTON

CIVILIAN

MAY 19 1943

RECEIVED
CONSERVATION CORPS
May 18, 1943

The Director,
Civilian Conservation Corps,
Otis Building, 810–18th Street, N. W.,
Washington, D. C.

Dear Sir:

Reference is made to our letter of November 16, 1942, releasing CCC Camp S-63, Coburn, Pennsylvania, for other than War Department disposition.

The lessor of the camp site has submitted an offer of one hundred dollars ($100.00) for the property remaining on the camp site and will, upon acceptance of this offer, execute a supplemental agreement releasing the Government from all obligations for restoration of the camp site and any claim arising out of the use and occupation by the Government of the premises.

The cost of dismantling of remaining buildings and restoration of the camp site is estimated at twelve thousand, nine hundred and forty—four dollars ($12,944.00). The value of material that can be salvaged is estimated at five thousand, seven hundred and thirty dollars ($5,730.00). The offer submitted is less than similar proposals on other camps. However, the lessor is not interested in the retention or use of the buildings, but intends to sell them to others under agreements requiring a certain amount of restoration of the premises.

The offer of the lessor will be accepted not later than June 1, 1943. The release of this camp for other than War Department disposition is, therefore, rescinded as of that date.

For the Chief of Engineers:

Very respectfully,

J. H. MILLER,
Major, Corps of Engineers,
Assistant; Repairs & Utilities Branch,
Construction Division.

Disposition letter for the camp

w/a H.R.

HISTORICAL RECORD OF CCC CAMP BUILDINGS

Leased 58.2 Acres, Fed, Owned None Acres. Date Completed May 19__, Dist. No. 1 ; State Pennsylvania; County Centre ; Camp ; S-58

Tel. No. 2R23 ; Telet. Stat Bellefonte, Pa.; Railroad Pennsylvania ; R.R. & Freight Stat Coburn, Penna. ; Post Office Coburn, Pennsylvania

Dist. & Direct. of Camp From R.H. 7 mi. north ; Condition & Type of Road of Highway 1.4 mile improved road, 5.6 mile dirt road poor

CONDITION TO BE FILLED IN BY CORPS AREA
Abandoned : Reoccupied : Salvage
Date : Date : Date

SOURCE OF WATER SUPPLY Spring
Spring, Well or City Spring
WATER STORAGE
Reservoir or Tank, Kind
Capacity 1000 gal. tank
WATER PUMP IF USED
Type, Capacity, How driven and
Type Of Machine Fairbanks Morse
Z Style. Gasolim 1000 gal. per hr.
Potability of Water, whether normal
or Chlorinated Chlorinated

SOURCE OF ELECTRICITY
City, A.C. or D.C. d.c.
CAMP GENERATOR
Capacity (KW) A.C. or D.C.
Type & size of Engine 5 HP D.C.
H type 4 cylinder
FIRE PROTECTION
No. Fire Extinguishers 24
No. Fire Buckets
No. Water Containers 16
City Fire Asst. Yes or No yes

SEWAGE DISPOSAL
City Connection
Septic Tank & Exc Pits 150 yds. to
natural drainage
GARBAGE & TRASH DISPOSAL
Incinerator
TYPE OF LATRINE
Officers & Foresters Septic Tank
Enrollees Pit 16' Stool

Turned over to:
Date

Cost of R.A. Bldg. $2199.22
Cost of Fed. Bldg. Unknown
Total $2199.22

Camp Bldg. No.	Designation of Building	Dimension of Building	Type of Construction Masonry or Frame	Type of Construction Rigid or Portable	No. of Rooms	Capacity	How Heated Coal, Wood, Gas.	No. of Heating Units	No. of Ranges	Water Connection - yes or no	Sewer Connection - yes or no	No. of Sinks	No. Lavatories	Capacity Hot Water Heater	Bldg. Owned or Leased	Cost of Building	Present Condition Good None	Excess to need of Corps Area	REMARKS
1	Barracks No. 1	111' x 21'	Frame	Rigid	"	58	Coal	2	"	No	No	"	"	"	owned		Good	None	
2	Barracks No. 2	111' x 21'	"	"	"	38	"	2	"	No	No	1			"		"	"	
3	"	"	"	"	"	38	"	2	"	No	No	1			"		"	"	
4	"	"	"	"	"	38	"	2	"	No	No	1			"		"	"	
5	Ho. supply & O.H.	21' x 70'	"	"	3	19	"	3	"	Yes	Yes	2	1	150	"		"	"	
6	Infirmary & O.H.	21' x 120'	"	"	4	284	"	2	"	Yes	Yes	16		500	"		"	"	
7	Mess Hall	21' x 120'	"	"	1	29	"	1	"	Yes	No				"		"	"	
8	Bath House	21'6" x46'	"	"	3		"		"						"		"	"	
9	Pump House	9' x 12'	"	"	1		"	1	"	Yes	No				"		"	"	
10	Oil House (Army)	12' x 10'	"	"	1		"		"						"		"	"	
11	Recreation Bldg.	21' x 111'	"	"	7	350	"	3	"	Yes	Yes	1	1		"		"	"	
12	Generator House	12' x 15'	"	"	1		"	1	"	Yes	No			40	"		"	"	
13	Latrine	20' x 14'7"	"	"	1		"	1	"			1	1		"		"	"	
14	Tech. Ser. Qtrs.	11'78"x21'5"	"	"	6	24	"	3	"	Yes	No	1			"		"	"	C.C. Curtin
15	Officers Quarters	21' x 40'	"	"	5	4	"	2	"	Yes	No				"		"	"	
16	Garage (Army)	30' x 24'	"	"	1		"	1	"	No	No				"		"	"	
17	Office T.H.	20' x 51'	"	"	3		"	1	"	No	No				"		"	"	
18	Blacksmith Shop	25' x 31'	"	"	1		"	1	"	No	No				"		"	"	
19	Shop and Tool Rm.	24'x14'16"	"	"	2		"	1	"	No	No /				"		"	"	
20	Garage T.S.	35' x 50'	"	"	1		"	0	"	No	No				"		"	"	
21	Garage& Store rm	104' x 24'	"	"	1		"	0	"	No	No				"		"	"	
22	Oil House T.S.	12' x 14'	"	"	1		"		"	No	No				"		"	"	

H. F. CURTIN
1st Lieut. Inf. Res.,
Commanding

HR 37/308

Camp structures inventory form

The final disposition of the camp returned the camp lands and all of its buildings into the hands of the original land owner. The land owner would soon thereafter start selling off the buildings. The camp buildings were in turn sold by the owner to many different buyers.

Many a story is told by locals about how numerous "cabins" and other structures situated throughout the Poe Valley region were constructed using lumber salvaged from the Poe Valley CCC camp structures. This is most likely a certainty, as this was common practice in the disbandment of CCC camp structures throughout the district.

Jim Homan, a classmate of mine attending one of our gatherings, shared this story: "My father, when a young man, helped his father disassemble one of the camp structures and rebuild the salvaged lumber as a hunting camp located in Renova, PA."

While penning this chapter I found a "camp for sale" item in a local real estate magazine. The camp for sale information sheet listed the typical information about the camp, including the location being Poe Valley. The listing also included the marketing promotion line, "The origin of this camp was the reconstruction of the 'pump house'" from the Poe Valley Civilian Conservation Corps camp.

As the general economy in America was strengthening and World War Two was ever massing, the Civilian Conservation Corps program was shrinking quickly throughout the country. Consolidation and closing of camps was occurring throughout the state and the entire program in all districts.

At this same time, an alternate plan was proposed by Army administrators for occupancy of Poe Valley nearing the end of the program. In June of 1941 this proposal was to disband Company 1333 by transferring in a black veterans' company from Camp S-113 Purvis.

America was a segregated nation all through the Civilian Conservation Corps era. "Locals quickly voiced objection to the proposed plan for this transfer as they noted this would be the second black camp in their all white county," as was reported by Senator Joseph Gufrey to Director McEntee. (Chronicled in *At Work in Penn's Woods* by Joseph Speakman.)

The proposed disbandment of Company 1333 and transfer of the black veterans' camp did not occur in Poe Valley.

CHAPTER 14

INSIGHTS INTO ENROLLEE LIFE AFTER CAMP

A wise man who assisted in getting the first several reunions organized, suggested we try to get some background information on his fellow enrollees. This wise man was enrollee veteran Samuel Wise. He put together an enrollee history form, which was distributed at the second annual reunion held in 1984. He received twenty-four history forms from fellow reunion attendees. During the preparation of this book, these forms surfaced from one of the boxes of things collected over the years. I again read through the information contained in these forms and found it striking to find so many parallels of the insights into the life tracks these men would take. Herein, I share these insights with readers who are learning more about the life and times of Camp S-63.

Of these twenty-four veteran history forms, the following is known: Nineteen of twenty-four served more than one six-month enrollment in the CCC, eighteen of twenty-four continued their education while in CCC camp, three of twenty-four advanced to the position of barrack assistant leader or barrack leader while in camp, twenty-one of twenty-four married, twenty of twenty-four had children, twenty-two of twenty-four were a member of the Armed Forces in World War Two, and three of twenty-four worked for a railroad company.

Occupations these men noted were coal miner, heavy equipment operator, foundry worker, aircraft manufacturing, telephone company lineman, dairy farming, Pennsylvania Department of Agriculture, Delaware Department of Environment, US Army officer, US Naval career, Pennsylvania State Police, packaging plant manager, General Motors Corporation, Pennsylvania Department of Corrections, furniture manufacturing, and church pastor.

So many times, I admonish myself for not having taken the time to write down the many stories and experiences the veterans shared while attending reunions. For the most part, the information contained within this book regarding a veteran-specific story are written from memory. One of the common stories shared by veterans during these gatherings was how their experience in camp would be most formidable in the positive development of their life track. Many told how the guidance and tutelage of the foremen would be remembered for a lifetime and had a significant impact on their personal and spiritual development as adults, fathers, and grandfathers.

On more than one occasion a veteran told how a particular foreman or commander had helped "put them on the straight and narrow."

At recent gatherings, where the extended family of veterans are in attendance, they share many stories off how their fathers, uncles, or grandfathers had been so influential to the positive in the development of the family unit and felt much of this was a result of the short yet highly influential CCC experience.

During the 2016 Poe Valley CCC gathering, I was presenting various uncaptioned photos of enrollees in camp life settings. I stopped on one such photo depicting a mess hall setting with three enrollees in kitchen aprons and commented that I would like to know if anyone could identify any individuals in the photos to please let me know. From the audience I heard a hand call out "I can tell you who the guy on the left is." The voice was that of Judith Korpics, daughter of veteran John Balaban. Judith went on to tell how she was researching her father's involvement in the Poe Valley camp and recently learned of the gatherings on the Internet and made the trip to Poe Valley from her home state of Virginia. Judith and I later met to share stories. She showed me numerous photos depicting her father and camp activities. She gifted me an original 1934 Christmas menu, wherein all enrollees, technical personnel, and military members in camp were listed. These names are provided in Chapter 6.

After learning more about enrollee Balaban, I asked Judith to write a biography of her father and allow me to place the information in this book. I shortly after received her father's CCC life track included herein and written in Judith's voice:

THE BALABAN STORY

Mess Sergeant, John Balaban, of CCC Company 1333 of Poe Valley Camp S-63 Coburn, Pennsylvania, was my father. He was a quiet, dignified, good man, who spoke with pride about serving in Roosevelt's CCC camp. His daily life and the raising of his four children reflected the many values taught to the CCC boys. He taught his children responsibility to yourself, others, and especially family. Respect for yourself and others was expected. Dignity and personal hygiene and a good work ethic were emphasized verbally and through example. Conservation of our natural resources was expected and when ignored was followed by a teaching moment. Waste was intolerable.

Responsibility and love of family with respect for parents was evident when he joined the CCC in 1933. He was a twenty-two-year-old man, who had worked in the Pennsylvania coal mines beside his father since he was a boy of fourteen. He recognized responsibility to family, and the CCC gave him a chance to help his father, mother, five younger brothers, and a sister at home in southwest Pennsylvania.

Judith's CCC father, John Balaban

Responsibility and responding to the needs of others and our country was evident throughout his life. During the Cold War, I can remember him as a Civil Patrol member in our community. He went to weekly meetings to help prepare us in case of an air attack by Russia. Thanks to the CCC, he knew first aid and about water purification. Caring for the welfare of others and the exercising of good judgment is seen again as he pulls away a cavalier miner, anxious to test his fate, just before the ceiling collapses. One edition of the *Poe Valley Ravin* refers to him as altruistic. He did truly wish the best for everyone. He was an unselfish man.

The Wandering Wonderer.

I wander and I wonder. I wander here and I wander there. I wonder this and I wonder that.

For one thing I wonder if it were our new student cooks who necessitated the construction of a new latrine. Whether the appointment of these cooks and the building of the latrine was a coincidence or not I do not know, but you can find after every meal a full house up there. Speaking of up there, I have heard several proposals of having a trolley system set up leading up to our sort-of isolated out-house. I'll bet those guys in number two don't take any more CCC pills.

I wonder why Alex isn't first in chow line anymore. Well, he says he found it sort of fatiguing and embarrassing to chisel everyday so he's getting around that difficulty by establishing permanent residence in the kitchen. I wonder how the mess fund is holding out with him and "Fats" within close range of our edibles.

I wonder why they don't ship those damn understudies out. Understudies galore, you stumble over them wherever you go. To top it all even the Hospital orderlies have an understudy. Well, it just shows to go you what a profound art, "loafing", is.

I wonder if G.K. Dannenhauer has run across this one:-"Those of the human family who are domiciled in vitreous places of abode are admonished against hurling petrified substances" To you Dannenhauer, it means:- "People who live in glass houses shouldn't throw stones.

I wonder what has consensus of opinion is regarding the new officers. There are Lieutenant Coates, and Lieutenants Corey and McClellan. Laying all jesty aside we must say that have come into a good camp with a good company, and may we hope that with our help they may make this a better camp. Of the old officers only Lieutenant Carroll remains. It was with regret that we saw the others leave and it will be with even greater regret that we shall see Lt. Corey go. (But still the world goes around.)

Twinkle, twinkle little star How I wonder where you are.

Ask Beatty. "Twinkletoe" Beatty the pool-shark and butter-fiend. Lot of us want to be first in the chow line but Beatty likes to be last. Did you ever try to take a bone away from a dog. Try taking butter away from Beatty,"Twinkletoe Beatty," to you. Gr-r-r-r-r-. Where's Harpo.

I wonder how some of our Romeos are getting along over on yonder side of the mountain, There is our platonic lover Whalen, and the altruist himself, Balaban. Gee, it's grand to be in love. Ask Babyface Schonn, sweet innocence himself.

Thusly I wander and I wonder and anyone wishing to accompany me in any of these verbal sprees, just address your correspondence to the,

"WANDERER"

- 10-

Dad's records reveal he applied for Emergency Conservation Work on October 31, 1933, and was enrolled on November 29, 1933. He had been unemployed since 1929. He was at Fort

Meade, Maryland, from November 29 to December 11, 1933. On December 12, 1933, he arrived at Camp 63 Coburn, PA, where his duties included "kitchen patrol." From April to May 1, 1934, his work was cooking, and from May 2, 1934, to August 3, 1935, he was mess sergeant with a performance rating of "excellent." Leadership positions usually meant more money for the family, but it meant so much more to him. Many pictures from that period show his pride in himself and his position and the comments at the bottom of those

pictures show the family's pride in him. Dad told one of my brothers that he "learned how to make leg of lamb in the CCC." He must have taught Mom, and she taught me.

Family and responsibility to the job can be seen throughout his life. He went to work even if he was sick. He disliked laziness. "Always give your best" even if it is picking weeds in the yard. No "goldbricking" allowed! Respect your tools by cleaning them before you put them away. No sleeping past eight A.M. He taught through example. Recognizing his responsibility to family, he and our mother sent four children to college, and that involved great sacrifice and discipline.

Discipline and living a disciplined life was evident in our family. Meals were at designated times, and we came to the table as "presentable," clean, tidy, and orderly. We could go out to play after homework was finished. Good grades and behavior were expected. You might say our household was a softer version of camp life. We thrived in that orderliness.

CCC taught self-discipline as an attribute for every man, but humans sometimes slip. The rules say no alcoholic beverages in camp, but liquor did get smuggled in via the payroll pouch. The payroll was stuffed into the shirt. Not much alcohol could make it into camp that way, and only an officer could pull that off. I do remember Dad telling the boys that "the Army can make a man of you and give you a skill, or you can leave a drunken bum. You get what you put into it."

I would say Dad enjoyed his time in the CCC. He was always a serious man, certainly not quick to smile. The pictures of him from the camp reveal a man I never knew. He appears very happy and pleased with himself, but he did not have a wife and four children in 1935.

My brother John, the oldest son, says one of the officer's told Dad that an officer in Camp S-63 had been involved in the Army's attempt to capture Poncho Villa. I wonder if he was one of these officers?

There is no doubt that the CCC greatly influenced Dad's life. He left Camp S-63 August 3, 1935. He had found employment, and shortly after he met my Mom. The CCC influenced that first meeting in Pittsburgh, PA. When he was introduced to my mother, she was very impressed by his appearance, especially his shiny shoes and his dignified personality. Her sister thought he was conceited. (See photos on page 278.)

They were married May 21, 1937, in Oakland, California. They worked for a chain called Margaret Burnham, and Dad was a chef/cook. Mom was a waitress. Again, the CCC had an influence on their lives. A mess sergeant was in charge of ordering supplies and would have a good idea of what a ration of food costs. Mom said, "Dad could quickly give a district manager a plate breakdown (cost)," and Dad's performance resulted in their being transferred to Reno, Nevada, to "get one of the stores out of the red."

Of their four children, I am the oldest, born in 1941, and the three boys were born in 1943, 1948, and 1952. We were raised with love, discipline, and high expectations for success. We always knew we were college bound and that as long as we were serious students, they would help us. My brother John became a dentist, brother Frank an endodontist, and brother Paul and I (Judy) are pharmacists. We and his dear wife, Peggy, were my proud and dignified CCC father's pride and joy in life. We miss both of them.

Veteran Lester A. Auman was born in Coburn, PA, and entered into the CCC on July 12, 1938, at the age of twenty. He remained in camp until October 11 of the same year when he received his Certificate of Discharge. His time in camp was less than the standard six-month hitch, as he departed to accept employment back home. For many enrollees, this was most common to separate from service in the CCC prior to completion of the six-month enrollment period to accept employment back home. Lester married and had two children, two grandchildren, and one great-grandchild, and like so many of his fellow enrollees served in the US Army during World War Two. After service in World War Two he resided in nearby Millheim, PA, was employed in local industry, and retired from The Pennsylvania State University, where he served as a campus patrolman.

Georgene Searfoss, Lester's daughter shared the following:

> My mother's maiden name was Edna Stover and lived in Millheim, PA, where the enrollees came to socialize during their weekend free time. For nearly two years with apparent family approval, Edna dated Poe Valley CCC enrollee John "Jack" Guilich. The family anticipated Edna might well become Mrs. John Guilich. In the summer of 1941 "Jack" told Edna he was planning to depart service in the CCC and return home to the Clearfield/Phillipsburg, PA, area and be a "rum runner." Edna promptly broke up with young "Jack," not wanting to take up with a rum runner. Not long after the breakup, a close friend, who by this time lived across the street from Edna, told her he cared for her; not long thereafter, Edna Stover would become Mrs. Lester Auman.

Veteran Charles Fryer was born in Coburn, PA, and signed on in the early stages of the program. After successfully serving out his hitch in the CCC, he enlisted in the US Army in 1935 and became a veteran of World War Two. During the war, he earned two Bronze Stars for valor and the French Croix de Guerre. He received a battlefield commission to second lieutenant while serving with the Reconnaissance Platoon of the 630th Tank Destroyer Battalion during the famed Battle of the Bulge. He continued his military service and retired from the US Army with the rank of captain.

In 1948 Charles returned home to Coburn, PA. He married his German sweetheart, Elizabeth Maier. He and Elizabeth resided in his hometown and had two sons. Charles became the postmaster of the Coburn Post Office and retired from that position in 1985. Growing up in Coburn myself, it was a certainty I would know Mr. Fryer. My older brother and I went to school and played with his two sons and attend the same church as the Fryer family. I interacted and spoke with Mr. Fryer often. He, like so many who had answered the call to duty during World War Two, did not casually speak about his time in war. It would be many years later while hosting a Poe Valley CCC reunion when I learned of his involvement and part in World War Two and the famed Battle of the Bulge.

Veteran Donald A. Walker living in Wingate, PA, was seventeen years old when he signed on the CCC in 1940 and was assigned to the Poe Valley camp where he served for twelve months. Don easily remembered he planted trees, worked with surveying crew, and "had" to work hard pulling "gooseberry bushes" while in camp. After successfully completing his time in camp, he returned home and like so many other fellow enrollees served in the US Army during World War Two. After his military service, he returned to Wingate, PA. He then married and raised three children. Donald went to work in heavy industry for the Cerro Metal Corporation in Bellefonte, PA, and retired after thirty-four years of employment.

Veteran Kenneth Harter was living in his hometown of Aaronsburg, PA, after graduating high school. Opportunity for full-time employment was most limited. Needing to help support his family was most important to Kenny, as his father had passed when he was ten years old, leaving his mother to be the sole provider for the family. Enrolling into the CCC in 1939 would be the choice he made to have full-time employment. Kenny, as he was known, served twelve months in the Poe Valley camp only a few miles from his hometown. After his enrollment, he returned home. Like so many of his fellow enrollees, he joined the US Army, becoming a combat soldier in the European theatre of war during WWII. On April 12, 1945, he was gravely wounded and left for dead on the battlefield. A buddy learning of his fate went back to check up on him to find him still alive. Sergeant First Class Harter was sent to several hospitals in Europe being treated for extensive wounds and broken bones before being sent back to the states for continuing hospital care. Refusing to allow recommended amputations, Sergeant Harter spent more than three years in military hospitals. While in hospital after hospital his determination and shear will to meet the rigors of rehabilitation and therapy resulted in his returning back to his hometown under his own power with the help of a brace and a crutch that remained part of his daily routine for the rest of his life. Sergeant Harter repeatedly told his doctors and care providers in the various military hospitals where he was being treated, "I walked into this man's Army and I am going to walk out of it too." And so he did.

After returning home, Kenny, having married prior to shipping out for war, resided with his wife in Millheim, PA, the next town over from his hometown of Aaronsburg. Here he built a new home, became the father of one daughter, and took on the occupation of "court crier" in the county courthouse. After retirement, Kenny and his wife maintained their home in Millheim, PA, spending winter months in Florida, and enjoyed traveling.

Veteran Malcomb D. Kuhnes living in Blanchard, PA, was seventeen years old when he signed on the CCC in 1938 and was assigned to the Poe Valley camp where he served for twelve months. Malcomb remembered he was assigned to Foreman Bailey Auman's crew, loading trucks by hand for road construction and eventually became a driver of one of these trucks. After satisfactorily completing his time in camp, he returned home and like so many other fellow enrollees served in the US Army during World War Two. After his military service he returned to his hometown of Blanchard, PA. He then married and raised three children. Malcomb after other employment went to work in the aircraft manufacturing industry for Piper Aircraft in Lock Haven, PA, retiring after twenty-five years of employment.

Veteran William A. Robinson living in Port Matilda, PA, was seventeen years old when he signed on the CCC in 1940 and was assigned to the Poe Valley camp where he served three consecutive six-month hitches. One of the reasons William joined the CCC was the allure of being able to travel while in the CCC. Travel did not happen in the CCC, as he was assigned to the Poe Valley camp located "pretty much just over the mountain" from home. He easily remembered being assigned to fire duty, to which he had to maintain fire in the coal-fired pot belly stoves to keep the barracks warm.

After satisfactorily completing his hitch in the CCC, in June of 1940 he immediately joined the US Marine Corps. In the Marine Corps his wish to travel was fulfilled. Again, like so many fellow CCC veterans he saw action in World War Two at the Marshall Islands in the South Pacific and Chosen Reservoir during the Korean War. William retired after twenty-three years of military service having attained the rank of master sergeant. While in the service of the US Marine Corps, he earned six Good Conduct Medals, a Korean Service Medal, a United Nations Service Medal, and the National Defense Service Medal.

William married, raised two children, had five grandchildren, and six great-grandchildren. After retiring from the Marine Corps, William returned to his hometown where he was employed by the State College Water Authority. Family, hobbies, and working with the Boy Scouts were thoroughly enjoyed by William.

William's achievements noted above were attained upon successful completion of the "seventh grade." William's grandson Gerald Hoy shared the following about his grandfather's formal education level with the following family story: "After completing the seventh grade Pap told us the principal of the Port Matilda School told him not to come back."

Veteran Randall Boob living in Coburn, was seventeen years old when he signed on the CCC in 1938. He was assigned to the Poe Valley camp where he served for twelve months, receiving his satisfactory discharge in June of 1941. Randall remembered easily how tough it was to get a long-term, good-paying job when he was seventeen years old. He had heard many stories about the CCC where he would be able to get a fair wage for at least six months, thus luring him to "join up." Foreman Bailey Auman, also from Coburn, knew of Randall's experience driving the milk route truck on occasion back home and put young Randall into the driver's seat of a dump truck. Randall drove truck most of the time during his CCC experience, supporting road building and road improvement work.

Soon after his separation from CCC service, America became fully involved in World War Two. Young Randall like so many his age joined the military, serving in the US Army Air Force. Randall was assigned to the famed 8th US Army Air Force and became a crewman on a B-17 heavy bomber group based in England and flew thirty-seven missions over heavily fortified enemy territory.

After serving his country in World War Two, Randall returned home. Here he married and became the father of one daughter. Occupations including dairy farming, employment with the nearby Pennsylvania State University, and the Borough of Bellefonte carried Randall into retirement. As of this writing, Randall is now ninety-five years young and remains as one of the few known remaining veterans who has attended several reunions and gatherings in Poe Valley.

Veteran Elwood L. Ward living in Bellefonte, PA, was twenty-two years old when he signed on the CCC in 1939 and was assigned to the Poe Valley camp where he served for nineteen months, receiving his satisfactory discharge in July of 1941. Elwood married after his service in World War Two in the US Army Air Force, where he attained the rank of sergeant. After the war, he settled on a dairy farm in the Brush Valley area of Central PA, only a few miles from his hometown and the Poe Valley CCC camp where he served. Here he and his wife Winifred raised three sons and a daughter, had eight grandchildren, and six great-grandchildren.

While in camp, Elwood was known as "Tex" due to his tall, lean stature. Photos depict "Tex" as being most capable at the swinging of ax felling trees. The June 1940 camp newsletter tells us Elwood achieved the rank of barrack leader, thereby earning an additional $15.00 a month. In addition to duties performed in camp, while holding the rank of barrack leader, Elwood, on separate occasions, was detached to the CCC New Cumberland Army Depot training rookies and served as a train guard.

During his time in camp, "Tex" apparently had a good eye for both fast and curve balls having a .333 batting average while playing left field on the camp baseball team.

Veteran Norman Wingard living right off of the Millheim-Siglerville Pike Road leading into Poe Valley was seventeen years old when he signed on the CCC in 1938 and was assigned to the Poe Valley camp where he served for twelve months. Norman choose to join up with the Civilian Conservation Corps like so many of his peers, as this would provide gainful employment at a time when there were no jobs to be had. Norman many times told his family he remembered being assigned to Foreman Bailey Auman's crew, performing road construction work and placed rock on the dam.

After satisfactorily completing enrollment, he received his discharge in 1940 and returned home and worked in the farming community. He married in 1941 and became father to three children. Like so many other fellow enrollees, Norman was drafted and served in the US Army in the Philippines during World War Two. After his military service, he returned back home where he settled and worked his own farm with his wife and children. Norman, in addition to working his own dairy farm, worked full time for thirty-three years as a metal worker for the Cerro Copper and Brass Company in nearby Bellefonte, PA.

Norman was proud of having served his country during time of war and was equally proud of being part of the CCC and shared many stories with his family of his times in the camp. One of Norman's stories was shared with me by Norman's wife Pauline and goes something like this: Norman told her the dances held in camp were popular, attended by the local girls providing opportunity for the boys to meet and talk to the girls and share a few dances. Certainly, anything other than fruit punch was not to be served to drink at these dances. With laughter in her voice, she told the story Norman had shared about the boys being issued long overcoats with large, deep pockets. The deep pockets in the coats were a good place to hide bottles of beer that had been "slipped" into the camp during these dances. The prospect to sneak a few sips of beer while away from Mom and Dad allowed for some of the enrollees a chance to get some one-on-one time to talk with a particular gal. I have often wondered if the chaperones ever caught on and would eventually conduct coat searches before allowing entrance into the dance hall.

In addition to the memories told by Norman, the family cherishes having Norman's CCC issue footlocker.

Enrollee Norman Wingard's CCC footlocker (now a family keepsake)

Little is known about Veteran Frank Berenty beyond his service in the Civilian Conservation Corps. His name, however, is noted two separate times in the *Poe Valley Ravin* newsletters.

The December 1940 issue reports Frank will be discharged on December 23, 1940, due to the expiration of his term of enrollment. The February 1941 issue reports a separate story about Frank.

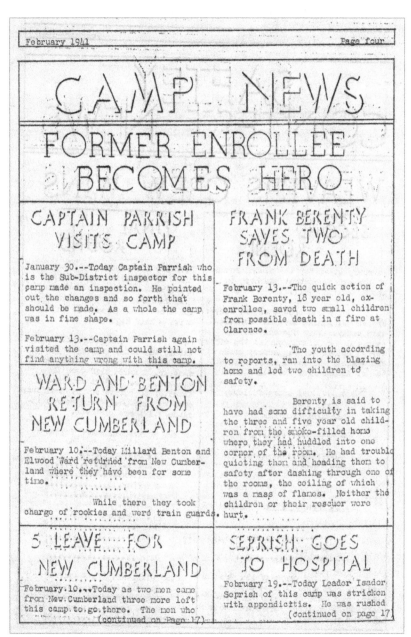

(continued on Page 17)

Enrollee Frank Berenty story

The similarities of military service, marriage, raising children, employment, and service to others noted in these few insights provides what I found to be a typical description for the life paths so many other veterans of the Poe Valley CCC camp followed. The veterans of the Poe Valley CCC camp, like their counterparts from the more than 4,000 camps nationwide, made up a significant percentage of the men of the "greatest generation." Many served their country in time of war. It is just now becoming better known the contributions these veterans provided for the betterment of our state and national parks and conservation of our natural resources, all the while bettering themselves through their service in the CCC. These veterans took skills learned and confidences gained while in camp throughout their life track. They would seek and maintain gainful employment, further their education, marry, build and maintain homes, raise families, and be a positive part and influence in all of life's aspects at home and all across America.

CELEBRITY IN CAMP

Numerous enrollees in the Civilian Conservation Corps would go on in life to gain celebrity status. Several enrollees in the camps around America who achieved fame were test pilot Chuck Yeager, boxer Archie Moore, and actors Raymond Burr, Walter Mathau, and Robert Mitchum.

Camp S-63 Poe Valley would, for six months in 1934, have its own soon-to-be celebrity in Enrollee Martin Filchock from Grinestone, PA. Martin had a gifted talent to draw cartoons of every type. He was known to draw a cartoon sketch for his bunkmates (depicting almost anything they wanted) for the princely sum of a penny, and sometimes he would get a whole nickel for a large-sized, hand-drawn cartoon. He had several of his cartoons published in the CCC national newsletter *Happy Days* while in camp. He was known to post a cartoon around the camp depicting a funny condition in his own effort to lighten the spirit of his fellow enrollees during a troubled time.

I easily remember sitting with my nephew reading with him a children's magazine; within the magazine was a cartoon known as "Check and Double Check" published in the Mom-approved children's magazine *Highlights for Children*. This cartoon had two identical-looking sketches side by side; the reader was then to find the few minor differences in the two sketches. I later learned this cartoon was created by Martin Filchock, the Poe Valley enrollee cartoonist.

Mr. Filchock was unable to attend any reunions, however, corresponded with me on numerous occasions. I had the pleasure to meet and visit with Mr. Filchock at his home in Martinsville, Tennessee. During this visit, he shared his life story, his time in Poe Valley, his hitch in the service, serving in the Army during World War Two, his marriage, and pride in being the father of a daughter who became a medical doctor.

He then told me of his times with a few of his friends, famed cartoonists Hank Ketchum and Charles Shultz. He went on to tell me, maybe, he had not made the kind of money his friends did but he was able to "pay the bills." Mr. Filchock lived to be 100 years old and worked his craft right up until near the time of his passing. His work was known to have been published in virtually every magazine of the time, such as *Saturday Evening Post*, *Good Housekeeping*, *Readers Digest*, and the like excepting his one true desire to be published in the *New Yorker*.

I received copies of the only documents held in the National Archives on the Poe Valley camp. Among the copy received were two cartoon sketches that had been published in the nationally distributed Civilian Conservation Corps *Happy Days* newsletter. When I looked at the cartoon, I quickly realized I had seen a copy of this cartoon before. Yes, among my grandfather's documents was indeed a copy of the same cartoon. I have often wondered how the copy was made and ended up in my grandfather's possessions (see next page).

Enrollee Martin Filchock's cartoon published in the CCC *Happy Days* newsletter

Reunions allowed me to get first-hand stories of camp life. Mostly these stories were being swapped between veterans who enjoyed telling their individual remembrances. I realize now much of what I have shared herein came from eavesdropping while the veterans shared their experiences while in camp. Most of the planning and execution of the reunions was in the hands of my wife, my mother, and myself; unfortunately, we did not have backgrounds in event planning and subsequently did not have roving photographers filming and/or recording conversations during the events. I did take a few photos myself and several group photos of the veterans attending the event. Many years ago, I also was not well-organized and photographs have been lost along the way. Fortunately, one of the group photographs is among my collection and is depicted here.

1984 CCC REUNION GROUP PHOTO

Front Row Kneeling: Gervis Corman, John Hettinger, Joe McCreery, Tim Wion, John Hazzard, Andrew Alexander, John Milton, Lester R. Bastress, James Murphy, and John Heckman.
Second Row Sitting: George Mandell, Nevin Crater, Herbert Moltz, Malcomb D. Kunes, Harold Corman, Carl Fomich, Ray Hazel, Robert Huber, Wylie Henry, James Savage, Henry Gramley, Nevin Walter, William Poorman, Cordes McCloskey, and Kenneth Harter.
Third Row: Donald Beyer, Lawrence Ammerman, Dale Bechtol, Howard Wykoff, Sam Wise, George Letrick, Joe Comitz, William T. Koren, Howard J. Boyer, William Harrhy, George Beckwith, Don Walker, Raymond Beckwith, Robert Thompson, Richard Berkstresser, Clair Hetrick, and Ebon Stricker.

CLOSING

Although unable to credit the quote, one of the comments I remember hearing from one of the Camp S-63 veterans attending a reunion was the following comment. I believe it to be so fitting of the time: "The forests were a place and I needed a place."

What I learned while listening to the many comments shared by the veterans during reunions was how much these young men gained from their brief time spent in the CCC camp. From these comments and later research, I also learned how much the public at large all across the nation gained from such a brief time period in America's history.

My grandfather left the Department of Forest and Waters after seven years of service and returned back home where he built a successful International Harvester Farmall Implement dealership, the Farmers Supply Company in Millheim, PA. This dealership was in part a result of his time in the "three Cs," where in addition to numerous duties, he performed maintenance work on crawler tractor equipment manufactured by the International Harvester Company and Caterpillar Tractor Company. This experience provided him introduction to the opportunities with the International Harvester Company.

Like my grandfather, so many others who had been part of the Civilian Conservation Corps in Poe Valley went on to be successful in life, in part, due to their experiences, learned skills, and knowledge gained while in the Civilian Conservation Corp.

My grandfather did not speak in terms of personal achievement or self-performance. He was known, not to describe accomplishment in the singular, such as I did this or I did that. He typically spoke about the accomplishment of others in his work. He spoke often about the completion of tasks that had been satisfactorily performed under his direction, these things the boys completed, as though he were not even part of it. He always spoke in the positive when telling any CCC story about "his boys." I do not remember him ever speaking in harsh words about any enrollee, even though I am certain there were a few "bad apples" to manage. I am also certain one of the reasons for this was my grandfather's ability to find ways to bring out the best in those he was assigned on a day-to-day basis.

My grandfather was a successful businessman, a family man, served on the governing council in his hometown, was a key figure in organizing one of the state's first cable TV companies, cabinetmaker, hand-saw filler, a go-to man to help construct or reconstruct farm buildings in the region, and a well-known pinochle card player. Anyone, however, who knew my grandfather would tell you he would chat up the accomplishments of a bunch of "boys" either "back in Poe Valley" or "out at Parker Dam" and typically mention little if anything he was doing or had done.

Those accomplishments he spoke of remain today as the legacy to a time when for eight years hundreds of miles of roadways, hundreds of bridges and earthen masonry dams creating recreational lakes were built, and tens of thousands of acres of forests were reclaimed without one contract written for the execution of the work.

This work was carried out by young men, some being just teenagers having no prior experience in their work. They performed this work under the direction of foremen having skills and necessary experience to provide the needed guidance for satisfactory completion of the assigned tasks.

These boys along with their peers throughout the country were developing a sense of self-worth during a time when hope had seemed lost. Economic loss for the country during The Great Depression was a staggering dollar value. The gain, however, the country received during this same time period through the positive works of these boys in natural conservation measures by far exceeded those staggering losses if a dollar value could be assigned to the improvement and development of our national and state parks and the restoration of natural resources.

My grandfather's pride in what his boys had accomplished, is just now becoming understood by the people throughout this great land of ours where national parks, state parks, and state and national forests provide the recreational service and wealth of natural resources available to us all, thanks to the work of the foreman's boys.

A time when every little thing accomplished was not deemed with the response, "awesome" as it is today, I know the respect and admiration these boys received from their bosses was limited during those desperate times, yet I know my grandfather was not the only foreman to tell how proud he was of what his boys accomplished.

Seventy-seven years after the closing of Camp S-63 all that physically remains at the original campsite are the Officers' Quarters structure, forestry quarters structure, a stone monument in memory of Bernard Oyler, tiled flooring of the kitchen's Mess Hall, and several concrete slabs where maintenance and shop structures once stood. The camp incinerator constructed of stone in its deteriorated condition remains standing positioned approximately one mile east of camp.

These physical reminders take us back to a time when for eight and a half years a Civilian Conservation Corps company consisting of anxious, young enrollees, many just teenagers, along with military administrators, foremen, an educator, an engineer, a superintendent, and a forester lived the life resembling that which would be found on a small military encampment.

Here, the entire camp assembly including all facilities and the complete infrastructure was constructed and maintained and improved by these same individuals.

This camp, during their terms of enrollment, would be home for the many young boys growing up and maturing through The Great Depression. While in this remote site situated in the mountains of Central Pennsylvania, these young boys matured earnestly while performing the works of forestry management, roads and trails construction, bridge construction, fire tower and watchers cabin construction, and construction of a 660-foot-long dam and twenty-seven-acre lake shoulder-to-shoulder with their peers.

These young men accepted the challenge to strengthen their mental and physical self, their character, and the nation at large. They developed life-long relationships, strengthened family back home, and supported in dramatic fashion the development of much of today's Pennsylvania's State Park System.

The camaraderie developed in the Civilian Conservation Corps camp was indeed similar to that of those who served in the military.

During the eight-and-a-half-year period of time the Poe Valley camp was in operation, the accomplishments of this group of inexperienced young men have stood the test of time, wherein trails, roads, forest improvements, and the lake created by the construction of a combined earthen and masonry dam is today one of Pennsylvania's top-pick state parks. People from near and far come to enjoy the quiet and natural beauty of Pennsylvania's bountiful forests and specifically to enjoy the serenity and natural beauty of Poe Valley.

Long gone are the sights and sounds of camp life, where the many young men of Civilian Conservation Corps, Company 1333, Camp S-63 lived together in wooden barrack structures, ate together in the Mess Hall, played baseball, and hung out in the Recreation Hall after the day's work. Here they had also gathered in small groups to continue their education and share their differing life experiences.

For anyone reading this book, I invite you to visit Poe Valley, take a step back into time, and join up with a company of young men and envision yourself among the original group of Poe Valley campers.

After setting up your camp, walk the trails created by the day-long swing of ax and grub hoe, traverse the roads opened up by pick and shovel, walk among the trees, soak in the view of natural vegetation strengthened by untold hours of care, and take a refreshing dip into Poe Valley Lake created by the construction of the dam, including a sixty-foot-wide, hand-placed, stone-masonry spillway.

Then, after your rejuvenating camping trip, when you are back home where you had pulled the plug connecting you to our digital world to get away from the hectic lifestyles before the trip, I ask you to plug back into the digital world and go to the following website: https://youtu.be/ZOGUrbchYKE.

Now one more time I invite you to revisit Poe Valley, this time the visit will take you back more than eighty years ago to the camp where you will witness by motion picture camp life and see the camp facilities and see many of the enrollees going about their daily activities. This motion picture will also reflect the work project activities going on down at the dam construction site. The sounds you hear is the music these young men danced to when the girls and the orchestra came into camp for the annual commanders-sponsored dance.

THE MOTION PICTURE STORY

About two years ago John Eastlake, a friend and fellow Civilian Conservation Corps enthusiast who well-knows my interest in Poe Valley, contacted me and asked if I might know a J. E. Smith in reference to Poe Valley and the Civilian Conservation Corps. I was quickly able to tell him it was most likely Mr. John E. Smith who was the state forester assigned to the camp. He then told me he may have something I will be most interested in. He advised, Mr. Mike Wennin a fellow Civilian Conservation Corps enthusiast and executive director of the Lumber Heritage Region of Pennsylvania had made a find on eBay. It turns out a 16 mm film was posted for sale and acquired by the director. The film had the following notation on the film can, J. E. Smith, Poe Valley Camp, July 1936.

Mr. Wennin subsequently had the film digitized and graciously gave me a copy.

For anyone watching this motion picture, it will be my hope you will be able to have the moment I was able to experience while watching. The film depicts unknown administration personnel, known military personnel, known foreman, known Education Advisor and many enrollees all generally unknown moving about the camp and work activity areas in early fall 1936.

Opening scenes depict unknown administration personnel outside of the headquarters facility. Next seen are the camp foremen, and right there was my grandfather moving about the camp with his fellow foremen. After a few more scenes, there was my grandfather again, riding "shotgun" in a truck filled with his boys on their way to work for the day. I was immediately taken back more than forty-five years in my memory seeing my grandfather moving about. Seeing my grandfather in this moment brought me to tears. I truly cannot express the gratitude I have for the finding of this film.

The gift of this video provides me with the opportunity to watch my grandfather in a motion picture anytime I want to do so, something no one in our family would have prior to this one-in-a-million find.

After looking at the film, I was able to determine the origin of the film. The photographer was Mr. Drew Kolb. Mr. Kolb lived in Millheim, PA, and was the operator of the Millheim Theater. This same Mr. Kolb was the theater manager who was supportive of the Civilian Conservation Corps operations in Poe Valley. He brought a projector into camp in the early days to show movies to the enrollees as part of their recreational activities, he also allowed the use of the Millheim Theater to show training films to the enrollees. On more than one occasion Mr. Kolb in cooperation with the company commanders opened up the theater to show the boys a special showing when a special award had been earned by the enrollees in camp.

Please do enjoy a time long ago when life in Poe Valley included Civilian Conservation Corps, Company 1333, Camp S-63.

ABOUT THE AUTHOR

Bill Marcum is a Civilian Conservation Corps enthusiast, who for many years hosted reunions for veterans of Civilian Conservation Corps Company 1333. In recent years, in collaboration with the Penns Valley Area Historical Museum, Centre County Historical Society, and the Pennsylvania Department of Conservation & Natural Resources has hosted gatherings for veterans, extended family members of veterans, and fellow Civilian Conservation Corps enthusiasts to celebrate its legacy. In 2018, Bill and his wife Mary were presented the Jacqueline J. Melander Award by the Centre County Historical Society for decades-long work in preserving the history, stories, and artifacts of the Civilian Conservation Corps, Company 1333, Camp S-63, Poe Valley.

CPSIA information can be obtained
at www.ICGtesting.com
Printed in the USA
BVHW030455220921
617104BV00006B/112